Cognitive Behavior Therapy of DSM-5 Personality Disorders

The first edition of *Cognitive Behavior Therapy of DSM-IV Personality Disorders* broke new ground. It differed from other CBT books by offering brief but thorough user-friendly resources for clinicians and students in planning and implementing effective treatments. The third edition of this classic text continues this tradition by providing practitioners—both practicing clinicians and those in training—a hands-on manual of highly effective, evidence-based cognitive and behavioral interventions for these challenging disorders.

The beginning chapters briefly describe the changes between the DSM-IV-TR and DSM-5 and emphasize the best of the recent evidence-based CBT assessment and treatment strategies applicable to personality disorders. The book then guides clinicians in each step of the treatment process—from assessment to case conceptualization to selection and implementation of intervention. Case material is used to illustrate this process with the most recent developments from Behavior Therapy, Cognitive Therapy, Schema Therapy, Cognitive Behavioral Analysis System of Psychotherapy, Mindfulness-Based therapies, and Dialectical Behavior Therapy.

Len Sperry, MD, PhD, is Professor and Director of Clinical Training at Florida Atlantic University and Clinical Professor of Psychiatry and Behavioral Medicine at the Medical College of Wisconsin. He has practiced, taught and written about personality disorders and CBT for over three decades and has had extensive formal training in the diagnosis and treatment of personality disorders and in CBT. Among his 900+ professional publications are several articles, book chapters, and books on personality disorders and on CBT, including the *Handbook of the Diagnosis and Treatment of the DSM-5 Personality Disorders*.

Jon Sperry, PhD, is Assistant Professor of Psychology at Lynn University and a staff therapist at the Counseling and Psychological Services at Florida Atlantic University. He has extensive training in CBT, and practices, supervises, and consults on the use of CBT in the treatment of personality disorders and other disorders. He has published several articles and book chapters and is co-author of *Case Conceptualization: Mastering this Competency with Ease and Confidence*.

Cognitive Behavior Therapy of DSM-5 Personality Disorders

Assessment, Case Conceptualization, and Treatment

Third Edition

Len Sperry & Jon Sperry

Routledge
Taylor & Francis Group

NEW YORK AND LONDON

KH

Third edition published 2016
by Routledge
711 Third Avenue, New York, NY 10017

and by Routledge
27 Church Road, Hove, East Sussex BN3 2FA

Routledge is an imprint of the Taylor & Francis Group, an informa business

© 2016 Taylor & Francis

The right of Len Sperry and Jonathan Sperry to be identified as authors of this work has been asserted by them in accordance with sections 77 and 78 of the Copyright, Designs and Patents Act 1988.

First edition published by Brunner/Mazel 2008

Second edition published by Routledge 2006

Library of Congress Cataloging-in-Publication Data
Sperry, Len, author.
    [Cognitive behavior therapy of DSM-IV-TR personality disorders]
Cognitive behavior therapy of DSM 5 personality disorders : assessment, case conceptualization, and treatment / by Len Sperry & Jon Sperry.—
Third edition.
        pages cm
    Revision of: Cognitive behavior therapy of DSM-IV-TR personality disorders. 2nd ed. c2006.
    Includes bibliographical references and index.
    1. Personality disorders—Treatment.   2. Cognitive therapy.
I. Sperry, Jonathan J., author.   II. Title.
    RC554.S67 2016
    616.89'1425—dc23

ISBN: 978-0-415-84188-7 (hbk)
ISBN: 978-0-415-84189-4 (pbk)
ISBN: 978-0-203-76408-4 (ebk)

Typeset in Goudy
by Apex CoVantage, LLC

Printed and bound in the United States of America by Publishers Graphics, LLC on sustainably sourced paper.

11/17/16

Contents

Foreword

In 1998, in preparation for the publication of the first edition of his book on the Cognitive Behavioral treatment of personality disorders, Len Sperry both honored me and flattered me by asking me to write a foreword for the volume. I was, at first, in doubt if I could add anything useful and worthwhile. When I was able to read the manuscript, I was even more apprehensive. I regarded it as a *tour de force* in the treatment of this difficult and stigmatized group of patients. Len demonstrated his understanding of the population that was, at that time, grouped on Axis II of the DSM multi-axial diagnostic system. The first edition was comprehensive, focused, and clinically useful for the experienced CBT therapist, the general therapist, the novice therapist, and the student therapist. He offered a sound theoretical base, a conceptual framework for the treatment, and both treatment strategies and techniques for navigating the always challenging therapy of Axis II patients. I was hyperbolic in my statement in the foreword that this book "may just set the standard for other treatment texts."

In 2006, Len published a second edition and asked me to write a foreword. How could I say "no" to such an opportunity to be part of this project? I was wrong! In this second edition, Len demonstrated an even greater sophistication in challenging the therapeutic myth that these patients whose problems are coded on Axis II or include an Axis II component, are untreatable. This convenient excuse for therapeutic laziness, failure or disruption is made untenable because Len shows how to do the therapy. I recently asked a seminar group of 100 professionals that I was teaching about the treatment of individuals whose problems fell primarily in the Cluster B continuum whether they would rather have to inform parents that (a) their child was severely autistic, (b) severely intellectually delayed, or (c) had a Borderline Personality Disorder (BPD) (Yes, DSM-5 accepts the diagnosis for children.) The vast majority listed BPD as the most difficult to share and to then try to treat. It demonstrated the stigmatization, the lack of understanding, the lack of motivation, and the lack of skills for many professionals. A careful reading of treatment volumes on personality disorders would be most helpful. To the question, which ones should I read, Len Sperry's work is tops on the list as an integrated source. (With all due humility the volume by Beck, Freeman, and Davis [2004] is a strong second choice.)

Drs. Len and Jon Sperry have taken the reviews and critiques of the first two volumes and written a highly readable, useable, and valuable third edition. They have asked me to write a forward for the third edition. It may be like wearing your lucky tee-shirt when your favorite team is playing in the play-offs. Now what can I say? I have already praised the first two volumes. What superlatives can I use here? They have included the most up-to-date research in evidence-based treatment that demonstrate that focused treatment is effective. They have left few excuses for excluding the patient whose problems revolve around or are centered on personality disorders. They have expanded the treatment arsenal to include the contemporary CBT treatments involving mindfulness, Schema Therapy, Dialectical Behavior Therapy, and more traditional CT approaches. Len and Jon have still included their Adlerian roots in the process. They have structured and even call this volume a "hands-on" manual. It is certainly that and more.

I would still rate this newest contribution as one of the best sources for treatment work with patients suffering with personality disorders. I am still honored and flattered that they have given me the opportunity to be part of this project.

Art Freeman, EdD

Preface

Clinicians regularly encounter individuals with personality disorders. Some 50 percent of those evaluated in clinical settings meet criteria for a personality disorder (Zimmerman, Rothschild, & Chelminski, 2005), as do 10 percent of the general public (Torgersen, 2009). These disorders can greatly disrupt an individual's work, family, and social relationships. They are associated with high rates of family conflict, separation, divorce, child custody proceedings, job termination, homelessness, substance abuse, violence, and criminal behavior. The presence of a personality disorder complicates co-occurring medical conditions, as well as the prognosis of other mental disorders. They are associated with poor treatment compliance, increased use of medical and psychiatric services, and the likelihood of relapse and premature termination (Skodol, Bender, Gunderson, & Oldham, 2014). Needless to say, treating these disorders can be extraordinarily challenging, and sometimes exasperating, for clinicians.

The first edition of *Cognitive Behavior Therapy of the DSM-IV Personality Disorders* (1999) broke new ground as the first single-authored text to address the diagnosis, case conceptualization, and treatment of the DSM personality disorders from a cognitive behavior therapy perspective. It differed from other CBT books by offering a brief but thorough, user-friendly resource for clinicians and trainees in planning and implementing effective treatment of the most common personality disorders encountered in an outpatient setting. The second edition of *Cognitive Behavior Therapy of the DSM-IV-TR Personality Disorders* (2006) incorporated additional resources for diagnosing, planning and implementing effective CBT interventions. The third edition of *Cognitive Behavior Therapy of the DSM-5 Personality Disorders* promises to continue this tradition of user-friendliness and clinical utility. As in previous editions, this edition emphasizes case conceptualization and tailored CBT treatment interventions for Avoidant, Borderline, Dependent, Histrionic, Narcissistic, and Obsessive-Compulsive personality disorders. These are the most common personality disorders seen in clinical practice today.

A caveat about DSM-5. Major changes were expected in how DSM-5 would characterize the personality disorders. However, when it appeared in May, 2013, the same disorders and criteria from the previous edition were retained. The few specific DSM-5 changes involving the personality disorders, including an Alternate Model, are discussed in Chapter 1. Despite these minimal changes in DSM-5, clinical practice and the demands on clinicians have changed significantly since DSM-IV first appeared.

In fact, several exciting developments in both research and in clinical practice have occurred since the second edition of this book appeared. Many of these represent highly effective evidence-based practices. The timing of these developments could not be better. They come just at the time in this era of accountability when therapists are increasingly expected to provide evidence-based treatment to all their clients and patients, including those who are personality-disordered. Fortunately, research increasingly demonstrates that focused psychotherapeutic interventions are effective in the treatment of these disorders. In the past decade, several new treatment interventions and strategies for effecting changes with these disorders are available to clinicians.

Whereas it was once assumed that treatment even of milder personality disorders required years of intensive psychotherapy, published case reports and even prospective studies are indicating that shorter term treatment can be effective even with severe disorders, including borderline personality. Still, some clinicians remain convinced that most personality disorders are untreatable. A recently published prospective study greatly challenges that belief (Zanarini, Frankenburg, Reich, & Fitzmaurice, 2010). It followed nearly 300 individuals diagnosed and treated for borderline personality disorder over a 10-year period. The main results were that 87 percent achieved symptom remission and 50 percent achieved total recovery. This means that they no longer met diagnostic criteria for this disorder and were functioning reasonably well in daily life!

Other clinicians are more optimistic, yet are not aware of or do not utilize the best available evidence-based interventions that are proven to be effective. It has been observed that "[t]herapeutic nihilism has yielded to widespread, but very inconsistent, use of the spectrum of potentially valuable treatment modalities" (Skodol, Bender, Gunderson, & Oldham, 2014, p. 868). In contrast, clinicians who are aware of and do utilize the best available evidence-based treatments increase the likelihood of successful treatment among individuals with these disorders.

This book describes the most recent developments in the treatment of personality disorders from a cognitive behavioral perspective. It focuses on how clinicians can increase their effectiveness and efficacy in working with personality disordered individuals by adopting a focused and tailored treatment strategy. A basic premise underlying this book is that the most effective treatment is tailored treatment that is focused on both the stylistic or temperament dimensions and the schematic or character dimensions of personality and the degree of severity of the disorder.

This new edition emphasizes the increasing applicability and effectiveness of a variety of evidence-based cognitive and behavioral interventions with personality disordered individuals. These include: Cognitive Therapy,

Schema Therapy, Cognitive Behavioral Analysis System of Psychotherapy, Mindfulness-Based Cognitive Therapy, and Dialectical Behavior Therapy.

The book is intended as a "hands-on" manual for practicing clinicians as well as clinicians-in-training. It offers clinicians a hopeful perspective on the treatability of these disorders and provides highly effective treatment protocols for achieving positive treatment outcomes. We trust it will make a difference in the lives of those who are afflicted with these disorders.

Len Sperry
Jon Sperry

Part I

Cognitive Behavior Therapy and Personality Disorders

1   Cognitive Behavior Therapy and Personality Disorders

Basic Considerations

Whether or not clinicians are comfortable ascribing paradigm shift language to clinical practice, there is no denying that major changes in the treatment of the personality disorders have and are occurring. These changes involve not only radically different treatment methods, but also rather different perspectives, conceptualizations, criteria, and assessment methods. Many of these changes are based on clinical research on the personality disorders that has greatly increased in the past decade. This chapter begins by identifying a number of changes in conceptualizing, classifying, and treating the personality disorders. Then, it describes the four-stage treatment model that is basic to the evidence-based approach advocated in this book. Finally, it provides an overview of the remaining chapters of the book.

Changes in Conceptualizing Personality Disorders

Before 1980, personality disorders were typically conceptualized in "character language," such as the oral character or obsessive character. Although there was a biological tradition in the study of personality that emphasized temperament, the psychological tradition that emphasized character was in vogue for most of the 20th century. Descriptions of personality disorders in DSM-I and DSM-II reflected this emphasis on character and psychodynamics. Within the psychoanalytic community, character reflected specific defense mechanisms. Accordingly, from a character perspective, the obsessive-compulsive personality would be characterized by the defenses of isolation of affect, intellectualization, and rationalization.

Currently, personality disorders are conceptualized in a broader perspective that includes both character *and* temperament (Cloninger, Svrakic, & Przybeck, 1993; Stone, 1993). *Character* refers to the learned, psychosocial influences on personality. Character forms largely because of the socialization process, particularly regarding cooperativeness, and the mirroring process that promotes the development of self-concept and a sense of purpose in life (i.e., self-transcendence and self-responsibility).

Temperament refers to the innate, genetic, and constitutional influences on personality. Whereas character and schema reflect the psychological dimension of personality, temperament, or trait (or style, as it is used synonymously in this book) reflects the biological dimension of personality. Cloninger (2004) contends that temperament has four biological dimensions (novelty-seeking, harm-avoidance, reward-dependence, and persistence), whereas character has three quantifiable dimensions (self-directedness or self-responsibility, cooperativeness, and self-transcendence). Other researchers would describe impulsivity and aggressivity as additional dimensions of temperament (Costello, 1996). Another widely known of the temperament-based models is the Five Factor Model with its trait dimensions of neuroticism, extraversion, openness, agreeableness, and conscientiousness (Costa & McCrae, 1990). Section III of the DSM-5 provides a dimensional approach to the personality disorders that is based on these and other models. It consists of five temperament domains: negative affectivity, detachment, antagonism, disinhibition, and psychoticism (American Psychiatric Association, 2013). Accordingly, from a temperament perspective, the obsessive-compulsive personality would be characterized by inhibited emotional expression, behavioral inhibition, cognitive rigidity, and overconscientiousness.

Temperament and character can be assessed by interviews and self-report instruments. The relevance of distinguishing character and temperament for treatment planning is significant. Whereas insight-oriented psychotherapy might be focused on the character dimensions, psychotherapy can have little or no impact on temperament dimensions. However, the addition of focused skill training may sufficiently regulate or modulate temperament or style features such as emotional dysregulation, impulsivity, and distress intolerance.

Changes in the Classification of Personality Disorders

The DSM diagnostic system has undergone some major changes since the second edition of this book was published in 1996. Most of these changes have involved adding or removing diagnoses and criteria. These will be described in subsequent chapters. However, there are also some major changes in the structure of the DSM-5 (American Psychiatric Association, 2013), and these are briefly noted here.

The most obvious change in DSM-5 is the return to a single-axis diagnosis as it was in DSM-I and DSM-II. The multiaxial (5-axes) system was introduced in DSM-III and continued through DSM-IV-TR. Of particular relevance for the personality disorders were Axis II and Axis V. Axis II was added for the coding of personality disorders, while Axis V was added for coding the individual's current level of functioning and impairment on the Global Assessment of Functioning Scale. There were several reasons for eliminating the multi-axial system. Among these was an unexpected drawback to adding Axis II. The opportunity to specify a diagnosis of a personality disorder became problematic for many clinicians. Out of concern that the diagnosis of a personality disorder would stigmatize an individual, some clinicians refused to specify an Axis II diagnosis when it was present. This was complicated by the mistaken notion among therapists and third-party payors that personality disorders were untreatable. As a result, some individuals who were diagnosed with personality disorders encountered problems securing treatment. Today, however, individuals who met the criteria for a personality disorder diagnosis may now find it easier to navigate mental health treatment, since they are less likely to be viewed as having a diagnosis that is more difficult to treat than of other disorders.

By eliminating Axis V, the Global Assessment of Functioning (GAF) score is gone. GAF was the numeric measure used by clinicians to rate an individual's social, occupational, and psychological functioning and well-being. It is a subjective measure of the degree of adaptivity (well-being) or maladaptivity (impaired functioning) an individual demonstrates in dealing with various problems-in-living. In place of this largely unreliable measure of functioning and impairment, DSM-5 encourages the use of the World Health Organization Disability Assessment Schedule 2.0 (WHODAS 2.0). Nevertheless, GAF continues to be used by some clinicians. It provides a continuum (1–lowest to 100–highest) on which to rate overall functioning and well-being.

Clinicians can also utilize the *Level of Personality Functioning Scale* (LPFS) that is included on pages 775–778 in Section III of DSM-5 (American Psychiatric Association, 2013). The LPFS is an objective measure for quickly and accurately determining the presence of a personality disorder. It is described in detail in Chapter 2 and used throughout this book in all case examples.

Major changes were expected in how DSM-5 would characterize the personality disorders. It was anticipated that at least four of the DSM-IV-TR personality disorders would be dropped purportedly because of limited research support. In addition, the diagnosis of all personality disorders were expected to shift to a dimensional focus, rather than categorical focus as it had been in previous editions. However, when DSM-5 appeared in May 2013, the same criteria found in DSM-IV-TR were retained, and the anticipated changes appeared in Section III in a chapter entitled "Alternative DSM-5 Model for Personality Disorders." It appears that this, or some version of the "Alternative Model," may be incorporated in subsequent editions (DSM-5.1 or 5.2). For now, clinicians are expected to continue using the same criteria and the categorical method of making diagnoses to which they are already familiar. However, they have the option of using the alternate criteria specified in Section III.

Also retained in DSM-5 was the earlier DSM definition of a personality disorder as an "enduring patterns of inner experience and behaviors that deviate markedly from the expectations of the individual's culture, is pervasive and inflexible . . . is stable over time, and leads to distress or impairment" (American Psychiatric Association, 2013, p. 645). While previous diagnostic criteria have been retained, there has been some updating of description of the various disorders. However, there is one substantive change. The diagnosis of Personality Disorder Not Otherwise Specified (NOS) has been replaced with Other Specified Personality Disorder (301.89) and Unspecified Personality Disorder (301.9).

Changes in the Treatment of Personality Disorders

In comparison to previous approaches to generic treatment of personality, treatment methods today tend to be considerably more focused and structured, with the clinician taking a more active role. Many of these treatment approaches and intervention strategies are theory-based and have been researched in clinical trials in comparison with other treatment approaches and modalities.

Cognitive Behavior Therapies

For the last three decades, Behavior Therapy, Cognitive Therapy, and Cognitive Behavior Therapy (CBT) were the treatment of choice for the psychosocial treatment of personality disorders. While research did not consistently support the efficacy of these traditional approaches, it has for newer, more focused approaches such as Dialectical Behavior Therapy (DBT) and Mindfulness-Based Cognitive Therapy (MBCT). Interestingly, DBT and MBCT, along with Acceptance and Commitment Therapy (Hayes, 2004), constitute what is being called the "third wave" of Behavior Therapy (Hayes, Follette, & Linehan, 2004).

The first wave refers to traditional Behavior Therapy, which endeavors to replace problematic behaviors with constructive ones through counterconditioning and reinforcement. Cognitive therapy is the second wave of Behavior Therapy. It works to modify problem behaviors by changing the thoughts that cause and perpetuate them. In the third wave, treatment tends to be more experiential and indirect and utilize techniques such as mindfulness, dialectics, acceptance, values, and spirituality. More specifically, third wave approaches are characterized by "letting go of the attempts at problems solving, and instead standing back to see what it feels like to see the problems through the lens of non-reactivity, and to bring a kindly awareness to the difficulty" (Segal, Williams, Teasdale, & Williams, 2004, p. 55). Unlike the first and second wave, third wave approaches emphasize second-order change, i.e., basic change in structure and/or function, and are based on contextual assumptions including the primacy of the therapeutic relationship. These approaches appear to be particularly germane to treating personality disorders. Extended discussions of standard DBT and Radically Open DBT in the treatment of a wide range of personality disorders appears in Chapters 2 and 4 and are selectively referenced in Chapters 5–10.

Medication

Traditionally, the use of medication in the treatment of personality disorders was viewed as limited. Medication tended to be utilized only for a concurrent clinical disorder such as Bipolar Disorder or a target symptom like insomnia. This view is rapidly changing. Today, a growing number of psychopharmacologists believe that psychopharmacological treatment can and should be directed to basic dimensions that underlie the personality. Psychopharmacological research on treatment of selected personality disorders has grown rapidly in the past few years (Reich, 2002; Sperry, 2003). Until recently, medication treatment of personality-disordered individuals has been largely empirical, that is largely trial and error. The reason is that there are still no specific drug treatments for DSM-5 personality disorders except for avoidant and borderline personality disorder (Black et al., 2014; Silk & Fuerino, 2013).

Combined Treatment

There is growing consensus, among all segments of the mental health community, that effective treatment of the personality disorders involves combining treatment modalities and integrating treatment approaches (Sperry, 2006). In many treatment centers, this means individual therapy is combined with group therapy or psychoeducation groups, and it may include medication or other modalities. Combining medication with individual and group modalities tends to increase effectiveness. Such efforts to integrate various approaches, as well as to combine treatment modalities, would have been considered heretical just a few years ago. Now, integrating and combining treatments is an emerging consensus that reflects the immensity of the "paradigm shift" that is occurring (Beitman et al., 2003; Sperry, 2003).

An Effective Treatment Strategy

The treatment strategy proposed in this book is rather straightforward. Treatment must be specifically planned with regard to the four stages of the treatment process, and it must be specifically tailored on the basis of the individual's needs, style, level of readiness, and expectations of treatment. This section describes the stages of the treatment process and tailoring treatment.

Stages of the Treatment Process

The process of change and the types of interventions required for the effective treatment of the personality disorders is similar to the general therapeutic processes and interventions used with symptom disorders, but it differs in focus and emphasis. Beitman (1991; Good & Beitman, 2006) has articulated the general change processes and compatible interventions in both psychotherapy and psychopharmacotherapy. The Beitman model articulates four developmental stages of the treatment process: engagement, pattern search, change, and termination. As applied to the treatment of personality disorders, these stages need to be somewhat modified. The stages of engagement, pattern identification, pattern change, and pattern maintenance are described below and will be illustrated in subsequent chapters with regard to specific personality disorders.

Engagement

Engagement is the principal therapeutic process in the early phase of treatment. Engagement requires the individual to trust, respect, and accept the influence of the provider. The building of trust and respect results in psychological connection and commitment. The provider's empathic stance toward the individual is essential in establishing a working therapeutic relationship or therapeutic bond. Engagement is a prelude to psychotherapy and psychopharmacotherapy, and until it is achieved, little if any change is possible. This is not to say that unengaged individuals will not attend sessions—they might—but there is little likelihood that any positive movement will occur. One early indication that engagement has been achieved is the individual's willingness to collaborate and take increasing responsibility for making necessary changes in their lives.

By definition, collaboration means that both parties, not just one, take responsibility. It is for this reason that, from the very outset, the clinician must ensure that the first task of treatment is to develop a collaborative working relationship. In such a relationship, both clinician and individual agree to focus their energies on the same treatment goals and objectives. It is the individual's responsibility to pursue the mutually agreed on goals and objectives. And, when individuals sidestep or move away from an agreed upon goal, it is the clinician's responsibility to confront the diversion. Therapeutic confrontation is used to return to the treatment goal and refocus the individual on the here and now of the therapeutic transaction. The clinician might say: "Wait a minute! What's going on between us that influenced how *we* ended up here? *We* agreed to work on ____. What happened?" Emphasizing "we" is crucial in a collaborative effort because both need to accept responsibility. Typically, the manner in which the borderline individual deviates and moves away from the agreed-on treatment goal or objective then becomes the focus itself. Thoughts or discussion about a troubling relationship or a failure to achieve personal goals will result in a move away from goal to the extent they feel threatened. The clinician processes the focus sufficiently until goals are sufficiently realigned. By definition, personality-disordered individuals find it difficult to cooperate and collaborate, much less take responsibility for their own behavior.

Engagement involves a socialization process that culminates in a formal or informal treatment contract and includes elements such as fee, length of sessions, duration of treatment, and education about the treatment process. Even more important is clarification and negotiation of expectations, goals, and role behaviors and responsibilities for both the individual and clinician for the treatment process.

A critical task of the engagement stage is to assess the individual's readiness and motivation for treatment and, if necessary, increase it. Five levels of readiness for change can be noted (Prochaska & DiClementi, 1982). They are *precontemplation*, which means the individual denies illness or any need for treatment; *contemplation*, which means that though the individual accepts that they have an illness and may need treatment for it, they have not decided to make changes; *determination*, which means that the individual is planning on making changes but has not started the behavior change process; *action*, which means the individual has decided to and has begun making changes; and *maintenance*, which means sustaining the change and preventing relapse. Low readiness for treatment is noted in precontemplation and contemplation. It will be reflected in treatment resistance and noncompliance in various ways: missing or coming late for appointments, failure to take medication or complete intersession assignment, or minimal or no progress in treatment. If the individual does not possess sufficient treatment readiness, the provider's task is to focus on the readiness issue before proceeding with formal psychotherapy or psychopharmacotherapy. Motivational counseling is a potent strategy for increasing readiness for change (Miller & Rollnick, 2013).

Predictably, transference and countertransference issues emerge in the engagement stage in subtle and not-so-subtle ways. This is particularly true in the treatment of personality-disordered individuals. In the following chapter, transference and countertransference issues for specific personality disorders are noted along with suggested intervention strategies.

Pattern Analysis

Pattern identification involves the elucidation of the individual's maladaptive pattern that reflects their manner of thinking, acting, feeling, coping, and defending self. In the context of this book, *pattern analysis* refers to the individual's specific schemas or characterological features, styles or temperament features, pattern triggers, and levels of functioning and readiness for change. Various assessment strategies can be used to specify the pattern. These include a functional evaluation interview, personality testing, and the elicitation of early recollection or core schemas. To the extent that the clinician understands and appreciates this formulation—particularly the predisposing factors and perpetuating factors unique to the individual—confrontation tactics, interpretations, cognitive restructuring, and behavioral interventions will tend to be more focused and efficacious.

Pattern Change

The purpose of defining underlying maladaptive patterns is to modify or change them. With personality-disordered individuals, the therapeutic change focus must, of necessity, include both schemas and styles. The treatment goal and process of therapeutic change involves three tasks: (a) the disordered or maladaptive pattern is relinquished; (b) a more adaptive pattern is adopted; and (c) the new pattern is generalized—thoughts, feelings, and actions—and maintained. The general treatment strategy is to effect sufficient change or modulation in styles *before* attempting to change or modify schemas. Specific strategies for pattern change target specific disordered styles and schemas.

Disordered or maladaptive schemas are enduring, inflexible, and pervasive core beliefs about self and the world that greatly impact thoughts, beliefs, and behaviors. The goal of treatment is to effect some measure of change in these beliefs such that they are more flexible and functional. Treatment can either restructure, modify, or reinterpret schemas (Layden, Newman, Freeman, & Morse, 1993).

Disordered styles are either undermodulated or overmodulated, and the goal of treatment is to achieve some measure of modulation. The styles are unmodulated both because of temperament and failure to learn sufficient self-control. Self-control involves a number of personal and interpersonal skills necessary to function in day-to-day circumstances with some degree of competence. It is necessary to teach the individual the concept of modulation in the context of overmodulation and undermodulation. *Modulation* is the state in which thought precedes action, in which spontaneity is experienced without pretense or exaggeration, and in which coping with problems can lead to effective and responsible behavior.

Needless to say, many personality-disordered individuals never adequately learned these skills during their formative years. Thus, it is often necessary to reverse these specific skill deficits in the context of treatment. Either within an individual or group treatment context, these skills are learned and practiced.

Pattern Maintenance

As the new pattern becomes fixed in the individual's life, the issue of preventing relapse and recurrence needs to be addressed. As formal treatment sessions become less necessary, the issue of termination becomes the therapeutic focus. The elements of the termination process are relatively predictable when contrasted with the wide range of possibilities inherent in the pattern identification and change stages. Individuals—and providers—often have difficulty with separation. New symptoms or old ones may appear, prompting requests for additional sessions. Presumably, when difficulty with separation or abandonment is noted in the maladaptive pattern, treatment will have focused on this issue (Good & Beitman, 2006).

Overview of the Book

This book is divided into two parts. Part I introduces the reader to the paradigm shift that is occurring in the treatment of the personality disorders today. The four chapters in Part I provide the reader with an understanding and appreciation of CBT theory and interventions.

Part II describes an integrative and practical approach to the treatment of six personality disorders that are most commonly seen in clinical practice. These include the Avoidant, Borderline, Dependent, Histrionic, Narcissistic, and Obsessive-Compulsive. They are also considered the most treatable of the personality disorders. Treatability means that not only can these six disorders be effectively managed in outpatient settings, but in some instances might even be cured. The four remaining DSM-5 disorders (Schizoid, Schizotypal, Paranoid, and Antisocial personality disorders) are considered to be less treatable and less commonly seen in outpatient settings. Accordingly, they are not included in this edition. In short, the most common personality disorders seen in an outpatient setting are also the ones that are most treatable, and these six disorders are detailed in Part II.

There is a common outline of the six chapters in Part II. It provides the reader a "map" to compare the treatment process and its various phases across the various disorders. Although this new edition emphasizes the usefulness and effectiveness of cognitive-behavioral interventions in the context of individual treatment, various other modalities and intervention strategies are also described. These include medication, group therapy and other group interventions, family interventions, and couples therapy. Case material illustrates the process of treatment for each of these six disorders.

Here is the common outline for Chapters 5–10:

A. **Assessment**

  1. Behavioral
  2. Cognitive
  3. DSM-5 Description
  4. Prototypic Description

B. **Case Conceptualization**

C. **Treatment**

  1. **Engagement Strategies**

     Early Session Behavior
     Facilitating Collaboration
     Transference and Countertransference

  2. **Pattern Analysis Strategies**

     Triggers
     Schemas
     Style/Temperament

  3. **Pattern Change Strategies**

     Schema Change
     CBASP Strategies
     Style-Skill Change
     Medication
     Group Treatment
     Marital and Family
     Combined and Integrative

  4. **Pattern Maintenance and Termination Strategies**

     Termination Issues
     Relapse Prevention Strategies

D. **Case Example**

The first section, "Assessment," provides the key Behavioral and Cognitive features of the specific disorder. It gives the DSM-5 Description of each disorder as well as a Prototypical Description. A prototype is a brief description that captures the essence of how a particular disorder most commonly presents. Readers wanting further information are referred to the *Handbook of Diagnosis and Treatment of DSM-5 Personality Disorders, Third Edition* (Sperry, in press).

The second section, "Case Conceptualization," provides common Cognitive Therapy, Behavior Therapy, and other CBT conceptualizations for the disorder.

The third section, "Treatment," describes the treatment process and effective strategies for treating each of the personality disorders considered amenable to treatment. Engagement, pattern identification, pattern change, and pattern maintenance refer to the stages of the treatment process from which specific effective strategies have been derived to guide treatment.

The subsection on "Engagement" describes relationship factors that are likely to be encountered with individuals manifesting this disorder. Specific behaviors that are likely to be manifest in the initial session are described. Specific challenges that the clinician must face in facilitating a working alliance or therapeutic collaboration are noted, as well as the most common transferences and countertransferences.

The subsection on "Pattern Analysis Strategies" describes optimal criteria, schemas, and style/skills dimensions for each disorder. The optimal single criterion for each disorder is given. Obviously, the diagnosis of personality disorders would be easier if clinicians had only one criterion to remember for each personality disorder. *Schemas* refer to the individual's core beliefs about self and world. Schemas reflect the characterological dimension of the disorder. *Style* refers to the temperament or stylistic dimension of the personality disorder, whereas *skills* refer to the type and level of self-regulation skills and social skills and skill deficits most characteristic of a particular personality disorder.

The subsection on "Pattern Change Strategies" describes several therapeutic interventions and methods for changing schemas or modifying characterological dimensions of the particular disorder. It also provides a number of treatment methods for modifying the stylistic or temperament dimensions that are under- or overmodulated for a given disorder. Typically, treatment is initially directed at modulating or regulating dysregulated dimensions of temperament that increase the individual's readiness and availability to engage in therapeutic change directed at a character dimension of the disorder. Finally, other modalities that are useful and necessary for treatment effectiveness are briefly described.

The subsection on "Pattern Maintenance and Termination Strategies" offers specific suggestions and directions on terminating the treatment process and preventing relapse. Although premature termination is common among personality-disordered individuals, it is less common when treatment is tailored. Nevertheless, planned termination of treatment is particularly difficult with certain personality disorders. More so than with symptom disorders, a tailored relapse prevention plan is an absolutely essential treatment strategy with personality disorders.

The "Case Example" section translates the many concepts, insights, and strategies previously described into clinical practice. An in-depth case example illustrates how engagement strategies, pattern analysis strategies, pattern change strategies, and pattern maintenance and termination strategies were used in an actual case. These are actual cases. Therefore, to ensure confidentiality, details of each case have been modified.

Summary

This chapter has described a number of developments—which some consider a paradigmatic shift—occurring in the treatment of the personality disorders today. This discussion has emphasized changes in the conceptualization, classification—including the DSM-5 changes, and treatment of the personality disorders. Conceptualizing and assessing personality disorders in terms of the dual dimensions of character and temperament set the stage for introducing the cognitive-behavioral approach to schema or character change and style or temperament change. The chapter then delineated a four-stage treatment approach—engagement, pattern analysis, pattern change, and pattern maintenance. Finally, it described the remaining chapters of the book, emphasizing Chapters 5–10.

2 Cognitive Behavior Therapy and Personality Disorders
Assessment, Case Conceptualization, and Treatment

In this age of accountability, effective clinical practice presumes that clinicians will conduct a focused clinical assessment and develop a case conceptualization based on it. This case conceptualization becomes the basis for making treatment decisions and implementing interventions tailored to the individual's need and expectations. This expectation of accountability holds for all clinicians including those working with difficult-to-treat individuals—such as those with personality disorders.

This chapter describes the clinical value of a comprehensive Cognitive Behavioral assessment. The first section focuses on the dimensions of a functional assessment. The next section delineates the components and elements of an integrative Cognitive Behavioral case conceptualization. The clinical value of a compelling case conceptualization is in serving as a "bridge" connecting assessment to treatment. Finally, the third section describes how treatment interventions are selected to achieve specific treatment targets. The overall goal of the integrative Cognitive Behavioral Therapy (CBT) approach described here is in achieving positive clinical outcomes in the personality-disordered individuals most commonly treated in outpatient settings. Case material illustrates the discussion.

Assessment

Effective treatment of personality-disordered individuals is greatly aided by a comprehensive assessment. Typically, this will include a diagnostic assessment, which leads to a DSM-5 diagnosis or diagnoses, and a focused functional assessment (Sperry, Carlson, & Kjos, 2003). At a minimum, such an assessment will specify behavior excesses and deficits, strengths, protective factors and risk factors, and level of functioning. A clinically useful functional assessment identifies the individual's maladaptive pattern, which includes both maladaptive cognitions and schemas, and temperament or style dimensions. Its purpose is to inform the case conceptualization and to establish treatment targets. The following case material illustrates the clinical value of a comprehensive functional assessment.

Clinical Illustration

Two individuals presented for clinical treatment at the same time. Both were attractive single females in their late twenties. Both were college graduates, both had similar presenting complaints, and both had the same diagnosis: Borderline Personality Disorder. Beyond these commonalities, there were some identifiable differences. Most notable were the vastly different treatment interventions that were selected as appropriate and effective with one but not with the other.

Keri Andrews

Ms. Andrews was brought to the emergency room of a local hospital by her boyfriend with agitation, dysphoria, and a laceration to her left wrist. Apparently, her boyfriend was late in returning from an out-of-town business trip and Keri, thinking he was never going to show up for the candlelight dinner she had prepared for him, became increasingly agitated, believing he was out with another woman, and slashed her left wrist. He arrived at her apartment 20 minutes later and immediately transported her to the nearest hospital emergency room. This was only the second time in her life that this 28-year-old woman had acted out impulsively. Three years ago she had also lacerated her wrist in similar circumstances with a previous boyfriend. She reported a stable work history for the past 6 years following college graduation. Recently, she was promoted to district manager. Keri described having four relatively close friends, including her roommate, whom she had known since her college days. She reportedly relates well with her coworkers, including her male boss. Although she maintains regular contact with her family, she admits that her relationship with her mother is sometimes strained. Her Global Assessment Functioning score on admission was 40, with the highest level in the past year estimated at 71. In the emergency room, she received a sedative and had her wrist sutured.

Table 2.1 maps four style or temperament dimensions and two functional dimensions. These dimensions are described in detail in the next subsection.

Table 2.1 Keri: Functional Assessment and Style Profile

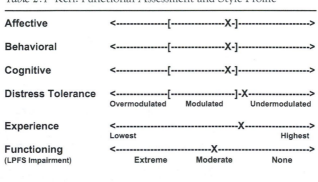

KEY:
[----------] = modulated or optimal range of Well-Being
(LPFS Impairment) = assessed with *Level of Personality Functioning Scale (LPFS)*

For now, it is notable that Keri is assessed as falling in the optimal control range, with only distress tolerance in the overcontrol range. This assessment reflects that while Keri is for the most part able to control or modulate her feelings, behavior, and thought processes, she is sensitive to certain negative emotional states, i.e., abandonment fears, for which she is relatively intolerant and which resulted in her self-harming behavior.

Cindy Jansen

Ms. Jansen also presented in the emergency room with wrist lacerations. She had been brought in by an ambulance called by her landlady. Apparently, after having her social security disability check stolen from her mail box and being "dumped"—her words—by her off-again, on-again boyfriend, she proceeded to get drunk and slash both her wrists. In the emergency room, she was so angry and combative that she had to be restrained while her wrists were being sutured. Medical records showed she had a long history of episodes of psychiatric treatment with three psychiatrists and two social workers, including various medication trials and three prior suicide attempts (two involving overdosing on prescribed antidepressants). Compliance with those appointments during those episodes of care as well as compliance with prescribed medications was poor. She noted that following graduation from college—after 7 years of trying various majors—she worked at several jobs. In most of the positions she held, she was underemployed, particularly in the past 3 years. She had started receiving social security disability some 18 months before her latest suicide attempt. She indicated that she had never really gotten along with her family, except for her father. Although she felt quite close to him as a child, he became increasingly emotionally distant from her during her adolescence and continuing to the present. She reported having no real friends, and, except for a small dog, feels rejected by everybody. In the emergency room, her Global Assessment Functioning score was estimated to be 28, with her highest level in the previous year at 42.

In terms of six style and functional dimensions in Table 2.2, it is noted that, unlike Keri, Cindy has been assessed as falling in the undercontrol range on all

Table 2.2 Cindy: Functional Assessment and Style Profile

	Overmodulated	Modulated	Undermodulated
Affective	<------------[------------------]-------------X----->		
Behavioral	<------------[------------------]-------------X----->		
Cognitive	<------------[------------------]-------------X----->		
Distress Tolerance	<------------[------------------]-------------X----->		

	Lowest		Highest
Experience	<----X-->		

	Extreme	Moderate	None
Functioning (LPFS Impairment)	<----------X-->		

four style dimensions. This means that besides having considerable difficulty controlling her feelings, behaviors, cognitions, she is also highly intolerant of emotional distress in her life. Because of her very low ratings on learning from past experiences and her overall functioning in non-distressing situations, it is not surprising that her clinical presentation is more acute and serious than Keri's presentation. The Case Conceptualization and Treatment sections of this chapter will continue this discussion of the treatment interventions selected for both Keri and Cindy. For now it can be said that the therapy planned for Cindy is considerably different than the therapy planned for Keri.

In short, both women shared some demographic similarities including meeting diagnostic criteria for Borderline Personality Disorder. Nevertheless, their clinical histories and results of functional assessments were quite different. Most notable are the extent of differences on affective style, behavioral style, cognitive style, distress tolerance, and the functional capacity to learn from experience, However, as each case illustrate, knowledge of the DSM diagnosis alone would be of little value in making key treatment decisions. Instead, these cases highlight the clinical value of assessing style and functional dimensions.

The Dimensions of a Functional Assessment

While some individuals are rather consistently anxious and worrisome, others are commonly relaxed and carefree. Some are consistently withdrawn while others are typically outgoing. Such enduring traits reflect an individual's unique temperament or traits, or, as some researchers refer to them, "temperament traits," a designation that reflects the predominance of a biological basis or heritability. For example, genetic studies indicate that impulsivity has an 80% heritability rate (Crowell, Beachaine, & Linehan, 2009). It has also been established that temperament and traits have both a biological and an environmental basis (Paris, 2012). In this book we use the shorthand designation of "style" instead of the designation "temperament traits." Rather than describing specific emotions, behaviors, or thoughts, these styles reflect what individuals "are like most every day throughout much of their lives" (Widiger, 2012, p. 13).

Currently, personality disorders are being conceptualized as including both temperament and character. Neurobiological and biosocial formulations of personality disorders have increasingly attracted attention among clinicians and researchers and have generated a considerable amount of research as well. Millon (1996) and Cloninger, Svrakic, and Przybeck (1993) hypothesized that temperament and neurotransmitters greatly influence personality development and functioning. Like many others, both Stone (1993), a psychoanalyst, and Cloninger (2004), a neurobiological psychiatrist, described personality as the confluence of both character and temperament.

Character refers to the learned, psychosocial influences on personality. Character forms largely because of the socialization process, particularly regarding cooperativeness, and the mirroring process that promotes the development of self-concept and a sense of purpose in life (i.e., self-transcendence and self-responsibility). Another way of specifying the characterological component of personality is with the term *schema*. Whether in the psychoanalytic tradition (Horowitz, 1988; Slap & Slap-Shelton, 1991) or the Cognitive Therapy tradition (Beck, Davis, & Freeman, 2015; Young, Klosko, & Weishaar, 2003) schema refers to the basic beliefs individuals use to organize their view of self, the world, and the future. Whereas the centrality of schema has historically been more central to the cognitive tradition and the Cognitive Behavioral tradition than to the psychoanalytic tradition, this apparently is changing (Stein & Young, 1992). Schema and schema change and modification strategies are central to this book.

Temperament refers to the innate, genetic, and constitutional influences on personality. Whereas character and schema reflect the psychological dimension of personality, temperament (or style, as it is used synonymously in this book) reflects the biological dimension of personality. Cloninger (2004) contends that temperament has four biological dimensions (novelty-seeking, harm-avoidance, reward-dependence, and persistence), whereas character has three quantifiable dimensions (self-directedness or self-responsibility, cooperativeness, and self-transcendence). Other researchers would describe impulsivity and aggressivity as additional dimensions of temperament (Costello, 1996).

Temperament and character can be assessed by interviews and self-report instruments. The relevance of distinguishing character and temperament for treatment planning is significant. Whereas insight-oriented psychotherapy might be focused on the character dimensions, psychotherapy will have little or no impact on temperament dimensions. For example, in the case of Cindy, who exhibited high levels of emotional dysregulation and impulsivity, individual psychotherapy would be insufficient to effect change. However, the addition of focused skill training and the structured milieu of the intensive outpatient program would likely be sufficient to modulate and better control her emotions, thoughts, and behaviors so that she could then profit from individual and group therapy directed at the character dimensions. On the other hand, Keri's temperament was sufficiently modulated in three of the four style dimensions such that focused psychotherapy could be the primary treatment directed at the character issues, while distress tolerance interventions could help temper the one-style dimension that was slightly undercontrolled.

Styles tend to be polar or "either or" by nature. This means that the absence of one characteristic feature of a style implies the presence of its polarity or polar opposite. For example, the polar opposite of impulsivity is inhibition. Four styles are useful in assessing and planning treatment for individuals with personality disorders. The first three of these styles were key factors in informing treatment in the first and second edition of this book. Because of its increasing research base and clinical utility, a fourth, distress tolerance has been added to this edition. This section describes the six dimensions of what I call the ABCDEF model for assessing style and functional capacity.

A = Affective Style

Affective style is the characteristic and predicable way in which an individual reacts emotionally to situations, particularly stressful situations. Affective style is also known as emotional style. Affective style has two polarities: emotional dysregulation and emotional constriction. Emotional dysregulation occurs when individuals experience a threatening situation and react with such intense and overwhelming emotion that completely overrides their cognitive controls. In contrast, emotional constriction manifests as limited emotional expression or alexithymia, the inability to identify and label one's feelings (Taylor & Bagley, 2012).

B = Behavioral Style

Behavioral style is the characteristic and predicable way in which an individual reacts behaviorally when stressed or challenged. Interpersonal style is closely related to behavioral style and is the characteristic way an individual reacts to others. Behavioral style has two polarities: behavioral inhibition and behavioral disinhibition. Disinhibition is reduced control over one's actions and responses. In contrast, inhibition is tight control over one's actions and responses (Bo, Stringer, & Clark, 2012). The polarities of interpersonal style are social withdrawal and relational enmeshment or overinvolvement (Sperry, 2006).

C = Cognitive Style

Cognitive style is the characteristic and predicable way in which individuals gather, perceive, think about, use, and recall information. It refers to the information processes methods that are used to make the decisions rather than about the specific decisions made. Methods of problem solving are also components in cognitive style and differing cognitive styles can be used to describe different personality types. Like other style dimensions, cognitive styles have polarities. They are rigidity or inflexibility and impulsivity. Cognitive rigidity is strong resistance to changing one's attitudes and opinions. Impulsivity is the tendency to react quickly without consideration of the consequences (Bo et al., 2012). It should be noted that cognitive style differs from cognitive ability, which is measured by aptitude or intelligence tests.

D = Distress Tolerance Style

Distress tolerance style is the characteristic and predicable way individuals react to negative emotional states. It is the capacity to tolerate or withstand such negative emotion without engaging in impulsive behavior as well as persisting in goal-directed behavior despite the distress (Lynch & Mizon, 2011). Like other style dimensions, distress tolerance has two polarities: distress intolerance and distress overtolerance. Distress intolerance is the inability to withstand distress by habitually attempting to change or escape aversive emotional or physical experience, such as pain. In contrast, distress overtolerance involves tolerating high distress that results in adverse long-term consequences. For example, an employee may tolerate ongoing but inadvertent mistreatment by another employee out of fear of the consequences of objecting to it (Lynch & Mizon, 2011).

E = Experience

The first of the two functional assessment dimensions is failure to learn from experience. Failure to learn from experience is one of the key behavioral characteristics of the psychopath identified by Cleckley in his classic book, *The Mask of Sanity*, originally published in 1941 (Cleckley, 1976). The Mental Health Foundation of the United Kingdom defines personality disorders as a group of conditions characterized by an inability to get along with others and to learn from experience. Failure to learn from experience is an error in thinking that is common in young adolescents. Fortunately, most grow out of it. However, most with moderate to severe personality disorders do not outgrow it and it continues to expand to all aspects of their lives. The basic error in thinking is reflected in Albert Einstein's famous definition of "insanity" as doing the same things repeatedly and expecting different results. This inability to learn can be assessed and gradated on a continuum from low to high. Fortunately, focused psychotherapy can increase the capacity to learn from experience. Cognitive Behavioral Analysis System of Psychotherapy (CBASP) and Radically Open Dialectical Behavior Therapy are two therapeutic approaches that directly foster learning from experience.

Learning from experience should yield non-distorted outcomes that are healthy and flexible in nature. For examples, an individual learns that she can get burnt by touching a hot stove. This is an example of positive learning from experience. On the other hand, learning from experience can be maladaptive. In a treatment session, after therapeutically processing a specific issue and asked what she learned from it, the client says: "I really shouldn't trust men." In such situations, when the client's conclusion is non-therapeutic, the therapist must help the client understand the reasons for her response and then foster adaptive learning from that experience.

F = Functioning

The second functional assessment dimension is global functioning. Of the six dimensions of the ABCDEF model, this is the broadest of measures of an individual's overall functioning and well-being. It utilizes the *Level of Personality Functioning Scale* (LPFS) from Section III of DSM-5. This scale is how a clinician evaluates an individual in terms of Criteria A for determining if a personality disorder is present in the Alternate DSM-5 Model for Personality

Disorders. It consists of four components: identity, self-direction, empathy, and intimacy. There are for levels for identifying an individual's current overall level of global functioning: little or no impairment, some impairment, moderate impairment, severe impairment, and extreme impairment. A determination of at least a level of "moderate impairment" is required for a diagnosis of personality disorder. This is equivalent to a Global Assessment of Functioning (GAF) rating of 60 or below (Skodol, Bender, Gunderson, & Oldham, 2014). As noted in Chapter 1, clinicians can use the personality disorder criteria in either Section II or Section III of DSM-5. They can use the LPFS, the GAF, or the WHODAS scale that replaces the GAF in DSM-5. In this book, because "it was set empirically to maximize the ability of clinicians to identify personality disorder pathology accurately and efficiently" (Skodol et al., 2014), the LPFS is used in every case example to determine global functioning.

Styles and Self-Control

Self-control is the capacity to remain in control of one's behavior, emotions, and cognitions, while inhibiting impulses and delaying gratification (Baumeister, Vohs, & Tice, 2007). Researchers have described different types of self-control with regard to clinical disorders and personality disorders: undercontrol, optimal control, and overcontrol (Lynch & Cheavens, 2008).

These correspond to three types of modulation: undermodulation, modulation, and overmodulation. In the first and second editions of this book, styles were related to these three types of modulation. Figure 2.1 portrays the relationship of these three types of modulation to well-being. Note that modulation is situated between the extremes of undermodulated and overmodulated, and that the more modulation increases, the greater the level of well-being. This edition continues the use of undermodulation, modulation, and overmodulation, although the designations undercontrol, optimal control, and overcontrol could be used.

Table 2.3 portrays the ABCDEF model of style dimensions and functional capacity. Included are the four dimensions of style: affective style, behavioral style, cognitive style, and distress tolerance. It also includes the functional levels of experience and overall functioning.

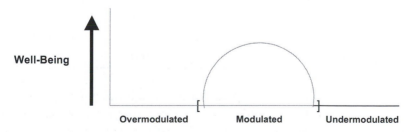

Figure 2.1 Well-Being in Relation to Types of Self-Control

Table 2.3 ABCDEF Style and Functional Assessment Profiles

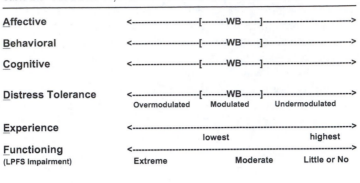

KEY:
[---WB---] = modulated or optimal range of Well-Being
ABCD = Style Assessment
EF = Functional Assessment
(LPFS Impairment) = assessed with *Level of Personality Functioning Scale (LPFS)*

Table 2.4 ABCDEF Style and Functional Assessment Profiles

Affective   <-----------------------[--------WB------]---------------------------->

                       constricted   dysregulated/labile

Behavioral   <-----------------------[--------WB------]---------------------------->

                       inhibited   uninhibited

                       withdrawn/isolative   overly involved

Cognitive   <-----------------------[--------WB------]---------------------------->

                       rigid/ruminative   impulsive

Distress Tolerance <-----------------------[--------WB------]---------------------------->

                       overtolerant   intolerant

Experience   <--->

                       lowest   highest

Functioning   <--->

(LPFS Impairment)   **Extreme**   **Moderate**   **Little or No**

Table 2.4 portrays the polar anchors for the ABCDEF model. For example, emotionally constricted represents the overcontrol end of the continuum while labile and emotionally dysregulated represents the under-controlled end.

Case Conceptualization

While the term "case conceptualization" is relatively new, Cognitive Therapy and Behavior Therapy were among the first therapeutic approaches to advocate for and to use case conceptualizations. Starting in the 1980s both Cognitive therapists and Behavior therapists used them although they were originally referred to as case formulations (Tarrier, 2006).

Common to most case conceptualization models, including the analytic, constructivists, interpersonal, psychodynamics, and systemic approaches, are the constructs of pattern and self-other schemas. This is not to suggest that all approaches to case conceptualization are the same. Actually, there are elements that are unique in every approach, as well as elements that are common among the approaches. Accordingly, a truly integrative approach to case conceptualization captures the *common elements* of the various approaches while retaining the distinctive or *approach-specific* elements of each approach (Eells, 2007, 2010).

Case Conceptualization: Diagnostic, Clinical, Cultural, and Treatment Formulations

A case conceptualization is a way of summarizing diverse information in a brief, coherent manner for the purpose of better understanding and treating of the individual. Furthermore, a case conceptualization consists of four components: diagnostic formulations, clinical formulations, cultural formulation, and treatment formulations (Sperry, 2010; Sperry & Sperry, 2012).

A *diagnostic formulation* is a descriptive statement about the nature and severity of the individual's psychiatric presentation. The diagnostic formulation aids the clinician in reaching three sets of diagnostic conclusions: whether the patient's presentation is primarily psychotic, characterological, or neurotic; whether the individual's presentation is primarily organic or psychogenic in etiology; and whether the individual's presentation is so acute and severe that it requires immediate intervention. In short, diagnostic formulations are descriptive, phenomenological, and cross-sectional in nature. They answer the "What happened?" question. For all practical purposes the diagnostic formulation lends itself to being specified with DSM-5 criteria.

A *clinical formulation*, on the other hand, is more explanatory and longitudinal in nature, and attempts to offer a rationale for the development and maintenance of symptoms and dysfunctional life patterns. Clinical formulations answer the "Why did it happen?" question. Just as various theories of human behavior exist, so do various types of clinical formulations exist: psychoanalytic, Adlerian, cognitive, behavioral, biological, family systems, biopsychosocial, or some combination. In this book, Cognitive Behavioral case conceptualizations are emphasized.

A *cultural formulation* is a systematic review and explanation of cultural factors and dynamics that are operative in the presenting problems. It answers the "what role does culture play?" question. More specifically, it describes the client's cultural identity and level of acculturation. It provides a cultural explanation of the client's condition, as well as the impact of cultural factors on the client's personality and level of functioning. Furthermore, it addresses cultural elements that may impact the relationship between the individual and the therapist, and whether cultural or culturally sensitive interventions are indicated.

A *treatment formulation* follows from the diagnostic, clinical, and cultural formulations and serves as an explicit blueprint governing treatment interventions. Rather than answering the "What happened?" or "Why did it happen?" questions, the treatment formulation addresses the "What can be done about it, and how?" question.

The most useful and comprehensive case conceptualizations are integrative ones that encompass all four components: diagnostic, clinical, cultural, and treatment formulations (Sperry & Carlson, 2014; Sperry & Sperry, 2012). The format of the following chapters of this book will highlight integrative conceptualizations. The diagnostic formulation will emphasize DSM-5 criteria. The clinical formulation will emphasize Cognitive Behavioral explanations, while the treatment formulations will suggest Cognitive Behavioral treatment goals and methods.

Basic Premises and Elements

In the opinion of many clinicians and researchers, case conceptualization is one of the most challenging clinical competencies to master (Eells, 2010; Sperry & Sperry, 2012). The perceived difficulty in developing an effective case conceptualization may be one reason why many therapists neither develop nor use case conceptualizations, or they lack confidence in their ability to conceptualize cases. My experience is that both experienced therapists and trainees can easily and confidently begin to master this competency in as little as 2–3 hours of formal training. The training approach involves learning an integrated model of case conceptualization based on common and distinctive elements; that emphasizes the element of pattern, i.e., maladaptive pattern.

Two basic premises underlie this integrative model. The first premise is that individuals unwittingly develop a self-perpetuating, maladaptive pattern of functioning and relating to others. Inevitably, this pattern underlies the individual's presenting issues. Effective treatment always involves a change process in which the client and therapist collaborate to identify this pattern, break it, and replace it with a more adaptive pattern. At least two outcomes result from this change process: increased well-being and resolution of the client's presenting issue.

The second premise is that pattern recognition and pattern change is at the heart of the case conceptualization process. Pattern is the predictable, consistent, and self-perpetuating style and manner in which individuals think, feel, act, cope, and defend themselves (Sperry, 2006; Sperry, Brill, Howard, & Grissom, 1996).

Pattern change involves three processes: (1) identify the maladaptive pattern, (2) relinquish the maladaptive pattern and replace it with a more adaptive pattern, and (3) maintain the adaptive pattern (Beitman & Yue, 1999).

The integrative case conceptualization described in this chapter is comprised of some 17 elements that are identified in Tables 2.5 and 2.6. Table 2.5 lists and defines 12 elements that are common to most case conceptualization models. Table 2.6 lists and identifies five elements that are specific and unique to a given model or approach. For instance, maladaptive cognitions and maladaptive behaviors are unique to the CBT model. Taken together, these 17 elements represent an integrative case conceptualization (Sperry & Sperry, 2012).

Full-Scale vs. Concise Case Conceptualizations

Full-scale case conceptualizations include all or most or all of these 17 elements. As such, a full-scale case conceptualization represents all four formulations: diagnostic, clinical, cultural, and treatment formulations. In contrast, a concise case conceptualization includes fewer elements. At a minimum, a concise case conceptualization should include presentation, precipitant, pattern, treatment goal(s), and treatment intervention(s). To the extent that a concise case conceptualization is clinically useful it must provide a reasonably compelling explanation for an individual's behavior and level of functioning.

Table 2.5 Common Elements of an Integrative Case Conceptualization

Presentation	presenting problem and characteristic response to precipitants
Precipitant	triggers that activate the pattern resulting in the presentation
Pattern: maladaptive	inflexible, ineffective manner of perceiving, thinking, acting
Perpetuants	triggers that activate one's pattern resulting in the presentation
Cultural identity	sense of belonging to a particular ethnic group
Acculturation &	level of adaptation to the dominant culture; stress-rooted
acculturative stress	acculturation including psychosocial difficulties
Cultural explanation	beliefs regarding cause of distress, condition, or impairment
Culture vs. personality	operative mix of cultural and personality dynamics
Treatment pattern	flexible, effective manner of perceiving, thinking, acting
Treatment obstacles	predictable challenges in the treatment process anticipated from the maladaptive pattern
Treatment–cultural	incorporation of cultural intervention, culturally sensitive therapy or interventions when indicated
Treatment prognosis	prediction of the likely course, duration, and outcome of her condition with or without treatment

Table 2.6 Signature Elements of Cognitive-Behavioral Case Conceptualizations

Predisposition	maladaptive behaviors: deficits and excesses maladaptive beliefs and schemas temperament-style factors re: overcontrol and undercontrol
Treatment Goals	reduce maladaptive beliefs and behaviors develop more adaptive beliefs and behaviors
Treatment Focus	troublesome situations triggered or exacerbated by maladaptive beliefs and/or behaviors
Treatment Strategies	**Basic treatment strategy:** identify and modify specific maladaptive beliefs and behaviors **Common strategies:** support; cognitive restructuring; replacement; exposure; skill training/psychoeducation
Treatment Interventions	Socratic questioning; examining the evidence; cognitive restructuring, including disputation; self-monitoring and Automatic Thought Record cognitive and behavioral replacement; thought stopping; behavioral activation; exposure; social skills training; behavioral rehearsal and enactment; stress reduction and relaxation

Because of its explanatory power, a case conceptualization, no matter how brief, cannot be considered merely a case summary.

Strengths and Protective Factors

This integrative case conceptualization model accounts for strengths and protective factors as well as deficits and risk factors (Sperry, 2014). The influence of client strengths and protective factors on Predisposition can be clinically useful in a Cognitive Behavioral case conceptualization in order to balance strengths and protective factors with deficits and risk factors.

Benefits of an Integrative Approach

It has been said that few, if any, case conceptualization approaches are sufficiently comprehensive while at the same time being relatively easy to learn and use (Eells, 2007). Some approaches are overly detailed in their attempt to be complete, while others leave out key factors for the sake of brevity. According to Eells (2007), the benefits of an integrative approach are that it includes key factors that are common to most approaches, while at the same time highlighting factors unique to a specific approach. For instance, it would be expected that an integrative approach would highlight Cognitive Behavioral constructs like core beliefs, schemas, and behavior deficits and excesses, but also include factors or elements common to other approaches such as presenting symptoms, precipitants, cultural factors, prognosis, etc. In contrast, a Cognitive Behavioral case conceptualization that only included core beliefs, schemas, and behavior deficits and excesses would be quite limited clinically because it leaves out key elements that experts and master therapists consider essential to effective treatment (Sperry & Carlson, 2014).

Case Conceptualizations: Explanatory, Tailoring,
and Predictive Power

A clinically useful case conceptualization has three characteristics. First, it provides a high level of **explanatory power**. Explanatory power means that the case conceptualization provides a compelling explanation for the presenting problem that answers the question of why the individual acted the way he or she did. Second, it provides a high level of **tailoring power**. Tailoring power refers to the selection of treatment interventions that are the "best fit" to the individual's style and functional profile, and extent of symptom severity, level of functioning, and whether it is an internalizing or externalizing disorder. The selected interventions must also match the presenting problem and the clinical, diagnostic, and cultural formulations and have a high likelihood of being successful for effecting change. Third, a clinically useful case conceptualization also provides a high level of **predictive power**. Predictive power is the anticipation of both the most likely obstacles and facilitators to treatment success (Sperry & Sperry, 2012). All three are essential for effectively and competently planning and guiding the treatment process.

Case Conceptualization: Case Example

The process of constructing a Cognitive Behavioral case conceptualization is illustrated here. Following background information, there is an assessment paragraph that identifies key information germane to this model. Then, a table summarizes the nine elements from the diagnostic, clinical, and cultural formulations and the eight elements of the treatment formulation for that specific case. Finally, a narrative integrating this information is provided in a case conceptualization statement. The first paragraph reports the diagnostic and clinical formulation, the second paragraph reports the cultural formulation, and the third reports the treatment formulation.

Case of Geri

Geri is a 35-year-old, African American female who works as an administrative assistant. She is single, lives alone, and was referred by her company's human resources director for evaluation and treatment following three weeks of depression and social isolation. Her absence from work prompted the referral. Geri's symptoms began soon after her supervisor told her that she was being considered for a promotion. As a child, she reports isolating and avoiding others when she was criticized and teased by family members and peers. She is highly acculturated, and believes that her depression is a result of work stress and a "chemical imbalance" in her brain.

Cognitive-Behavioral Assessment

Besides diagnostic assessment information, the Cognitive-Behavioral assessment added the following: Geri mentioned that her family was demanding, critical, and emotionally distant throughout her childhood. She stated that her parents provided her with very little emotional support as a child and she rarely speaks with them today. Her younger brother reportedly would laugh and call her fat and ugly. Neighborhood kids and classmates at school would also tease her and make fun of her, and she adds that all she can remember about teachers is that they criticized her. Since childhood, she has been very shy in most interpersonal relationships and she avoids talking to others when possible. An assessment of maladaptive behaviors and cognitions identified the following: among behavioral deficits was social withdrawal. Also noted were prominent social skill deficits in relational skills and friendship skills. Regarding maladaptive cognitions, she made the following statements: "It's safer not to trust anyone"; "If people got to know me better, they wouldn't like me"; and "Getting close to others isn't worth the risk." She also stated that "I'd rather be safe and alone than get a promotion and a raise." Table 2.7 describes the results of the diagnostic and Cognitive-Behavioral assessment summarized for the key elements of a full-scale case conceptualization.

Full Case Conceptualization

Geri's increased social isolation and depressive symptoms *(presentation)* seem to be her reaction to the news of an impending job transfer and promotion, given her history of avoiding situations in which she might be criticized, rejected, and feel unsafe *(precipitant)*. Throughout her life, she found it safer to avoid others when possible and conditionally relate to them at other times; as a result she lacks key social skills and has a limited social network *(pattern)*. Geri's overt problems are understandable when viewed as a consequence of her core beliefs. Her self-view involves core beliefs about being inadequate and vulnerable to negative evaluations of others. Her worldview involves core beliefs about life being unfair and unpredictable, and others being critical, rejecting, and demanding. These are reflected in maladaptive schemas that include defectiveness and social isolation. Her maladaptive behaviors consist of shyness and avoidance in situations which she perceives as unsafe and prefers social isolation to engagement with others. In the past, Geri preferred to avoid social situations because it protected her from the possibility of making mistakes and being rejected. Her beliefs are consistent with an avoidant personality pattern in which she tends to perceive situations as threatening and unsafe and subsequently withdraws from others to feel safe. Behaviorally, this pattern of avoidance manifests itself in shyness, distrust, and social isolation, and since early life, this pattern has resulted in skill deficits including assertive communications, negotiation, conflict resolution, and friendship skills. In short, her pattern can be understood in light of demanding, critical, and emotionally unavailable parents, the teasing and criticism of peers, and her response of withdrawal and avoidance behavior which limited the learning of adaptive relational skills *(predisposition)*. This pattern is maintained by her shyness, the fact

Table 2.7 Case of Geri: Case Conceptualization Elements

Presentation	increased social isolation and depressive symptoms
Precipitant	her reaction to an impending job promotion and transfer out of a close-knit work group
Pattern-maladaptive	disconnects when feeling unsafe
Predisposition	*Maladaptive cognition:* views herself as inadequate and frightened of rejection, and views the world as rejecting and critical but wants safe relationships; *Maladaptive schemas:* defectiveness and social isolation
	Maladaptive behaviors: history of being teased, criticized, rejected; social isolation and avoidance behavior which limited learning relational and friendship skills
	Protective factors/strength one trustworthy friend and Geri's dog; religious convictions; anticipation that she will qualify for a return-to-work accommodation re: psychiatric disability
Perpetuants	maintained by her shyness, living alone, and generalized social isolation
Cultural identity	African American conflicted about limited ethnic ties
Acculturation & acculturative stress	highly acculturated; no obvious acculturative stress
Cultural explanation	depression results from job stress and chemical brain imbalance
Culture vs. personality	personality dynamics are significantly operative
Treatment pattern	connects while feeling safer
Treatment goals	reduce maladaptive beliefs and behaviors; develop more adaptive beliefs and behaviors
Treatment focus	troublesome situations triggered or exacerbated by maladaptive beliefs and/or behaviors
Treatment strategy	identify and modify specific maladaptive beliefs and behaviors; cognitive restructuring; replacement; exposure; skill training and psychoeducation; medication
Treatment interventions	Socratic questioning; examining the evidence; cognitive restructuring, including disputation; self-monitoring and Automatic Thought Record; cognitive and behavioral replacement; thought stopping; behavioral activation; exposure; skills training
Treatment obstacles	"test" practitioners; likely to resist group therapy; overdependence on therapist; difficulty with termination
Treatment-cultural	gender may be an issue so assign supportive female practitioners
Treatment prognosis	good, if increased social connections, skills, and returns to work

that she lives alone, her limited social skills, and that she finds it safer to socially isolate (*perpetuants*).

She identifies as middle-class African American but is not involved with that community (*cultural identity*). She and her parents are highly accultur-ated, and there is no obvious acculturative stress (*culture-acculturation*). She believes that her depression is the result of stresses at work and a "chemical imbalance" in her brain (*cultural explanation*). There are no obvious cultural factors that are operative. Instead, it appears that Geri's personality dynam-ics are significantly operative in her current clinical presentation (*culture v. personality*).

The challenge for Geri is to function more effectively and feel safer in relat-ing to others (*treatment pattern*). Treatment goals include reducing depres-sive symptoms, increasing interpersonal and friendship skills, and returning to work and establishing a supportive social network there (*treatment goals*). The treatment focus is to analyze troublesome situations triggered or exacer-bated by her maladaptive beliefs and behaviors (*treatment focus*). The basic treatment strategy will be to identify and modify specific maladaptive beliefs and behaviors and utilize support, cognitive restructuring, replacement, expo-sure, and skills training as primary strategies (*treatment strategy*). Initially, behavioral activation will be used in conjunction with medication to reduce her clinical depression and energize her sufficiently to be able to participate in therapy and be ready to return to work, and she will be referred for medica-tion evaluation along with medication monitoring, if indicated. Increasing relational and friendship skills are best accomplished in a psychoeducation group, and individual therapy will be useful in transitioning her to such a group. Her maladaptive beliefs will be processed with guided discovery, and she will be taught to self-monitor thoughts, behaviors, and feelings and to challenge them with the Automatic Thought Record. Geri is eligible for a work accommodation under the American for Disabilities Act. Presumably, she can return to the safety of her former work setting with a promotion and/ or raise. Accordingly, this treatment goal can be facilitated by the therapist consulting with her work supervisor and Human Resources director about such an accommodation (*treatment intervention*). Some obstacles and chal-lenges to treatment can be anticipated. Given her avoidant personality struc-ture, ambivalent resistance is likely. It can anticipated that she would have difficulty discussing personal matters with practitioners, and that she would "test" and provoke practitioners into criticizing her for changing or canceling appointments at the last minute, being late, and that she might procrasti-nate, avoid feelings, and otherwise "test" the practitioner's trustability. Once trust in the practitioner is achieved, she is likely to cling to the practitioner and treatment and thus termination may be difficult unless her social sup-port system outside therapy is increased. Furthermore, her pattern of avoid-ance is likely to make entry into and continuation with group work difficult. Therefore, individual sessions can serve as a transition into group, including having some contact with the group practitioner who will presumably be accepting and nonjudgmental. This should increase Geri's feeling of safety and make self-disclosure in a group setting less difficult. Transference enactment is another consideration. Given the extent of parental and peer criticism and teasing, it is anticipated that any perceived impatience and verbal or nonverbal indications of criticalness by the practitioner will activate this transference. Finally, because of her tendency to cling to others with whom she trusts, increasing her capacity to feel more confident in functioning with greater independence and increasing time between the last 4–5 sessions can reduce her ambivalence about termination (***treatment obstacles***). Treatment progress does not seem dependent on cultural or even culturally sensitive interventions at this time. However, gender dynamics could impact the therapeutic relationship given her strained relationship with her father and limited involvement with men ever since. Accordingly, female practitioners for both individual and group therapy appear to be indicated in the initial phase of treatment (***treatment-cultural***). Assuming that Geri increases her self-confidence, relational skills, and social contacts in and outside therapy, as well as returns to work, her prognosis is adjudged to be good; if not, it is guarded (***treatment prognosis***).

Case Conceptualizations for Keri and Cindy

Unlike the full-scale case conceptualization for the case of Geri, this section includes brief case conceptualizations for the cases of Keri and Cindy.

Concise Case Conceptualization: Keri

Keri's agitation, dysphoria, and wrist cutting (***presentation***) was her reaction to believing that she was stood up by her boyfriend whom she presumed was with another woman (***precipitant***). Fearing abandonment, she drives others away with unrealistic demands for closeness (***pattern***). This is a mild externalizing pattern with "moderate impairment" on the Level of Personality Functioning Scale. Keri's suicide gesture is understandable when viewed in light of her beliefs and biological vulnerability. She views herself as vulnerable and neglected, and views others as potentially rejecting. While she would like to believe that others are caring and concerned, she finds that some are untrustworthy and invalidating. When under increased stress, she is most likely to experience feelings of abandonment. She is particularly sensitive and finds it very difficult to tolerate such negative emotional states (***predisposition***). Given her relatively high functioning, a course of psychotherapy was mutually agreed upon with the goal of reducing her distress intolerance and examining her beliefs and needs for closeness in close, intimate relationships (***treatment goals***). CBASP focused on replacing self-harming cognitions and behaviors with more life-affirming ones will be used along with self-soothing and other distress tolerance enhancing strategies (***treatment interventions***).

Concise Case Conceptualization: Cindy

Cindy's anger, combativeness, and wrist cutting (**presentation**) was her reaction to a missing social security disability check and being "dumped" by her boyfriend (**precipitant**). Fearing abandonment she drives others away with unrealistic demands for closeness (**pattern**). This is a strong externalizing pattern with "extreme impairment" on the Level of Personality Functioning Scale. Cindy's suicidal behavior is understandable when viewed in light of her beliefs and biological vulnerability. She views herself as defective, vulnerable, and neglected, and views others as dangerous, unpredictable, and rejecting. She is also biologically vulnerable to impulsivity, emotional dysregulation, acting out behaviors, and distress intolerance. Throughout her life, she has experienced others as untrustworthy and hurtful, even though she wanted to believe that others could be caring and nurturing. When under increased stress, she experiences intense feelings of abandonment and rage. The result is repeated destructive relationships and a fragile sense of self (**predisposition**). Given her low level functioning, long history of psychiatric treatment, and three prior suicide attempts, a referral was made for intensive outpatient treatment with the goal of decreasing her undercontrolled style and increasing her self-control and resilience (**treatment goals**). Dialectical Behavior Therapy with group skills training in mindfulness, emotion regulation, distress tolerance, and interpersonal effectiveness are interventions aimed at increasing her self-control and resilience. Individual therapy (CBASP) would focus on increasing her capacity to learn from experience, and replacing her self-defeating thoughts and behaviors regarding relationships with more adaptive ones (**treatment interventions**).

It is noteworthy that both women have the same DSM-5 diagnosis: Borderline Personality Disorder, and the same maladaptive pattern: fear of abandonment leads to driving others away with unrealistic demands for closeness. On the other hand, both have been assessed with very different style profiles, i.e., biological vulnerabilities, relational histories, as well as very different overall levels of functioning. Not surprisingly, their case conceptualizations, including treatment plans, differ considerably.

Treatment

This is a book primarily about the Cognitive Behavioral treatment of the most common personality disorders seen in outpatient settings. Chapter 3, "Cognitive Behavior Therapy and Personality Disorders: Interventions: I," describes the character dimension of personality and its evolution and transformation into "schema" language. Schema is discussed with regard to the cognitive-behavioral and psychodynamic traditions, and several schemas commonly noted among personality-disordered individuals are described. These schemas will be referred to repeatedly throughout Chapters 5–10. Next, new CBT approaches with particular relevance to personality disorders are described. These include Schema Therapy, Cognitive Behavioral Analysis System of Psychotherapy, Mindfulness-Based Cognitive Therapy, and similar "third wave" approaches that emphasize mindfulness and acceptance. Also included are new developments in Cognitive Therapy and Dialectical Behavior Therapy, including Radically Open Dialectical Behavior Therapy.

Chapter 4, "Cognitive Behavior Therapy Personality Disorders: Interventions: II," continues the discussion of Chapter 3. It briefly describes the temperament dimension in personality and its revival in the formulation and treatment of personality disorders. Sixteen specific treatment interventions targeted to modifying styles are described. It seems that clinicians who attempt to provide effective treatment to patients with moderate to severe personality disorders must have sufficient capability to use these or similar interventions. Because many of these interventions are not commonly used by clinicians, each is described in some detail, along with key references for additional information. These interventions will be referred to repeatedly throughout Chapters 5–10.

Table 2.8 provides a brief glimpse of some of the specific interventions described in Chapter 4 as they relate to the ABCDEF style profile.

Table 2.8 Therapeutic Interventions Targeted to Style Profile

Affective

<----------------------------------[--------WB-------]--------------------------->
RO-DBT: Emotion Regulation Training   *DBT: Emotion Regulation Training*
Emotional Awareness Training   *Anger Management Training*

Behavioral

<----------------------------------[--------WB-------]--------------------------->
RO-DBT: Interpersonal Effectiveness   *DBT: Interpersonal Effectiveness*
Assertiveness Training   *Symptom Management Training*

Cognitive

<----------------------------------[--------WB-------]--------------------------->
RO-DBT: Core Mindfulness   *DBT: Core Mindfulness*
Cognitive Flexibility Training   *Sensitivity Reduction Training*

Distress Tolerance

<----------------------------------[--------WB-------]--------------------------->
RO-DBT: Distress Tolerance Skills   *DBT: Distress Tolerance Skills*

Experience
<--->
               CBASP

Functioning<-->
                    CBASP
                    Problem Solving & Self-Management Training
                    Relapse Prevention
                    Stress Reduction/Mindfulness/Relaxation
                    CT: Cognitive Restructuring & Schema Therapy

Key:
DBT = Dialectical Behavior Therapy group skill training module
RO-DBT = Radically-Open Dialectical Behavior Therapy group skill training module

Treatment Interventions for Keri and Cindy

Based on the functional assessment of each case, the treatment goals and interventions specified in the case conceptualization are considerably different. Table 2.9 visually portrays these treatment recommendations in terms of their respective style profiles.

Table 2.9 Treatment Plan and Targeted Therapeutic Interventions: Cases of Keri and Cindy

---

Keri

Affective   <---------------[----------------X-]---------------------->

Behavioral <---------------[----------------X-]--------------->

Cognitive   <---------------[----------------X-]--------------->

Distress   <---------------[-------------------]-X------------------->
Tolerance   self-soothing

Experience <--------------------------------------X-------------------->
                             CT, CBT, CBASP

Functioning <--------------------------------------X-------------------->
                             CT, CBT, CBASP

Cindy

Affective   <---------------[-------------------]---------------X------>
                             DBT: emotion regulation

Behavioral <---------------[-------------------]---------------X------>
                             DBT: interpersonal
                                  effectiveness

Cognitive   <---------------[-------------------]---------------X------>
                             DBT: core mindfulness

Distress   <---------------[-------------------]---------------X------>
Tolerance   *DBT: distress tolerance skills*

Experience <-----X--->
                             CT, CBT, CBASP

Functioning <------------X--->
                             CT, CBT, CBASP

Concluding Note

Competency in working effectively with individuals diagnosed with personality disorders is increasingly expected of psychotherapists today. A Cognitive Behavioral approach to assessment, case conceptualization, and treatment relevant to personality disorders was described and illustrated in this chapter. The ABCDEF assessment model was described and illustrated. It complements the assessment of maladaptive beliefs and schemas. Two cases of individuals with the same personality disorder diagnosis were followed throughout the chapter to illustrate the clinical value of style-function assessment and the need for vastly different treatments based on their Style Assessment. An integrative model of case conceptualization was also described and illustrated. It incorporates both common elements and Cognitive Behavioral specific elements. A detailed case example illustrated this integrative case conceptualization approach. Presumably, the use of the ABCDEF assessment model and style profile, and the integrative case conceptualization model can increase a therapist's competence and confidence as well as treatment outcomes.

3 Cognitive Behavior Therapy and Personality Disorders

Interventions: I

This chapter sets the stage for the Cognitive Behavioral treatment (CBT) of specific personality disorders [covered in Chapters 5–10] by emphasizing CBT interventions particularly effective in modifying schemas and basic character structure. It begins by discussing the constructs of character and schema. It then articulates how the construct of schema is understood in two psychological traditions, the psychodynamic and the cognitive behavioral. The remainder of the chapter is an overview of recent major developments in the understanding and treatment of the personality disorders within the cognitive behavioral tradition. Besides reviewing revisions in Cognitive Therapy, Schema Therapy, and Dialectical Behavior Therapy, it introduces two newer approaches, Cognitive Behavioral Analysis System of Psychotherapy and Mindfulness-Based Cognitive Therapy, which shows considerable promise in the treatment of the personality disorders. Furthermore, Cognitive Coping Therapy and Structured Treatment Interventions are briefly noted.

Character

Character refers to the learned, psychosocial influences on personality. Because character is essentially learned, it follows that it can be changed through such processes as psychotherapy. Largely because of the influence of Freud and his followers, psychotherapy and psychiatric treatment focused almost exclusively on the dimension of character to the point at which personality essentially became synonymous with character. Character forms largely because of the socialization process, particularly regarding cooperativeness and the mirroring process that promotes the development of self-concept and a sense of purpose in life (i.e., self-transcendence and self-responsibility). Character can be assessed both by structured interview and by self-report inventories. On the *Temperament Character Inventory* (Cloninger, Svrakic, & Przybeck, 1993), character is measured by three character dimensions: cooperativeness, self-directedness (also called self-responsibility), and self-transcendence. Healthy personality reflects positive or elevated scores on these three dimensions, whereas personality disorders reflect negative or low scores on them. Furthermore, individuals with low scores on one or more of the character dimensions and increased dysregulation of one or more of the temperament dimensions typically experience either considerable distress or impairment in life functioning or both. For example, the borderline personality disorder would likely rate high in two temperament dimensions but low in character dimensions of self-directedness and cooperation.

Schema

Another way of specifying the characterological component of personality is with the term *schema*. Whether in the psychoanalytic tradition (Horowitz, 1988; Slap & Slap-Shelton, 1991) or the cognitive therapy tradition (Beck, 1964; Beck, Davis, & Freeman, 2015; Young, Klosko, & Weishaar, 2003), schema refers to the basic beliefs individuals use to organize their view of self, the world, and the future. Although the centrality of schema has historically been more central to the cognitive tradition and the cognitive behavioral tradition than to the psychoanalytic tradition, this apparently is changing (Stein & Young, 1992). Schema and schema change and modification strategies are central to this book. The remainder of this chapter reviews some different conceptualizations of schema and then describes several different schemas useful in clinical practice.

Adler first used the term *schema of apperception* in 1929 to refer to the individual's view of self and the world. For Adler, psychopathology reflected the individual's "neurotic schema" (Adler, 1956, p. 333) and these schemas were central to the individual's life-style. Recently, the use of the term *schema* and *schema theory* has emerged as central in the various subdisciplines of cognitive science, as well as by various psychotherapy schools' convictions (Stein & Young, 1992). This section describes the psychodynamic and cognitive behavioral traditions of schemas.

Psychodynamic Tradition

Whereas classical psychoanalysts focused on libidinal drives, modern analysts have focused instead on relational themes, emphasizing the self, the object, and their interaction, while a number of ego psychology and object relations theorists have emphasized schema theory. Many have contributed to the development of schema theories in the psychoanalytic tradition (Eagle, 1986; Horowitz, 1988; Inderbitzin & James, 1994; Slap & Slap-Shelton, 1991; Wachtel, 1982).

A representative example of these theories is the model described by Slap and Slap-Shelton (1991). They described a schema model that contrasts with the structural model devised by Freud and refined by the ego psychologists, and that, they contend, better fits the clinical data of psychoanalysis than the structural model. Their schema model involves the ego and sequestered schema. The ego consists of many schemas that are loosely linked and integrated with one another and relativity accessible to the consciousness. These schemas are based on past experience but are modified by new experience. This process forms the basis of adaptive behavior. Sequestered schemas are organized around traumatic events and situations in childhood that were not mastered or integrated by the immature psyche of the child. These schema remain latent and repressed. To the extent that these sequestered or pathological schemas are active, current relationships may be cognitively processed according to these schemas, rather than treated objectively by the more adaptive schemas of the ego. Essentially, current situations cannot be perceived and processed in accord with the reality of the present event but rather as replications of unresolved childhood conflict.

Treatment consists of helping the patient to describe, clarify, and work through these sequestered, pathological schema. These schemas are exposed to the client's mature, adaptive ego to achieve integration. Patients are helped to recognize how they create and recreate scenarios that reopen their pathologic schemas. The repeated demonstration and working through of the traumatic events that gave rise to the pathological schemas engenders a greater degree of self-observation, understanding, and emotional growth.

Cognitive Behavioral Tradition

Like the psychodynamic tradition, the cognitive behavioral tradition is quite heterogeneous. Common to this tradition is the belief that behavior and cognitions influence each other. Approaches within this tradition include stress-inoculation and self-instructional training (Meichenbaum, 1977), rational emotive therapy (Ellis, 1979), and cognitive therapy (Beck, 1976). Because cognitive therapy has taken the lead in articulating schema theory in the cognitive behavioral tradition, it will be highlighted. The rest of this chapter and the remainder of this book emphasize the cognitive behavioral treatment of the personality disorders.

Schema Assessment

There are various ways of assessing schemas. Basic to a schema is the individual's self-view and worldview. From an Adlerian perspective, schemas are central to an individual's lifestyle (Adler, 1956). Lifestyle, as well as schemas, can be assessed with a semi-structured interview that includes the elicitation of early recollections or early memories. The process begins by asking the patient: "What is, your earliest memory?" or "Think back as far as you can and tell me the first thing you remember." An early recollection must be distinguished from a report. An *early recollection* is a single, specific event that is personally remembered by the individual, whereas a *report* can be an event that occurred more than once or for which the patient was told about the event by another, or by seeing it in a photo, home movie, or video. Additional memories from early and middle childhood are then elicited. From these memories the clinician searches for patterns related to the patient's view of self, that is,

"I am strong, defective, unloved," and the patient's worldview: "The world puts too many demands on me, is a scary place, and is unfair." These views can be summarized and interpreted to reveal the individual's lifestyle themes or schemas (Eckstein, Baruth, & Mahrer, 1992).

In the cognitive therapy tradition, schemas are typically identified or derived from the interview process (Beck et al., 2015). Young (Young et al., 2003) describes several methods for assessing schemas. The evaluation interview is critical in identifying schemas: In this interview, the clinician elicits presenting symptoms and problems and attempts to formulate a connection between specific symptoms, emotions, life problems, and maladaptive schemas.

During the course of inquiry about life events and symptoms, the clinician endeavors to develop hypotheses about patterns or themes. Issues of autonomy, connectedness, worthiness, reasonable expectations, and realistic limits are probed to ascertain if any of these present significant problems for the patient. It can be quite useful to inquire about "critical incidents" by asking the patient to describe a situation or incident that they consider indicative of their problem (Freeman, 1992a). The clinician listens for specific triggers, patterns indicative of schemas, and specific behavioral, emotional, and cognitive responses. As themes and patterns emerge, the clinician formulates them in schema language, that is, view of self and view of the world and others. Because schemas are predictable and recurring phenomenon they can be "triggered" in the interview through imagery and discussing upsetting events in past or present. This process of triggering confirms the clinician's hypothesis about the presence of a specific schema.

In addition to the clinical interview, a number of schema inventories are available including the *Life History Assessment Forms*, the *Young Schema Questionnaire*, the *Young Parenting Inventory*, the *Young-Rygh Avoidance Inventory*, and the *Young Compensation Inventory*. Imagery assessment is another method of assessment and confirming operative schemas. See Young et al. (2003) for a description of these inventories.

The most commonly utilized of these inventories is the *Young Schema Questionnaire* (Young & Brown, 1994, 2001). The long version includes 205 items and is preferable in clinical practice while the short version contains 75 items and is utilized primarily used in research studies. Both utilize a 6-point Likert scale. Preliminary reliability and validity data has been reported on both clinical and non-clinical populations (Schmidt, Joiner, Young, & Telch, 1995; Young & Brown, 2001).

Cognitive Behavioral Approaches With Personality Disorders

Since the publication of the first edition of this book, there have been a number of promising developments in CBT involving the treatment of the personality disorders. This section will briefly survey these developments particularly in Cognitive Therapy, Dialectical Behavior Therapy, Schema Therapy and

Cognitive Behavioral Analysis System of Psychotherapy, and Mindfulness Training: DBT and Mindfulness-Based Cognitive Therapy.

Cognitive Therapy

Cognitive therapy with personality disorders was originally presumed to be similar to cognitive therapy with depression in that both focused on a cognitive formulation or case conceptualization, utilized a collaborative relationship, took a problem-solving approach, and actively helped clients to learn new skills in problem situations (Beck, 1997; Beck et al., 2015). However, because personality-disordered individuals characteristically have dysfunctional schemas and ingrained interactional patterns, treatment needed to be modified. Unlike clients with symptom disorders, personality-disordered clients have difficulty complying with treatment protocols including homework. Their maladaptive beliefs and behavior patterns were found to be extremely resistant to change solely with cognitive interventions. Besides presenting with problems and symptoms that were often pervasive, vague, and chronic, these clients often had difficulty forming a therapeutic alliance. Accordingly, the original model of cognitive therapy needed revision, and Beck and his associates have recently offered a revised or reformulated model.

The third edition of their text, *Cognitive Therapy of Personality Disorders* (Beck et al., 2015) provides a fuller and reformulated model of personality disorders and its treatment. Notable is the emphasis on identifying and modifying maladaptive schemas. Beck acknowledges the difficulties in establishing an effective therapeutic relationship with these clients and provides suggestions for focusing more than the usual amount of attention on the therapist-patient relationship (Beck et al., 2015). He also suggests not relying primarily on verbal interventions and beginning with interventions that require a minimal degree of client self-disclosure. Furthermore, he advocates helping clients to deal adaptively with aversive emotions. Similarly, he considers limit setting to be essential to treatment progress (Beck et al., 2015). In addition, the reformulated model of cognitive therapy with personality-disordered clients recognizes the need to address the developmental history issues, and utilizes specialized techniques. Finally, mindful of the proclivity for clients to relapse, the reformulated model also incorporates relapse prevention techniques (Pretzer & Beck, 2004).

The following sections on Schema Therapy, Dialectical Behavior Therapy, Cognitive Behavioral Analysis System of Psychotherapy, and Mindfulness Training: DBT and Mindfulness-Based Cognitive Therapy continue the discussion of Cognitive Therapy by indicating how they are similar to and different from it.

Schema Therapy

Schema Therapy was developed by Young (1990) to help personality-disordered clients who failed to respond adequately to CBT. While Young finds that recent revisions of cognitive therapy for personality disorders by Beck and his colleagues (Beck et al., 2004) are more consistent with Schema Therapy formulations, he contends that there remains significant differences between these approaches, particularly Beck's primary emphasis on conceptual change and the range of treatment strategies. Like Beck's reformulated model, Schema Therapy has also evolved over the past three decades. It appears that while Schema Therapy is applicable to all personality disorders, Young has emphasized its application to borderline personality disorder (Klosko & Young, 2004; Young et al., 2003). The following paragraphs overview the current model of Schema Therapy theory and practice.

Schema Therapy is a broad, integrative model that shares some commonalities with object relations therapy, experiential therapy, DBT, interpersonal therapy as well as cognitive therapy and other forms of CBT. Despite these similarities, Schema Therapy differs from these approaches with regard to the nature of the therapy relationship, the general style and stance of the therapist, and the degree of therapist activity and directiveness (Young et al., 2003).

Theory

Four central concepts in the Schema Therapy model are: early maladaptive schemas, schema domains, coping styles, and schema modes. Each is briefly described below.

Early maladaptive schemas are broad, pervasive themes or patterns regarding oneself and one's relationships with others that are dysfunctional to a significant degree. Schemas comprise memories, emotions, cognitions, and bodily sensations. They begin as adaptive and relatively accurate representations of the child's environment, but can become maladaptive and inaccurate as the child grows up. Schemas considerably influence how individuals think, feel, act, and relate to others. They are triggered when individuals encounter environments reminiscent of the childhood environments that produced them. When this happens, the individual is flooded with intense negative affect. Young reviews research on the brain systems involved with fear conditioning and trauma that he contends provides a biological basis for early maladaptive schemas.

Early maladaptive schemas are the result of unmet core emotional needs. These schemas appear to emerge from aversive childhood experiences such as abuse, neglect, and trauma in early life. In addition, temperament and cultural influences are factors. Young and his associates have delineated 18 Early Maladaptive Schemas. Considerable empirical support exists for these schemas (Young et al., 2003).

Schema domains reflect the basic emotional needs of a child. When these needs are not met in childhood, schemas develop that lead to unhealthy life patterns. Currently, the 18 early maladaptive schemas have been grouped into five broad schema domains. Table 3.1 provides a capsule description of these schemas and domains.

Table 3.1 Maladaptive Schemas and Schema Domains

DISCONNECTION AND REJECTION

Abandonment/ instability:	The belief that significant others will not or cannot provide reliable and stable support.
Mistrust/Abuse:	The belief that others will abuse, humiliate, cheat, lie, manipulate, or take advantage.
Emotional deprivation:	The belief that one's desire for emotional support will not be met by others.
Defectiveness/Shame:	The belief that one is defective, bad, unwanted, or inferior in important respects.
Social Isolation/ Alienation:	The belief that one is alienated, different from others, or not part of any group.

IMPAIRED AUTONOMY AND PERFORMANCE

Dependence/ Incompetence:	The belief that one is unable to competently meet everyday responsibilities without considerable help from others.
Vulnerability to Harm or Illness:	The exaggerated fear that imminent catastrophe will strike at any time and that one will be unable to prevent it.
Enmeshment/ Undeveloped Self:	The belief that one must be emotional close with others at the expense of full individuation or normal social development.
Failure:	The belief that one will inevitably fail or is fundamentally inadequate in achieving one's goals.

IMPAIRED LIMITS

Entitlement/ Grandiosity:	The belief that one is superior to others and not bound by the rules and norms that govern normal social interaction.
Insufficient Self-Control / Self-Discipline	The belief that one is incapable of self-control and frustration tolerance.

OTHER-DIRECTEDNESS

Subjugation:	The belief that one's desires, needs, and feelings must be suppressed in order to meet the needs of others and avoid retaliation or criticism.
Self-Sacrifice:	The belief that one must meet the needs of others at the expense of one's own gratification.
Approval-Seeking/ Recognition-Seeking:	The belief that one must constantly seek to belong and be accepted at the expense of developing a true sense of self.

OVERVIGILANCE AND INHIBITION

Negativity/Pessimism:	A pervasive, lifelong focus on the negative aspects of life while minimizing the positive and optimistic aspects.
Emotional inhibition:	The excessive inhibition of spontaneous action, feeling, or communication—usually to avoid disapproval by others, feelings of shame, or losing control of one's impulses.
Unrelenting Standards/ Hypercriticalness:	The belief that striving to meet unrealistically high standards of performance is essential to be accepted and to avoid criticism.
Punitiveness:	The belief that others should be harshly punished for making errors.

Treatment

In general, the basic goals of Schema Therapy with personality-disordered individuals are the following: identify early maladaptive schemas to validate the client's unmet emotional needs, to change dysfunctional beliefs and maladaptive schemas to more functional ones, to change maladaptive life patterns and coping styles, and to provide an environment for learning adaptive skills. When treating borderline disorder, very specific treatment goals are specified (Klosko & Young, 2004). These goals are described in Chapter 6 of this book, which describes the treatment of the Borderline Personality Disorder.

Schema Therapy has two phases: the assessment and education phase and the change phase. In the first phase, therapists help clients identify their schemas, understand the origins of their schemas in childhood, and relate their schemas to their current problems. In the change phase, therapists integrate several interventions, including cognitive, experiential, behavioral, and interpersonal strategies, to heal schemas and replace maladaptive coping styles with healthier behaviors (Young et al., 2003). With borderline disorder, three stages of treatment are specified (Klosko & Young, 2004). See Chapter 6 for the stages of treatment.

It is worth noting that Schema Therapy is a theory-intense approach, which requires considerable training and experience to practice it appropriately and effectively. Furthermore, just as Young has criticized Beck's reformulated model of cognitive therapy for personality disorders, Young's model is not without criticism from the other side: "Although this modification of cognitive therapy [Young's revised model of Schema Therapy] was a plausible approach to understanding and treating personality disorders, it has the disadvantage of adding considerable complexity" (Pretzer & Beck, 2004, pp. 302–303).

Dialectical Behavior Therapy

Originally developed for the treatment of borderline personality disorder (Linehan, 1993), Dialectical Behavior Therapy (DBT) has been modified and extended for use with other personality disorders as well as symptom disorders such as mood disorders, anxiety disorders, eating disorders, and substance use disorders (Lynch & Cuper, 2012; Marra, 2005; Lynch & Cuper, 2012). DBT is an outgrowth of behavior therapy but is less cognitive than traditional CBT because DBT assumes that cognitions, per se, are less important than affect regulation. Accordingly, DBT places more emphasis on emotion regulation rather than maladaptive thought processes. While it recognizes that cognitions are a factor in behavior, they are not a necessary mediating factor. Rather, cognitions are more likely to serve to "make sense" of behavior and emotional events after the fact (Marra, 2005).

Theory

There are numerous similarities between DBT and traditional CBT, particularly cognitive therapy. Both require a collaborative stance between client and therapist. Both utilize learning principles, analyze triggers and environmental prompts, explore schemas and emotions, and utilize modeling, homework, and imagery. Furthermore, both recognize the importance of empathic responding.

There are a number of differences between cognitive therapy and DBT in the treatment of personality disorders. Essentially, cognitive therapy posits that the same techniques used in eliciting and evaluating automatic thoughts during depression or anxiety disorders are used in treating personality disorders (Beck et al., 2015).While cognitive therapy contends that dysfunctional feelings and behaviors are due to schemas that produce consistently biased judgments and a tendency to make cognitive errors through attributional bias, DBT focuses instead on how schemas are initially formed. Accordingly, therapists utilizing DBT explore schemas and the underlying dialectic conflicts that produced them rather than performing "collaborative experiments" to prove their limited usefulness. Rather than utilizing cognitive restructuring, the DBT therapist attempts to connect belief systems to underlying affect and need, and then assist clients to reinterpret their belief systems based upon greater awareness of their feelings and needs.

Instead of utilizing "guided discovery" to dispute and revise maladaptive beliefs, "DBT analyzes both the affective and cognitive inference processes to determine how the schema was formed in the first place. This involves identifying deprivational emotional states in early development that could have produced fixation or perseveration and attentional constriction that could serve protection from threatening internal or external cues, as well as broadly examining the effects of negative reinforcement through emotional escape and avoidance strategies or inadequate psychological coping skills that could have been rewarded through the partial reinforcement effect" (Marra, 2005, p. 141).

Finally, DBT differs from the cognitive therapy of personality disorders by adopting a non-pejorative interpretation of pathology. Instead, the DBT therapist sees behavior and strategy as operant behavior. Like others, the personality-disordered client is attempting to avoid harm and seek pleasure but has difficulty successfully obtaining the desired outcome due to the emotional vulnerability. Nevertheless, the DBT therapist assumes that inadequate compromises between competing and contradictory needs and desires form the basis of their personality structure and helps them achieve their needs in a non-pejorative way.

Treatment

Linehan (1993, 2014) specified four primary modes of treatment in DBT: individual therapy, skills training in a group, telephone contact, and therapist consultation (Linehan, 1993, 2014). While keeping within the overall model, group therapy and other modes of treatment may be added at the discretion of the therapist, providing the targets for that mode are clear and prioritized. The individual therapist is the primary therapist and the main work of therapy is carried out in the individual therapy sessions. Between sessions, the client should be offered telephone contact with the therapist, including off-hours telephone contact, although the therapist has the right to set clear limits on such contact. The purpose of telephone contact is not psychotherapy but rather to give the client help and support to find ways of avoiding self-injury as well as for relationship repair where the client feels that she has damaged her relationship with her therapist and wants to put this right before the next session. For the client to learn that self-injury calls are not acceptable and to avoid reinforcing such calls—and after ensuring her immediate safety—no further calls are allowed for the next twenty-four hours.

Skills training is usually carried out in a group context, ideally by someone other than the individual therapist. In the skills training groups clients are taught skills considered relevant to the particular problems of personality-disordered individuals. There are four groups of skills: core mindfulness skills, interpersonal effectiveness skills, emotion modulation skills, and distress tolerance skills (Linehan, 2014).

Core Mindfulness Skills. These skills help individuals focus their mind and attention on the present and attend to what is happening in the here and now in a calm manner. They help individuals slow down and focus on doing what is needed to care for themselves in the present moment. Individuals learn the value of a "wise mind" instead of succumbing to intense emotions and acting in a destructive way.

Interpersonal Effectiveness Skills. These skills help individuals understand what their needs are in their relationships and develop more effective ways of dealing with others in order to get their needs met in a healthy way. This involves respecting the self and others, listening and communicating effectively, coping with interpersonal conflict, repairing relationships, and assertiveness.

Emotion Modulation Skills. These skills help individuals understand the function of emotions and how to not be overwhelmed by them. They focus on decreasing emotional intensity and provide strategies so individuals can ride out strong emotions without acting on them. These skills include learning to identify and label current emotions, identifying obstacles to changing emotions, reducing emotional reactivity, increasing positive emotions, and changing emotions.

Distress Tolerance Skills. These skills help individuals develop acceptance of the current situation as well as crisis survival skills to decrease the likelihood of engaging in problematic behavior. They teach individuals to soothe themselves in healthy ways when feeling upset rather than becoming overwhelmed by emotions or hiding from them. In addition, reality acceptance skills focus on fully accepting reality and responding to painful aspects of life in a more adaptive manner.

Stages of Treatment. Following an initial period of pre-treatment involving assessment, commitment, and orientation to therapy, DBT consists of four stages of treatment (Linehan, 2014). Stage 1 focuses on "severe behavioral dyscontrol." The goal of this stage is to increase behavioral control and targets suicidal behaviors, self-harm, and severe therapy interfering behavior like substance abuse. Stage 2 focuses on "quiet desperation" with the goal of increasing emotional experiencing in those dealing with issues like post-traumatic stress and other residual disorders not addressed in stage 1. Stage 3 focuses on "problems of living." The goal of this stage is to work through concerns of ordinary happiness and unhappiness. Stage 4 focuses on "incompleteness," where the work is on increasing the capacity for joy, freedom, and spiritual fulfillment. The targeted behaviors of each stage are brought under control before moving on to the next phase. Therapy at each stage is focused on the specific targets for that stage, which are arranged in a definite hierarchy of relative importance.

Core Strategies. The core strategies in DBT are "validation" and "problem solving." Attempts to facilitate change are surrounded by interventions that validate clients' behavior and responses in relation to the client's current life situation, and that demonstrate an understanding of their difficulties and suffering. Problem solving focuses on the establishment of necessary skills. Other treatment modalities include contingency management, cognitive therapy, exposure-based therapies, and medication.

Practicing DBT

The provision of DBT therapy is easier to accomplish in an inpatient, partial hospitalization or residential treatment setting rather than in outpatient practice. The reason is that, as described by Linehan (1993), DBT is best implemented with a treatment team in which one therapist provides psychosocial skill training, another provides individual therapy, others can provide a consultation function; and the therapists have access to a therapist consultation group for support. Recently, Marra (2005) has offered suggestions for adapting DBT treatment in private practice settings. While he recommends that skills training be provided by another therapist, he offers guidelines when that is not possible. Nevertheless, he encourages any private practice clinician who anticipates utilizing DBT to have access to a psychotherapy consultant if involvement in a therapist consultation group is not possible.

Research Support. Finally, empirical support exists for the effectiveness of DBT. Several randomized controlled trials that evaluated the overall effectiveness of comprehensive DBT treatment have been published (Koons et al., 2001; Linehan et al., 1991; Linehan et al., 2002; Linehan et al., 2006; Verheul et al., 2003). When evaluated against treatment-as-usual control conditions, DBT was superior. While most of this research focused on borderline personality disorders in females, some studies modified DBT for use in other populations and in various settings. These include studies with adolescents and adults in inpatient and forensic settings with various disorders including binge eating disorder, bulimia, anorexia nervosa, chronic depression, and other personality disorders. However, there is very little research on the use of DBT with males or minorities (Lynch & Cuper, 2012).

Cognitive Behavioral Analysis System of Psychotherapy

Cognitive Behavioral Analysis System of Psychotherapy (CBASP) is a form of CBT that was developed by McCullough (2000) and further elaborated (McCullough, Schramm, & Penberthy, 2015). Basic to this approach is a situational analysis which combines behavioral, cognitive, and interpersonal methods to help clients focus on the consequences of their behavior and to use problem solving for resolving both personal and interpersonal difficulties. CBASP was initially targeted for the treatment of clients with chronic depression. A national, multi-site study launched CBASP as an effective treatment. Clients who met criteria for chronic unipolar depression, usually meeting criteria for both major depressive disorder and dysthymic disorder, were randomly assigned to one of three treatment groups: medication only (nefazodone, with the trade name of Serzone), psychotherapy (CBASP) only, or a combination of medication and CBASP. While clients in all three treatment conditions improved significantly, those receiving the combined treatment improved the most. Over the 12-week study period, 55 percent of the medication-only group reported a positive response, and 52 percent of the CBASP-only group experienced a treatment response, whereas 85 percent of those who took both medication and received CBASP had a positive response to treatment (Keller et al., 2000).

Theory

A basic assumption of CBASP is that clients can learn to analyze specific life situations and then manage daily stressors on their own. The basic premise of CBASP is simple and straightforward: a therapist assists clients to discover why they did not obtain a desired outcome by evaluating their problematic thoughts and behaviors. In short, therapists assist clients in determining which thoughts and behaviors have gotten in the way of achieving what they wanted. Since there is often a mismatch between what a client wants and what actually occurs in the client's life, the CBASP approach can be utilized with a variety of distressing problems and presentations ranging from child behavior problems and couple's conflict to anxiety disorders and personality disorders, including borderline personality disorder (Driscoll, Cukrowicz, Reardon, & Joiner, 2004). Interestingly, McCullough (2002) noted his reservations to utilizing CBASP with adults with severe borderline personality disorder, particularly those with comorbid chronic depression.

Treatment

The overall goal of CBASP treatment is to identify the discrepancy between what clients want to happen in a particular situation and what has or is actually happening. By examining their specific circumstances, clients gradually discovers problematic themes and patterns in their lives as well as ways in which they can achieve what is desired.

There are two phases in CBASP treatment: elicitation and remediation. The elicitation phase consists of six steps which are framed by specific questions: How would you describe the situation? How did you interpret the situation? Specifically, what did you do and what did you say? What did you want to get out of the situation, i.e., what was your desired outcome? What was the actual outcome of this situation? And, finally: Did you get what you wanted?

During the remediation phase, behaviors and interpretations or cognitions are targeted for change and revised so that the client's new behaviors and cognitions will contribute to and result in their desired outcome. First, each of the client's interpretations of the situation is assessed to determine whether it helped or hindered the achievement of the desired outcome. Next, each of the client's behaviors is similarly analyzed to determine whether or not it helped or hindered in the attainment of the desired outcome (Driscoll, Cukrowicz, Reardon, & Joiner, 2004).

A modified version of this approach (Sperry, 2005, 2006, 2014) is particularly useful in working with personality-disordered individuals, particularly those who are assessed as low in learning from experiences on their ABCDEF profile. Such individuals have not had sufficient experience in learning from their mistakes because they too often engage in emotional thinking rather than in consequential thinking. This modified intervention strategy works by increasing consequential thinking. It focuses the individual's attention on the link between how their negative or self-defeating thoughts and behaviors result in the negative consequence (actual outcome) they end up with instead of the desired outcome that they really want. The strategy includes nine steps which begin with a cognitive and a behavioral analysis and proceed to processing their interpretations and behaviors in terms of their desired outcome or consequence.

The steps are first listed and then illustrated in the following case and transcription.

Step 1: Can you describe what happened?
Step 2: What was your interpretation of [your thoughts about] the situation?
Step 3: What were your behaviors? [What did you say, what did you do?] Your feelings?
Step 4: What were your expectations [what did you want or hope would happen]?

Step 5: What actually happened?

Step 6: Did your behaviors and thoughts help or prevent [hurt] you from getting what you wanted?

Step 7: It didn't sound like it did. Can we analyze this together to see what happened and what might be different?

Step 8: How did your behaviors [thoughts/interpretations] help get you what you wanted? OR How did your behaviors [thoughts/interpretations] prevent [hurt] you from getting what you wanted? OR Were your expectations realistic?

Step 9: What thoughts might have better helped you get what you wanted? OR What behaviors might better help you get what you want the next time a situation like this comes up? OR How can your expectations be modified to be more realistic?

Case Illustration

Jason is a 20–year-old single Caucasian male who is beginning his sophomore year of college. He presents for therapy because social anxiety is inhibiting his life in a various ways. Although he can participate in most solitary and family activities, he experiences considerable anxiety in situations in which he has to be around or interact with others. This includes being in class, going to the grocery store, having to speak in class, etc. This has been somewhat problematic since age 12 but has increased since he is away from home and in college where activities that he previously did not have to attend to, i.e., going shopping or speaking in class were not problems since his mother did most of the shopping and home-schooled him. His DSM-5 diagnoses are: Social Anxiety Disorder and Avoidant Personality Disorder.

This is their fifth session. For the three previous sessions the focus was on exposure to difficult, anxiety-provoking situations without talking to anyone in those situations. Jason was introduced to this modified version of CBASP in the previous session and he and the therapist agreed on an assignment that he would undertake and report on in their following session. The following vignette focuses on just one interpretation and one behavior related to that assignment at the beginning of this session. The therapist began by eliciting his thoughts and behaviors regarding the assignment.

Therapist:	So can we review your assignment from your last session? (Sure). It was for you to make eye contact with someone and greet that person. Is that right?
Jason:	Yeah. I went to the grocery store Friday night, and when I was going through the checkout line, I said hello to the grocery clerk and asked her how she was doing.
Therapist:	Okay, now on to Step 2. What were your interpretations or thoughts when you were in that situation?

Jason: One of my thoughts was "I'm not normal because I am here alone."

Therapist: Okay. So one of your interpretations in this situation was "I'm not normal because I am here alone." I see your SUDS rating for this thought was 90. This seems to be a good interpretation for us to focus on. Let's also look at your behaviors. What did you do in that situation?

Jason: While I was in the grocery store, I kept my head down the entire time and looked at the floor or nothing at all, except when I looked at the clerk and made eye contact with her.

Therapist: What else did you do?

Jason: I just pretty much kept my head down and did not talk to anyone except for when I asked the clerk how she was doing. So I said: "hi" and asked her how she was doing. I probably said it very softly.

Therapist: Did the clerk respond?

Jason: Yes she said she was doing fine. But then I couldn't think of anything else to say so I looked back down and didn't say anything else.

Therapist: So your behaviors in this situation were to keep your head down and look at the floor and not to talk to anyone except when you greeted the clerk.

Jason: Yes.

Therapist: So, what was your desired outcome?

Jason: To go to the grocery store and get my groceries without any stress.

Therapist: And what was the actual outcome?

Jason: I got my groceries but my SUDS was about 85 or 90. I was able to make eye contact with the grocery clerk and ask her how she was doing.

Therapist: Did you achieve your desired outcome then?

Jason: Sort of. I was able to make eye contact with the clerk and speak to her, but I wasn't able to talk to anyone else or even look at anyone else and I still experienced a lot of stress.

Therapist: It sounds like you may have actually had two desire outcomes then. One was to get your groceries without experiencing any stress. But it also seems like another desired outcome for you was to be able to make eye contact and greet a person while in the grocery store. Do you think that is true?

Jason: I guess so. I was able to look at the clerk and ask her how she was doing. But I still experienced a lot of anxiety while in the grocery store and I couldn't think of anything else to say to the woman at the checkout counter.

Therapist: Do you think that both going to the grocery store and not experiencing any stress are realistic desired outcomes for you that time?

Jason: No, it really wasn't.

Therapist:	What might have been a more realistic desired outcome for you at that time?
Jason:	It would have been to make eye contact with someone, say "hello", and ask the person how he or she is doing while trying to tolerate my anxiety a little better.
Therapist:	That does sound more realistic. (Pause). So, did you get the outcome you wanted?
Jason:	I suppose so. But I still wasn't able to think of anything else to say, and my SUDS level was about 90 when I spoke to the grocery clerk, which bothered me a lot.
Therapist:	Okay, then, let's go back through your interpretations to see which ones were helpful and hurtful to you in getting your desired outcome of making eye contact with someone and greeting the person, while tolerating any anxiety. Your first interpretation was, "I am not normal because I am here alone." Do you think that thought was helpful or hurtful to you in this situation?
Jason:	Hurtful.
Therapist:	Why?
Jason:	Because I kept my head down and didn't speak to anyone because they would look at me and think I was weird because I was alone and because I was talking to them.
Therapist:	Can you think of any thoughts, then, that you could replace the hurtful thought with that would be helpful to you in this situation?
Jason:	I am normal.
Therapist:	Good. How do you think that would have helped you?
Jason:	Well, if I kept telling myself that I was normal and was not weird for being there alone, and that it's okay to feel anxious, I may have been more likely to have kept my head up and made eye contact with someone. I probably would have been more likely to say hello to someone.
Therapist:	So telling yourself "I am normal and I am not weird for being here alone or feeling anxious" would have made it easier for you to keep your head up, make eye contact with others, and to talk to other people?
Jason:	Yes.
Therapist:	It seems, though, that in this situation you were able to do that. You made eye contact with the checkout clerk and greeted her.
Jason:	But I still felt a lot of anxiety, which really bothered me, and that made it harder to look up.
Therapist:	Do you think that your replacement thought would have made you feel less anxious, then, or help you accept the anxiety you felt?
Jason:	Probably. It would have been a lot easier for me.
Therapist:	So your interpretation "I am not normal because I am here alone" was hurtful to you because it made you keep your head down and not speak to anyone while you were in the grocery store, except

| | when you spoke to the clerk, and then you still experienced a lot of anxiety, which made you feel more uncomfortable. If you replaced that interpretation, then, with "I am normal and I am not weird for being here alone, and it's okay to feel anxious" you would have experienced less anxiety or been more accepting of it, and you would have been more likely to keep your head up and speak to others. Is that right? |

Jason: Yes.

Therapist: Then let's move to your behaviors. One of them was to keep your head down the entire time, except when you made eye contact with the clerk. Do you think this was helpful or hurtful to you in achieving the outcome you wanted?

Jason: Hurtful. I probably would have been more likely to make eye contact with other people and maybe even say hi if I didn't look down the entire time.

Therapist: But you were able to make eye contact and speak to the clerk. How was it hurtful, then?

Jason: While I was looking at the ground, I just kept thinking about how I wasn't normal and that I just wanted to leave.

Therapist: So keeping your head down actually made you think more negatively?

Jason: Yes. If I had my head up and looked at other people, I might have been distracted and not thought those things over and over again.

Therapist: Then, what behavior would have been helpful to you in this situation?

Jason: To keep my head up. I probably wouldn't have thought negatively as much and would have been more likely to make eye contact with others and to even speak to people in the grocery store.

Therapist: So in this situation, if you would have thought to yourself "I am normal and I am not weird for being here alone, and it's okay to feel anxiety" instead of, "I am not normal because I am here alone, and I shouldn't feel anxiety," and if you would have kept your head up instead of looking at the ground the entire time you would have been more likely to get your entire desired outcome, which was to make eye contact and greet someone while feeling less anxiety and better tolerating the anxiety you did feel, right?

Jason: Yes, that is right.

Commentary. This was Jason's first experience with analyzing and processing his interpretations and behaviors and their problematic consequences, and replacing them with more helpful and adaptive ones. Often, clients with chronic and difficult to treat clinical disorders with co-occuring personality disorders are not initially responsive to Cognitive Therapy or CBT that emphasizes cognitive restructuring. To the extent to which they rely on emotional thinking they are unlikely to learn from experience. However, many respond very positively to this intervention strategy which fosters consequential thinking and more adaptive functioning. Jason's increasing use of consequential thinking is even more apparent in the subsequent session. The transcription of that session appears in Chapter 5.

Mindfulness: DBT and Mindfulness-Based Cognitive Therapy

Mindfulness can be defined as paying attention in a particular way that is intentional, in the present moment, and nonjudgmentally (Kabat-Zinn, 1994). This awareness is based on an attitude of acceptance of personal experience that involves a commitment to living fully in the present moment. Training in mindfulness offers practice in "facing" rather than "avoiding" potential problems and difficulties. This is accomplished through meditative practices such as the body scan, mindful stretching, and mindfulness of breath, body, sounds, and thoughts. These practices teach the core skills of concentration; mindfulness of thoughts, emotions, feelings, and bodily sensations, as well as being present, letting go; and accepting life as it is. This leads to an "aware" mode of being characterized by freedom and choice, in contrast to a mode dominated by habitual patterns of automatic thinking and acting, or "automatic pilot" living. Accordingly, the goal of mindfulness training is to teach individuals how to respond to stressful situations "mindfully" rather than to react automatically to them.

There are several different approaches to acquiring mindfulness, but two, Dialectical Behavior Therapy and Mindfulness-Based Cognitive Therapy, have particular relevance in working with personality-disordered individuals. The contributions of each will be described.

Mindfulness in Dialectical Behavior Therapy

In DBT, mindfulness meditation is a necessary skill to be developed as well as an underlying attitude. Validation is a core strategy in DBT, used to counteract the effects of an invalidating environment and to foster self-validation. DBT therapists search to validate or acknowledge the "wisdom" of a patient's experience. This reflects the Buddhist principle of radical acceptance and the belief that everything is perfect as it is. Patients are encouraged to understand that all behavior can be understood in terms of their consequences. For example, in response to a patient who describes cutting his or her wrist in order to avoid shameful feelings, a DBT therapist might say: "It's not surprising that you would want to stop your painful feelings by cutting your wrists, since most of us don't like to experience painful feelings." DBT therapists model an attitude of acceptance toward self and others, and genuine acceptance is an essential element in effective treatment.

Mindfulness is taught as a core skill in the context of group skills training (Linehan, 1993). The training format consists of a year-long program with weekly 2-to 2.5-hour classes of about eight patients and two facilitators. Mindfulness skills make up the first of four skills modules and involve a series of meditative practices for cultivating awareness and acceptance. Patients learn to achieve mindfulness through learning "what" skills and practicing "how" skills. Instruction involves didactic and experiential learning as well as assigned homework. In contrast to MBCT, which prescribes a formal meditation practice, DBT often relies on informal mindfulness practice such as mindfulness of everyday activities (Linehan, 2014). This difference is based on the opinion that patients with severe personality disorders, such as borderline personality disorder, are less able to productively engage in lengthy sitting practice.

Mindfulness-Based Cognitive Therapy

Mindfulness-Based Cognitive Therapy (MBCT) was developed by Segal and colleagues (Segal, Williams, & Teasdale, 2002, 2013). It is considered one of the "third wave" CBT approaches. MBCT integrates aspects of Cognitive Therapy with components of Mindfulness-Based Stress Reduction (MBSR), which was developed by Kabat-Zinn (1994). MBSR is a widely used adjunctive to medical treatment for various clinical conditions as well as self-help technique for stress management and non-clinical conditions.

Thus, MBCT emphasizes changing the awareness of, and relation to, thoughts, rather than changing thought content. It offers participants a different way of living with and experiencing emotional pain and distress. The assumption is that cultivating a detached attitude toward negative thinking provides one with the skills to prevent escalation of negative thinking at times of potential relapse.

Usually, MBCT skills are taught by one instructor in 8 weekly 2- to 3-hour group sessions. In each session, participants engage in various formal meditation practices designed to increase moment-by-moment, nonjudgmental awareness of physical sensations, thoughts, and feelings. Assigned homework includes practicing these exercises along with exercises designed to integrate application of awareness skills into daily life. Specific prevention strategies derived from traditional Cognitive Therapy methods are incorporated in the later weeks of the program.

Finally, empirical support exists for the efficacy of integrating mindfulness meditation with Cognitive Therapy. A comprehensive review of 64 published empirical studies concluded that MBSR can help a broad range of individuals cope with clinical and non-clinical problems (Grossman, Niemann, Schmidt, & Walach, 2004). Even though it was noted that there were some methodological problems with the studies, it is interesting to note that both controlled and uncontrolled studies show similar effect sizes of 0.5 ($P < .0001$). A much smaller review of 13 studies (4 controlled and 9 uncontrolled) concluded that MBSR is probably more effective with non-clinical than with clinical problems (Bishop, 2002).

Other Cognitive Behavioral Methods

Cognitive Coping Therapy

Cognitive therapies (CT) and cognitive behavior therapies (CBT) have long been used in the treatment of personality disorders (Beck et al., 2015). Cognitive restructuring, wherein maladaptive beliefs or schemas are identified, processed, and challenged, is the most widely known and utilized treatment strategy associated with those approaches. Coping skills methods are commonly an adjunctive to cognitive restructuring. Typically, therapists using CT or standard CBT will first turn to cognitive restructuring to treat the presenting problem. Then they pull from coping skills therapy whatever specific skills are needed to achieve the planned treatment goals and outcomes (Sharoff, 2002). However, in complex cases, such as those with chronic depression or anxiety symptoms, low motivation for treatment, emotional lability, and histories of chronic relapse—characteristics common to many personality-disordered individuals—cognitive restructuring has limited utility. However, cognitive coping therapy has been developed as an alternative treatment to cognitive restructuring and appears to be a particularly promising and potent treatment strategy with personality disorders.

As described by Sharoff (2002), cognitive coping therapy is an active, directive, didactic, and structured approach for treating clients in a short time frame. It is a complete and self-contained approach to treatment that begins with assessing an individual's coping skills—in terms of skill chains, subskills and microskills—and then increasing skill competence in targeted areas as needed. Five key skill areas with representative treatment modalities include: *cognitive skills*—problem solving, self-instruction training and self-management; *emotion skills*—emotional containment and compartmentalization; *perceptual skills*—perspective taking, thought stopping, and psychological distance taking; *physiological skills*—meditation and relaxation training; and *behavior skills*—communication and assertiveness training.

Like other skill intervention strategies, described by Sperry (2006), the cognitive coping therapy approach is also a bottom-up approach that, when combined with top-down treatment strategies such as cognitive restructuring, therapeutic confrontation, or interpretation, can greatly enhance treatment outcomes with personality-disordered individuals.

Structured Treatment Interventions

Unlike schemas which reflect the psychological dimension of personality, temperament, i.e., the innate, genetic, and constitutional aspect of personality, reflects its biological dimension. Temperament plays an important role in the regulation and dysregulation of an individual's affective, behavioral, and cognitive styles (Sperry, 1999, 2003). While research shows that medication can modulate or normalize dysregulated behaviors, a similar modulating effect has also been noted for social skills training (Lieberman, DeRisi, & Mueser, 1989). Thus, it appears that social skills training is a relatively potent bottom-up treatment strategy for normalizing such limbic system mediated behaviors as impulsivity, aggressivity, and mood lability, to name a few. Sperry (1999, 2006) contends that personality-disordered individuals typically exhibit significant skill deficits, and that structured skill training interventions are useful and necessary in successful treatment of moderate to severe personality disorders. Skill deficits can be reversed by the acquisition of requisite skills in individual and group sessions through practice via modeling, coaching, role-playing, and graded task assignments.

Summary

This chapter described several CBT approaches and interventions that are particularly effective in modifying schemas and basic character structure. These approaches primarily effect change with a top-down strategy. Generally, this strategy can be reasonably sufficient in personality-disordered individuals who are high functioning, it is not in others. What is needed is a bottom-up approach which addresses temperament to complement the top-down strategy. In other words, effective change nearly always requires addressing both character and temperament factors. Because structured skills training is a potent bottom-up treatment strategy, it is commonly used—either alone or with medication—as an adjunct to standard CBT interventions like cognitive restructuring or cognitive and behavior replacement, as in CBASP. Several of these structured intervention strategies for modifying affective, behavioral, cognitive, distress tolerance styles are described in Chapter 4.

4 Cognitive Behavior Therapy and Personality Disorders

Interventions: II

This chapter sets the stage for the Cognitive Behavioral treatment of specific personality disorders [covered in Chapters 5–10] by emphasizing CBT interventions particularly effective in modulating temperament and style. As noted in Chapter 1, temperament primarily reflects the biological dimension of personality, whereas character and schema primarily reflect the psychological dimension of personality. Furthermore, personality-disordered individuals tend to be over- or undermodulated in terms of temperament, and irresponsible, uncooperative, and self-focused in terms of character (Cloninger, Svrakic, & Przybecki, 1993). Accordingly, effective treatment of personality disorders must address both of these disordered dimensions of personality. Unfortunately, therapeutic strategies that are effective in modifying character and schemas tend to be minimally effective in modulating temperament and style (Cloninger, 2004; Young, Klosko, & Weishaar, 2003). However, there are specific treatment interventions, particularly social skills training and other focused behavioral strategies, as well as medication, that are effective in modulating temperament.

This chapter begins with a brief explanation of how modulating temperament requires certain types of interventions. It then describes the dimensions of temperament in terms of its regulation and dysregulation of behavior. Next, it provides a brief overview of skills, skill deficits, and skill training and their role in regulating or modulating the temperament/style dimensions of personality-disordered individuals. This is followed by a listing of personality disorders classified as either internalization or externalization disorders. Finally, 16 intervention strategies useful in this modulation process are described. Resource citations are provided for each strategy. The reader will note that reference is made to these strategies in subsequent chapters of this book.

Neuroscience, Genetics, and Temperament Modulation

Recent findings in neuroscience and molecular genetics are providing valuable insights into the assessment and treatment of personality disorders (South, Reichborn-Kjennerud, Eaton, & Krueger, 2012). The fact is that psychological interventions can and do influence the brain. In noting the differential effect of medication and psychotherapeutic interventions on neuronal functioning and brain circuits, neuroscience researchers have come to conceptualize treatment process in terms of either "top-down" or "bottom-up" strategies (Sperry, 2006). "Top-down" refer to treatment efforts that are primarily focused on cortical structures and neural tracts (top), which also can influence subcortical circuits, particularly in the limbic system (down). Similarly, "bottom-up" refers to the treatment efforts that are largely focused on limbic circuits, which can also produce changes in cortical circuits.

Recent research suggests that the symptoms prominent in some personality disorders, like Antisocial and Borderline Personality Disorder, result from a failure of circuits in the prefrontal cortex to appropriately regulate the limbic system. Presumably, this malfunction begins early in life and likely is influenced by genetics, adverse experiences, and other environmental factors. The end result is disrupted brain development, and problems in the neural circuits that facilitate top-down control of the limbic system including the amygdala and hippocampus (Hooley, Cole, & Gironde, 2012).

There is increasing interest in efforts to normalize the expression of under- and overmodulated styles or temperament traits with behavioral interventions and medication (Reich, 2000, 2005; Sperry, 2006). For example, top-down treatment strategies typically utilize standard psychotherapies, i.e., cognitive restructuring and dynamic interpretations, to enhance cortical influences on limbic circuits. The goal is to undo negative learning, particularly maladaptive beliefs, and to increase the modulating or normalizing effects of emotional responses. Bottom-up treatment strategies typically involve the use of skill training and/or medication in order to modulate harmful and other overmodulated behavior patterns and emotional states by normalizing the activity of limbic structures (Hooley, Cole & Gironde, 2012). There is mounting evidence that skill-based interventions (as in Dialectical Behavior Therapy) are effective in regulating or moderating these circuits. Such interventions may actually be as or more effective than medication as bottom-up strategies (Fawcett, 2002). Besides the group skills training in Dialectical Behavior Therapy, it appears that other forms of social skills training (Lieberman, DeRisi, & Mueser, 1989) like cognitive coping therapy (Sharoff, 2002) and Cognitive Behavioral Analysis System Therapy (McCullough, 2000) also function as effective bottom-up treatments.

Dimensions of Temperament

Cloninger (2004) noted that temperament and character can be measured with biological markers and self-report instruments. On Cloninger, Svrakic, and Przybeck's (1993) *Temperament Character Inventory (TCI)*, individuals with increased dysregulation of one or more of the temperament dimensions typically experience considerable distress and impairment in life functioning. Just as schema—and its modification—is central to this book, so also is temperament and style—and their modulation. In fact, effective treatment for many personality-disordered individuals will require addressing both schema and style treatment targets.

Skills, Skill Deficits, and Skills Training

Effective functioning in daily life requires mastery of a number of requisite personal and relational skills. Most individuals begin learning these requisite skills in childhood and further refine them throughout the course of adolescence and early adulthood. Some individuals have the requisite skills but for conscious or unconscious reasons do not use them. Other individuals have never learned or sufficiently mastered these skills. This lack of learning or mastery of a basic requisite skill is called a skill deficit (Lieberman et al., 1989). It is a basic premise of this book that most personality-disordered individuals have skill deficits. Because of these deficits, these individuals experience, to varying degrees, dysregulation of one or more temperament dimensions that cause distress to themselves or others. The three temperament or style dimensions emphasized in this book are affective style, behavioral and relational style, and cognitive style. Over- or undermodulation of one or more of these styles can significantly affect the level of symptoms and overall level of functioning. In other words, requisite skills—including coping skills—have the effect of regulating or modulating temperament or style dimensions, whereas skill deficits make it more difficult, if not impossible, to modulate style dimensions.

Recall the case examples in Chapter 2. Both Keri and Cindy presented for treatment following a suicide gesture. Although both had the same diagnosis and level of education, Keri's Global Assessment of Functioning score was 40 (with 71 as the highest in the past year) and Cindy's was 27 (with 42 as the highest in the past year). Keri's high level of premorbid functioning suggested that she had mastered most requisite skills, including coping skills, to achieve her level of success. Cindy, on the other hand, had significant skill deficits, which explains why affective, behavioral/relational, and cognitive styles were so overmodulated.

Clinicians can effectively assist individuals in reversing such skill deficits by working with clients to acquire the personal and relational skills that they have not previously mastered. These skills can be learned directly in individual sessions through practice, that is, coaching and role playing, and through graded task assignments. When feasible, group treatment settings can be particularly useful for social skills training (Lieberman et al., 1989).

For those personality-disordered individuals with significant symptomatic distress and who exhibit significant functional impairment, traditional psychotherapeutic interventions are of limited use. However, medication and structured interventions called skills training are quite effective when temperament dysregulation is present. In addition, these structured interventions are effective when skill deficits are indicated.

Externalizing and Internalizing Personality Disorders

Researchers have proposed an internalization-externalization model for classifying behavior and disorders based on reactions to stress. Externalizing
behaviors are characterized by external actions such as emotional reactivity,
hostility, acting out, and impulsivity. In contrast, internalizing behaviors are
characterized by internal processes such as anxiety, depression, and somatiza-
tion. Temperament is thought to be the basis for this model. The model has
been applied to the personality disorders. Internalizing personality disorders
are associated with negative emotionality and constraint, while the externalizing personality disorders are associated with negative emotionality and a lack
of constraint. "Both internalizing and externalizing disorders involve emotional distress, expressed inwards (internalized) when people have normative
levels of constraint, and expressed outwards (externalized) when emotional
distress is accompanied by a lack of constraint" (Krueger & Tackett, 2003,
p. 122). Another way of conceptualizing the internalization-externalization
classification is in terms of two types of maladaptive coping: overcontrol and
undercontrol. Undercontrol reflects an externalizing style characterized by
emotionally deregulated and impulsive disorders, while overcontrol reflects an
internalizing style characterized by emotionally constricted, perfectionistic,
and rigid disorders (Lynch & Mizon, 2011). Table 4.1 lists personality disorders in terms of internalization or externalization.

Table 4.1 Classification of Personality Disorders (PD) as Externalizing
or Internalizing Disorders

Externalizing Disorders	Internalizing Disorders
Borderline PD	Avoidant PD
Antisocial PD	Obsessive-Compulsive PD
Narcissistic PD (overt)	Narcissistic PD (covert)
Histrionic PD	Dependent PD

Structured Treatment Interventions for Personality Disorders

The 16 structured interventions are detailed in Table 4.2. These interventions are referred to throughout the book. Each intervention is described in a
step-wise fashion that illustrates its application in the treatment setting. At
least one key reference or resource is provided for each of these interventions
so that the reader may pursue additional information on using these effective
therapeutic interventions.

Anger Management Training

The purpose of anger management training is to decrease the arousal and
expression of hostile affects, while increasing the individual's capacity to

Table 4.2 Structured Intervention Strategies
for Personality Disorders

---

 1. Anger Management Training
 2. Anxiety Management Training
 3. Assertiveness Training
 4. Distress Tolerance Training
 5. Emotional Regulation Training
 6. Empathy Training
 7. Impulse Control Training
 8. Interpersonal Skills Training
 9. Limit Setting
10. Mindfulness Training
11. Problem-Solving Training
12. Radical Openness Skills Training
13. Self-Management Training
14. Sensitivity Reduction Training
15. Symptom Management Training
16. Thought Stopping

---

tolerate and channel this energy in prosocial ways. This is usually a therapist-directed intervention that can be applied in individual or group treatment context. It is then practiced and applied by the individual. Collaboration between clinician and the individual tends to increase the individual's motivation and compliance. The intervention proceeds in the following fashion:

First, the clinician instructs the individual in the four sets of factors that determine the response of anger in that individual: (a) high-risk circumstances (external, contextual factors, such as individuals, places, or times of day that can potentially provoke an angry or rageful response in the individual); (b) internal triggering factors (internal factors, such as the individual's feelings, cravings, level of fatigue that render the individual more vulnerable to an angry response); (c) individual self-statements (specific beliefs that can render the individual more vulnerable to an angry response, or that can defuse an angry response); and (d) individual's coping skills that neutralize or exacerbate the effects of these internal and external factors.

Second, the clinician instructs/trains the individual in identifying the four sets of factors, and develops—with the individual—a checklist or form of the most likely factors for that individual. For example, the clinician asks the individual to describe a recent instance of a response of anger, and assists the individual in indicating the four specific factors. He had been stopped for speeding and for driving while under the influence of alcohol: (a) he left a tavern after four drinks and decided to drive home rather than take a cab (high-risk circumstance); (b) he was tired after a stressful day at work and was disinhibited and feeling bad that someone had just broken his car aerial (internal triggering factor); (c) he was thinking: "Why does this stuff always happen to me?" and "Nobody does this to my car and gets away with it" (self-statement); and (d) he is impulsive with a "hair-trigger" temper (coping skills) and speeds off angry and resentful.

Third, the clinician tells the individual to write down each incident in which he felt anger, the four factors, and what he did when he experienced that emotion (i.e., cursed and kicked the side of his car when he noticed the car aerial was broken). The individual then self-monitors these factors and responses between sessions with the form. During subsequent sessions, the clinician and individual review the form. They analyze the factors looking for commonalities and specifying coping skill deficits (i.e., he's mostly likely to be angry and disinhibited when he's tired, been stressed at work, or been drinking).

Fourth, the clinician works with the individual to specify alternatives to these high-risk circumstances (i.e., if he's been drinking he'll take a cab or ask a designated driver to get home). Then, the clinician helps the individual to specify a plan for reducing the various internal triggering factors (i.e., when he's tired and stressed out he can go jogging rather than go to the tavern).

Fifth, the clinician instructs and assists the individual to learn effective, alternative self-statements to cope with anger-provocation (i.e., "It's too bad this happened, but I don't have to go ballistic over it").

Finally, the clinician trains the individual in learning relaxation skills (i.e., controlled breathing and counting to 10 before acting when he sees that his car has been vandalized) and other coping skills such as assertive communication as an alternative to the anger and rageful responses.

Resources

Glick, B., & Gibbs, J. (2011). *Aggression replacement training: A comprehensive Intervention for aggressive youth* (3rd ed.). Champaign, IL: Research Press.

Potter-Efron. R. (2007). *Rage: A step-by-step guide to overcoming explosive anger.* Oakland, CA: New Harbinger Publications.

Anxiety Management Training

The purpose of anxiety management training is to decrease the arousal and expression of distressing affects, and to increase the individual's capacity to face and tolerate these affects. This is usually a therapist-directed intervention that can be applied in individual or group treatment context. It is then practiced and applied by the individual. Collaboration between clinician and the individual tends to increase the individual's motivation and compliance. The intervention proceeds in the following fashion.

First, the clinician instructs the individual in the determinants of the response of anxiety in that individual: (a) external triggering factors, such as specific individuals or stressful demands that can potentially elicit anxiety in the individual; (b) internal triggering factors, such as physiological responsivity and individual self-statements, that is, specific beliefs that can render the individual more vulnerable to anxiety, or that can neutralize it; and (c) individual's coping skills that neutralize or exacerbate the effects of these internal and external factors.

Second, the clinician instructs the individual in identifying the three sets of factors, and develops—with the individual—a checklist of the most likely factors for that individual. The clinician then asks the individual to describe a recent incidence of anxiety and assists the individual to specify the three specific factors. In the example of performance anxiety, the individual is (a) assigned to give a quarterly business report at a board of directors meeting (external trigger); (b) experienced moderate physiological reactivity during other public presentations: "I feel completely inadequate giving a speech to my superiors." "I know I'm going to screw up, and I'll be so embarrassed" [internal triggers]; and (c) prefaces the presentation by asking the group's indulgence saying she is a better accountant than public speaker (coping skills) and experiences feelings of inadequacy, dry mouth, sweaty palms, and heart palpitations while giving the presentation. Alternately, an anxiety survey can be used, and if there are more than one anxiety responses, an anxiety hierarchy survey can be used.

Third, the clinician tells the individual to write down each incident in which she has experienced anxiety, the three factors, and what she did when experiencing that emotion (i.e., she quickly excused herself after giving the report, experienced some relief, but concluded she had failed again). The individual then self-monitors these factors and responses between sessions with the form.

Fourth, during subsequent sessions, the clinician and individual review the checklist. They analyze the factors looking for commonalities and specifying coping skill deficit (i.e., she's likely to experience performance anxiety when addressing superiors, although she has no problem giving presentations to peers or inferiors).

Fifth, the clinician works with the individual to consider options when faced with external triggers (i.e., to inquire about submitting a written rather than verbal report, or having a colleague give the presentation, while she is present to field questions on the report).

Sixth, the clinician works with the individual to specify a plan for reducing the various internal triggering factors, that is, learning to reduce physiological reactivity by controlled breathing or other relaxation exercises, and specifying more adaptive self-statements, that is, "My worth as a person and as an employee doesn't depend on how well I can give speeches. This is only one small part of my job"; "I know this material cold—certainly better than anyone on board. I can get through this 5-minute talk and maybe even enjoy it."

Seventh, the clinician trains the individual in learning relaxation skills, such as controlled breathing 10 minutes prior to giving a presentation, and other coping skills as an alternative to the anxiety and self-deprecatory responses. Treatment progress is evaluated based on the individual's increasing capacity to face internal and external triggering factors with more adaptive coping behaviors. The individual's self-report of the absence of, or a significant reduction in, anxiety in such circumstances indicates the treatment has been effective.

Resources

Quick, E. (2013). *Solution focused anxiety management: A treatment and training manual.* Burlington, MA: Academic Press.
Suinn, R. (1991). *Anxiety management training: A Behavior Therapy manual.* New York, NY: Springer.

Assertiveness Training

The purpose of assertiveness training is to increase an individual's capacity for expressing thoughts, feelings, and beliefs in a direct, honest, and appropriate manner without violating the rights of others. More specifically, it involves the capacity to say "no," to make requests, to express positive and negative feelings, and to initiate, continue, and terminate conversations. Lack of assertive behavior is usually related to specific skills deficits, but it is sometimes related to interfering emotional reactions and thoughts. Assertiveness training proceeds in the following fashion.

First, the clinician performs a careful assessment to identify the following: situations of concern to the individual; current assertiveness skills; personal and environmental obstacles that need to be addressed, such as difficult significant others or limited social contexts; and personal and environmental resources that can be drawn on.

Second, the clinician formulates an intervention plan. If appropriate behaviors are available but not performed because of anxiety, the focus may be on enhancing anxiety management skills. Discrimination training is required when skills are available but are not performed at appropriate times. If skill deficits are present, skill training is indicated.

Third, the intervention is introduced. For skill training, the clinician teaches the individual specific skills via modeling, behavioral rehearsal, feedback, and homework. Modeling effective behavior in specific situations is accomplished by using one or more of the following methods: in vivo demonstration of the behavior by the clinician, written scripts, videotapes, audiotapes, or films. In behavior rehearsal, the individual is provided opportunities to practice the given skill in the clinical setting.

Fourth, the clinician provides positive feedback following each rehearsal in which effective verbal and nonverbal reactions are noted and specific changes that could be made to enhance performance are identified. Homework assignments involve tasks that the individual agrees to carry out in real-life contexts.

Fifth, the length of assertion training depends on the domain of social behaviors that must be developed and on the severity of countervailing personal and environmental obstacles. If the response repertoire is narrow, such as refusing requests, and the obstacles minor, only a few sessions may be required. If the behavior deficits are extensive, additional time may be required even though only one or two kinds of social situations are focused on during intervention. Assertiveness training can occur in individual sessions, group therapy, as well as in other small contexts such as support groups and workshops. Sank and Shaffer (1984) provided a detailed four-session assertiveness training module for use in a structured group therapy context.

Resources

Alberti, R. (2008). *Your perfect right: Assertiveness and equality in your life and relation-ships* (9th ed.). San Luis Obispo, CA: Impact Publications.
Michelli, D. (2013). *The assertiveness workbook: A teach yourself guide.* New York, NY: McGraw-Hill.

Distress Tolerance Skill Training

Distress tolerance is the capacity to perceive one's environment without demanding it be different, to experience one's current emotional state without attempting to change it, and to observe one's thought and action patterns without attempting to stop them. Thus, it is the ability to tolerate difficult situations and accept them. Typically, lower functioning individuals with borderline and histrionic personality disorders have difficulty tolerating distress. Distress tolerance training attempts to help the individual to develop skills and strategies to tolerate and survive crises and to accept life as it is in the moment. Among individuals with mood lability and impulsivity, the ability to tolerate distress is a prerequisite for other therapeutic changes. This intervention is usually introduced and demonstrated by the clinician. It is then practiced and applied by the individual. As such, it is a self-management intervention. Initially, the clinician may have to cue the individual to apply the technique within and between treatment sessions. The intervention proceeds in the following fashion.

First, the clinician assesses the individual's ability to distract themselves from painful emotional thoughts and feelings, and to soothe themselves in the face of worry, loneliness, and distress. Skill deficits in either or both areas are noted.

Second, based on this assessment, the clinician instructs the individual in one or both of the following essential skills and strategies: distraction and self-soothing methods. If distraction is a basic skill deficit, it becomes the focus of treatment. Distraction techniques include thought stopping, shifting attention by making a phone call, watching television or listening to music, jogging, comparing oneself to others who are less well off, and intense sensations; for example, placing one's hand in a container of ice water or flicking a thick rubber band on one's wrist to produce a painful but harmless sensation intense enough to derail the thought and impulse for wrist-cutting and other self-harmful behaviors.

Third, if self-soothing is a basic skill deficit, it becomes the focus of treatment. Self-soothing techniques include controlled breathing exercises—in which air is drawn in slowly and deeply and then exhaled slowly and completely—savoring a favorite food or snack, and listening to or humming a soothing melody. Acceptance skills include radical acceptance—complete acceptance from deep within, turning the mind toward acceptance—choosing to accept reality as it is, and willingness, versus willfulness.

Resource

Linehan, M. (2015). *Skill training manual for treating borderline personality disorder* (2nd ed.). New York, NY: Guilford.

Emotion Regulation Skill Training

Individuals who habitually exhibit emotional lability may benefit from help in learning to regulate their emotions. Emotion regulation skills can be extremely difficult to teach, because emotionally labile individuals often believe that if they could only "change their attitude" they could change their feelings. Labile individuals often come from environments where others exhibit cognitive control of their emotions, and show little tolerance of the individuals' inability to exhibit similar control. Subsequently, labile individuals often resist attempts to control their emotions because such control implies that others are right and they are wrong for feeling the way they do. Much of the labile individual's emotional distress is a result of such secondary responses as intense shame, anxiety, or rage to primary emotions. Often the primary emotions are adaptive and appropriate to the context. The reduction of this secondary distress requires exposure to the primary emotions in a nonjudgmental atmosphere. Accordingly, mindfulness to one's own emotional responses is essentially an exposure technique. This intervention typically proceeds in the following fashion.

First, the clinician assesses the individual's overall skill in emotional regulation, and then the sub-skills of identifying and labeling affects, modulating affects, and mindfulness.

Second, the clinician formulates a plan for reversing the skill deficit(s). Skill training can occur in either an individual or group treatment context. Although the skills of emotion regulation can be learned in an individual-treatment context, group context greatly facilitates these efforts. Skill training groups can provide a measure of social support and peer feedback that individual treatment cannot.

Third, the clinician, whether in an individual or a skills-group context, teaches, models, and coaches the individual(s) in the given sub-skill of emotional regulation. The first step in regulating emotions is learning to identify and label emotions. Identification of an emotional response involves the ability to observe one's own responses as well as to describe accurately the context in which the emotions occur. Identification is greatly aided if one can observe and describe the event prompting the emotion, can interpret the event that prompts the emotion, can differentiate the phenomenological experience, including physical sensations of the emotion, and can describe its effects on one's own functioning.

Similarly, emotional lability can be attenuated by controlling the events that triggered the emotions or by reducing the individual's vulnerability to lability. Individuals are more susceptible to emotional lability when they are under physical or environmental stress. Accordingly, individuals should be assisted in reducing such stressors by achieving a more balanced lifestyle. This includes appropriate nutrition, sufficient sleep, adequate exercise, reduction of substance use, and increased self-efficacy. Although these targets seem straightforward, making headway on them with labile individuals can be exhausting for both individuals and clinicians. Work on any of these targets requires an active stance by the individuals and persistence until positive effects begin to accrue.

Increasing the number of positive events in one's life is one approach to increasing positive emotions. Initially, this involves increasing daily positive experiences. Subsequently, it means making life changes so that positive events will occur more often. In addition to increasing positive events, it is also useful to work on being mindful of positive experiences when they occur, and unmindful of worries that the positive experience will end. Mindfulness to current emotions means experiencing emotions without judging them or trying to inhibit them, block them, or distract from them. The assumption is that exposure to painful or distressing emotions, without association to negative consequences, will extinguish their ability to stimulate secondary negative emotions. Whenever a individual already feels "bad," judging negative emotions as "bad" leads to feelings of guilt, anger, or anxiety, which further increases distress intolerance. Frequently, individuals can tolerate a painful affect if they can refrain from feeling guilty or anxious about feeling bad in the first place.

Fourth, the clinician works together with the individual to arrange for the individual to practice a given skill(s) both within and outside the treatment context. Within the treatment context, the use of role play can be particularly valuable in reinforcing the individual's newly acquired skill(s). Particular situations and relationships can be targeted for practice outside the treatment context.

Resource

Linehan, M. (2015). *Skill training manual for treating borderline personality disorder* (2nd ed.). New York, NY: Guilford.

Empathy Training

Empathy training is a technique for more directly enhancing the individual's empathic abilities. In empathy training, the individual is asked to think about and then communicate his/her understanding of the feelings and point of view of the other. These understandings are then checked out with the other individual and inaccuracies are corrected. Particular attention is given to the individual's understanding of what he/she has done or said that has aroused hurt feelings in the other, and what the other wishes would have happened instead of what did happen. The technique of empathy training is a powerful tool for interrupting projective identification and splitting. It often leads to greatly increased awareness of the feelings and needs of the other. This, in turn, greatly facilitates constructive negotiation and problem solving. Although there are various approaches to empathy training, the relationship enhancement approach has been demonstrated to be effective with personality-disordered individuals, including individuals with narcissistic personality disorder in a relatively short time—three to four sessions—particularly if empathy training takes place in the context of couples sessions. The intervention proceeds in the following fashion.

First, the clinician assesses the nature and extent of the individual's capacity to manifest the three skills of empathy: active listening, accurately interpreting interpersonal cues, and responding empathically.

Second, assuming an empathic deficit (i.e., in one or more of the three skills of empathy), the clinician begins the training by modeling the three skills of empathy. After being continually modeled by the clinician, the individual begins to develop empathic understanding and responding.

Third, the clinician begins to coach the individual on the given skill(s) beginning with non-relationship issues, and then moving to positive feelings before progressing to conflicts. The clinician teaches the individual to access the underlying vulnerability and the healthy needs that underlie his narcissistic defense. This is done through the dual process of empathic listening and the coaching of skilled expression of one's authentic feelings and point of view. The individual initially tends both to experience and express vulnerability in the form of anger, criticism, and blame. Empathic listening becomes a way of calming the individual's reflexive reactions and of creating a pause between emotions and the reflexive, harmful behaviors that have resulted from those emotions.

Fourth, empathy training also assists individuals in monitoring their emotional reactivity. Individuals typically experience that listening empathically and responding within the guidelines for effective expression feels supportive to them. They also begin to discover that when emotions are accurately observed and expressed subjectively with increasing consciousness of how meanings affect feelings, these emotions shift or even vanish quite rapidly. What often perpetuates anger, for example, is the lack of full attention to it on the part of the individual, and to the meanings and desires it reveals. When this attention neither inhibits nor defends the emotion, but instead maintains a compassionate and curious observer stance, change in feelings, meanings, and actions can occur quickly.

Resources

Guerney, B. (1988). *Relationship enhancement manual*. State College, PA: IDEALS.
Scuka, R. (2005). *Relationship enhancement therapy: Healing through deep empathy and intimate dialogue*. New York, NY: Routledge.

Impulse Control Training

Impulse control training is an intervention in which the goal is to reduce involuntary urges to act. This intervention is usually introduced and demonstrated by the clinician. It is then practiced and applied by the individual. As a result of applying this intervention, the individual increases self-control. This intervention involves three phases: assessment, training, and application. The intervention proceeds in the following fashion.

First, the clinician undertakes an assessment of the pattern of the individual's thoughts and feelings that lead up to self-destructive or maladaptive impulsive behavior. Once this pattern is understood, it is possible for the individual to find other ways to accomplish the same result that have fewer negative effects and are more likely to be adaptive.

Second, the clinician and individual examine the individual's thoughts and feelings leading up to self-destructive or maladaptive impulse behaviors. For example, the individual keeps a log of thoughts and feelings associated with each impulsive behavior.

Third, the clinician teaches the individual competing responses to impulses by inducing an urge to act impulsively, and then helping the individual to implement strategies to delay acting on that impulse for progressively longer periods of time, which can be cognitive (i.e., counting to 10 before acting or speaking when upset) or muscle relaxation (i.e., progressive relaxation). The most common competing responses are systematic distractions that are either internal or external. Internal distractions are thoughts that are incompatible with the impulses. For example, the individual's self-talk becomes: "This is actually funny, and I'm going to smile instead of fume." External distractions include a change in the environment that focuses the individual's attention. For instance, the individual is prompted to leave the room when a parent is shouting at him and in the past, he has the impulse to hit the parent.

Fourth, the clinician helps the individual practice and supplies feedback until the individual develops a reasonable level of mastery. The clinician teaches the individual to apply internal and/or external distractions to neutralize maladaptive impulses. For example, when the individual is around his father who is drinking, he avoids getting hooked into fighting by conjuring up an image of Charlie Chaplin walking with a drunken limp, and then telling his father he has to leave to meet a friend.

Finally, because self-destructive impulsive behavior can be particularly problematic, it is essential for the clinician to develop a clear understanding of a individual's motivation for self-destructive behavior by examining the thoughts and feelings leading up to the self-destructive impulses or behavior, and then by asking directly, "What were you trying to accomplish through this action?" Suicide attempts, self-mutilation, and other self-destructive acts can be the product of many different motives: desire to punish others at whom the client is angry, desire to punish oneself or obtain relief from guilt, desire to distract oneself from even more aversive obsessions, and so forth. Once the motivation is understood, it is possible for the individual to find other ways to accomplish the same result that have fewer untoward effects and are more likely to be adaptive. For example, it may be possible to substitute a minimally self-destructive behavior, such as marking oneself with a pen, for a more self-destructive act, such as wrist-slashing. This less destructive act can later be replaced with a more adaptive alternative. Not surprisingly, if the risk of the individual's performing seriously self-destructive acts is high, and the above-described interventions do not prove effective in the limited time available, hospitalization may be needed to allow sufficient time for effective intervention.

Resource

Linehan, M. (2015). *Skill training manual for treating borderline personality disorder* (2nd ed.). New York, NY: Guilford.

Interpersonal Skills Training

Interpersonal skills refer to a broad range of skills in relating socially and/or intimately with others. These include distress tolerance, emotional regulation, impulse control, active listening, assertiveness, problem solving, friendship skills, negotiation, and conflict resolution. Lower functioning personality-disordered individuals may have significant skill deficits, while higher functioning personality-disordered individuals tend to have better developed conversational skills. However, to be effective interpersonally requires much more than the capability of producing automatic responses to routine situations. It also requires skills in producing novel responses or a combination of responses when the situation demands. Interpersonal effectiveness is the capacity to appropriately respond assertively, to negotiate reasonably, and to cope effectively with interpersonal conflict. Effectiveness means obtaining the changes one wants, by keeping the relationship and one's self-respect. And, even if higher functioning borderline individuals possess adequate interpersonal skills, problems arise in the application of these skills in difficult situations. They may be able to describe effective behavioral sequences when discussing another person encountering a problematic situation but may be totally incapable of carrying out a similar behavioral sequence when analyzing their own situation. Usually, the problem is that both belief patterns and uncontrollable affective responses are inhibiting the application of social skills. These individuals often prematurely terminate relationships, or their skill deficits in distress tolerance make it difficult to tolerate the fears, anxieties, or frustrations that are typical in conflictual situations. Similarly, problems in impulse control and emotional regulation lead to inability to decrease chronic anger or frustration. Furthermore, a deficit in problem-solving skills makes it difficult to turn potential relationship conflicts into positive encounters. In short, interpersonal competence requires most of the other skills described in this chapter as well as others. The intervention proceeds in the following fashion.

First, the clinician must assess the individual's current relational skills and skill deficits. The skills to be assessed include distress tolerance, emotional regulation, impulse control, assertiveness, problem solving, active listening, friendship skills, negotiation, and conflict resolution. Specific skill deficits are noted.

Second, the clinician formulates a plan for dealing with the noted skill deficit(s). If there are global deficits, it might require referral to a group focused on social skills training. Such groups are invaluable in providing social support while individuals are learning personal and interpersonal skills.

Third, skill training begins either in an individual or group-treatment context. Usually the sequence involves modeling of a given skill, and then coaching to achieve increasing levels of mastery. Interventions that involve several modes of practice or enactment seem to be the most efficacious and time efficient. Video demonstration of the skills, role-play practice, and homework exercises are integral features of such an approach. Assuming that an individual who has been referred to a skills training group is also in individual treatment, the clinician assesses and monitors progress.

Fourth, the clinician works together with the individual to arrange for the individual to practice a given skill(s) outside the treatment context. This usually includes initiating conversations with strangers, making friends, making and going on dates. Assessment of the skill level is followed by additional modeling and coaching.

Resource

Linehan, M. (2015). *Skill training manual for treating borderline personality disorder* (2nd ed.). New York, NY: Guilford.

Limit Setting

Limit setting is an intervention designed to help individuals recognize aspects of themselves that are being defended against by resorting to a destructive, outer-directed activity or diversion. Personality-disordered individuals often have difficulty maintaining boundaries, as well as appreciating and anticipating the consequences, especially the negative consequences, of their actions. Limit setting is a therapeutic intervention that is quite useful in as well as outside treatment settings. The intervention proceeds in the following fashion.

First, the clinician observes or anticipates one of the following individual behaviors: treatment-interfering behaviors, such as coming late for sessions, missing a session, unnecessarily delaying or failing to make payment; harmful behavior to self or others, including parasuicidal behaviors; inappropriate verbal behavior (e.g., abusive language); dominating treatment by excessive or rambling speech; efforts to communicate with the clinician outside the treatment context (i.e., unnecessary phone calls); inappropriate actions (e.g., hitting or unwanted touching, breaking or stealing items); or failure to complete assigned therapeutic tasks (i.e., homework). For example, a fashionably dressed individual complained of financial hardships and requested a special reduced fee and payment schedule.

Second, the clinician begins implementing limit setting. The limit is specified in "if __ then __ " language. It is crucial that the clinician state the limit in a neutral, non-critical tone and nonjudgmental language. In the above example, rather than making special concessions to him, the standard fee arrangements were clearly explained. He was told that if he could not afford to be seen at the clinic, the clinician would be sorry but would assist him in finding lower cost treatment.

Third, the clinician explains the rationale for the limit. In the above example, it was further explained that allowing him to accumulate a sizable bill would not be in his best interest.

Fourth, the clinician specifies or negotiates with the individual the consequences for breaching the limit. In the above example, that clinician told the individual that if he would fall behind in payments by two sessions, according to clinic policy, he would need to wait until his balance was current before additional sessions would be scheduled.

Fifth, the clinician responds to any breeches of the limit setting. Because individuals can and do test limits—whether for conscious or unconscious reasons—more commonly in the early phase of treatment, limit testing should be expected. The clinician should be prepared to respond by confronting and/ or interpreting it; enforcing the consequences and discussing the impact of the breech on treatment; or predicting that such testing may reoccur. For example, in the above case, the individual did test the agreement once; the clinician expressed concern but upheld the limit. Thereafter, the individual kept up with his payments and his treatment continued.

Resource

Green, S. (1988). *Limit setting in clinical practice*. Washington, DC: American Psychiatric Press.

Mindfulness Training

There are at least two types of mindfulness training that have been found useful in working with personality-disordered individuals. The first one to be articulated, Dialectical Behavior Therapy (DBT) involves six skills, while Mindfulness-Based Cognitive Therapy (MBCT) involves four skills. The skill sets for both of these approaches are briefly described.

Dialectical Behavior Therapy

Mindfulness is the first, and most important, of four core skill sets that make up the psychoeducational component of DBT. These skills are usually taught in a group format by someone other than the individual's therapist. A recent adaptation of DBT for private practice allows individuals to learn the skills in a one-to-one or group setting (Marra, 2005). Linehan (1993) divides mindfulness skills into two categories: what skills and how skills. The what skills include: Observe—just notice without getting caught in the experience; Describe—put words on the experience; and Participate—become one with your experience; while the how skills include: Nonjudgmental—see but do not evaluate; One-Mindful—do one thing at a time; Effective—do what needs to be done in each situation. The reader will note that unlike mindfulness in MBCT, DBT does not include any formal meditation. That is because Linehan contends that sitting meditation exercises are too demanding for individuals with severe personality disorders, such as borderline personality disorder. Following is a brief description of the six mindfulness skills in DBT.

OBSERVE

Goal: The goal is to sense or experience something without describing or labeling the experience. It is noticing or attending to something without getting caught up in the experience and without reacting to it.

Activities for Skill practice: Encourage individuals to have a "Teflon mind" so that experiences, feelings, and thoughts that enter the mind slip right out. Develop exercises wherein individuals can practice observing. For example, have them close their eyes and watch their thoughts coming and going like clouds in the sky. Have them notice each feeling, rising and falling, like waves in the ocean. Or, have them take a walk and attend to every sensation they have through their senses—the feel as they step on the walkway or small pebbles on a path, the scents they smell, the hue of colors they see, the sounds of insects, animals and the wind.

DESCRIBE

Goal: The goal is to use words or thoughts to label what has been observed. Describing involves reporting facts without making judgment or evaluation, e.g., "It tasted sour" instead of "I didn't like the taste"; and "He told me what happened" instead of "He's not very honest."

Activities for Skill practice: Design exercises where individuals can have an experience and provide a running commentary. For example, when a feeling, inner sensation, or thought arises, they might say outloud to a person they are paired up with: "I'm feeling anxious right now" . . . or . . . " my stomach muscles are tightening" . . . or . . . "The thought 'I just can't do this exercise' has come into my mind." For homework, assign them a diary or journal exercise: have them describe in writing what is happening; putting a name on their feelings, i.e., calling a thought just a thought, and a feeling just a feeling without getting caught up in content.

The conveyor belt exercise: Have them imagine a conveyor belt. As thoughts and feelings come down the conveyor belt, sort them into categories. For example, there is one box for thoughts of any kind, one box for sensations in your body, and one box for urges to do something (e.g., stopping). Have them rate and log their efforts at developing this skill on a 1–10 scale, and review the log periodically.

PARTICIPATE

Goal: The goal is to entering wholly into an activity, becoming one with the activity. Participating means that individuals throw themselves fully into something 100 percent. It means becoming one with their experience, completely forgetting themselves. While it is spontaneous behavior to a certain extent, it is done from a mindful perspective.

Activities for Skill practice: Design activities in which individuals can get fully involved in the moment, while letting go of ruminating. For example, have individuals actively practice a social skill in which they have a deficit, e.g., for the individual who is shy and avoidant around others, have him or her practice making small talk, talking about the weather or an upcoming social or sports event. Practice is continued throughout the entire course so that the new skill is learned so it can be done without being self-conscious. Have them rate and log their efforts at developing this skill on a 1–10 scale, and review the log periodically.

NONJUDGMENTAL

Goal: The goal is to take a nonjudgmental stance when observing, describing, and participating. Judging involves any labeling or evaluation of something as good or bad, as valuable or not, as worthwhile or worthless. There is a difference between a judgment and a statement of fact. A statement of fact may seem to be a judgment because the fact is simultaneously being judged. For example: "I am fat" may simply be a statement of fact. But, if one adds (in thoughts, implication, or tone of voice) that the idea of being fat is bad or unattractive, then a judgment is added. The motto or mantra for this week should be: "Observe but don't judge."

Activities for Skill practice: Design exercises for class format so individuals can focus on the "*what*," instead of the "good" or "bad" or the "should" or "should not." You might have them listen to clips of dialogue from a popular TV show or movie and have them point out judgmental vs. nonjudgmental stance. It is useful to give them home assignments in which they can note in their diary or journal situations in which they did or could have practiced a nonjudgmental stance. Have them rate and log their efforts at developing this skill on a 1–10 scale, and review the log periodically.

ONE-MINDFUL

Goal: The goal is to focus on one thing in the moment—awareness of what you are doing. This means focusing attention only on one activity or thing at a time, bringing one's whole self into the task or activity. A motto or mantra for the course could be: Do one thing at a time. When eating—eat. When walking—walk. When bathing—bathe. When working—work. When in a group or one-on-one conversation—focus attention only on the person speaking. When thinking—think. When worrying—worry. Do each thing with all of your attention. If other actions, or other thoughts, or strong feelings distract one, let go, let go of distractions and get further in touch with your true self. The opposite of it is mindlessness, i.e., automatic behaviors without awareness, and distracted behavior, i.e., doing one thing while thinking about or attending to another instead of doing—again, and again, and again.

Activities for Skill practice: Design exercises for class format and for home assignments so individuals can practice one-pointed attention or concentration. If they find they are doing two things at once, stop and go back to one thing at a time. Point out that focusing on one thing in the moment does not mean that they cannot do complex tasks requiring many simultaneous activities. But, it does mean that whatever one does, one should attend fully to it, that is, to focus attention only on one activity or thing at a time, bringing one's whole self into the task or activity. Have them rate and log their efforts at developing this skill on a 1–10 scale, and review the log periodically.

EFFECTIVE

Goal: The goal is to focus on being effective. It means focusing on what works, and doing what needs to be done in each situation. It means limiting the use of evaluative comments such as "fair" and "unfair," "right" and "wrong," "should" and "should not." As Marsha Linehan puts it: "Don't cut off your nose to spite your face."

Activities for Skill practice: Plan exercises in which individuals can act as skillfully as they can, and meet the needs of the situation they are in. A useful home assignment is to have individuals maintain a log or diary of the instances in the past week in which they attempted to keep sight of their objective in specific situations and do what is necessary to achieve them. The goal is to accomplish one's objective without vengeance, useless anger, or righteousness. Have them rate and log their efforts at developing this skill on a 1–10 scale, and review the log periodically.

Mindfulness-Based Cognitive Therapy Approach

Mindfulness-Based Cognitive Therapy (MBCT) is another strategy for incorporating mindfulness into psychotherapy. It utilizes a skill-training group format to teach four sets of mindfulness skills in order to increase individuals' moment-to-moment awareness and to approach situations with an attitude of nonjudgment and acceptance. It involves intensive training both in a class format facilitated by an instructor rather than a therapist, and home practice. The four sets of meditative practices or skills are:

BODY SCAN

This skill guides individuals to shift attention throughout the body to explore directly sensations in the body, without having to change them or achieve any special state.

STRETCH AND BREATH

This skill involves a sequence of five simple standing stretches to bring body sensations into focus during each movement with focus on sensations of the breath.

YOGA

This skill involves simple stretches starting from a lying posture to allow individuals to explore sensations of the body in movement and stillness, and to explore the how the body has limits that can be respected without judgment and self-criticism.

SITTING MEDITATION

This skill guides individuals to focus in turn on the breath, the body, sounds, thinking, and emotions. Individuals learn to see their own thoughts and emotions from a new perspective, relating to them as they relate to sounds, discovering that thoughts often come and go as leaves on a stream or as white clouds passing across a blue sky.

Resources

Linehan, M. (2015). *Skill training manual for treating borderline personality disorder* (2nd ed.). New York, NY: Guilford.

Segal, Z., Williams J., & Teasdale J. (2002). *Mindfulness-based cognitive therapy for depression.* New York, NY: Guilford Press.

Segal, Z., Williams J., & Teasdale J. (2013). *Mindfulness-based cognitive therapy for depression* (2nd ed.). New York, NY: Guilford Press.

Problem-Solving Skills Training

Problem-solving skills training is a treatment intervention strategy through which individuals learn to use an effective set of skills to cope with distressing or troublesome personal and interpersonal situations. The goals of this form of social skills training are to assist individuals in identifying problems that cause their distress, to teach them a systematic method of solving problems, and to equip them with a method for approaching future problems. Problem-solving training is often a brief method of intervention that can be used in individual, couples, and group-treatment contexts. This is a clinician-initiated intervention that requires some training and practice by the individual to master this set of skills. This intervention proceeds in the following fashion.

First, the clinician assesses the individual's capacity to solve problems in terms of the five skills involved in problem solving. The five are problem identification, goal setting, generating alternative courses of action, decision making, and implementation of the decided course of action.

Second, the clinician explores with the individual the origin and nature of a specific problematic situation (i.e., problem identification). For instance, the individual notes that she runs out of money about one week before receiving her monthly paycheck, because of impulse buying during the first 3 weeks of the month.

Third, the clinician helps the individual to assess the problem, identify causative factors, and set realistic goals. In the above example, impulse buying is identified as the cause, and the goal set is to budget money to last the entire month, and to save 10% in a bank account.

Fourth, the clinician helps the individual to generate alternative courses of action. In terms of the example, alternatives are discussed. One is to develop a 30-day budget, a second is to ask the employer for a biweekly paycheck, and the third is to have an automatic paycheck deposit to a bank account.

Fifth, the clinician helps the individual choose a course of action with regard to its short- and long-range consequences. In this example, the individual decides that setting up a budget is the most realistic short- and long-term course of action.

Sixth, the clinician offers information and supports the individual's efforts to implement the course of action. In this case, the individual agrees to meet with a financial planner and sets up a monthly and annual budget plan, and also opens a savings account.

Resource

McKay, M., Davis, M., & Fanning, P. (2012). *Thoughts and feelings: Taking control of your moods and your life* (4th ed.). Oakland, CA: New Harbinger Publications.

Radical Openness Skills

Radical Openness Dialectical Behavior Therapy is an extension of standard Dialectical Behavior Therapy. The primary focus of standard Dialectical Behavior Therapy is to reduce severe emotional dysregulation and behavioral undercontrol, which are core issues in individuals with borderline personality disorder and other externalizing personality disorders. By contrast, the primary focus of Radical Openness Dialectical Behavior Therapy is to reduce behavioral overcontrol, rigidity, and emotional constriction and increase flexibility, openness to new experience, and encourage expression of emotions. These are core issues in individuals with obsessive-compulsive personality disorder and other internalizing disorders. Skills training is central to standard Dialectical Behavior Therapy and it is also central to Radical Openness Dialectical Behavior Therapy. However, there are some modifications in the skill modules of core mindfulness, distress tolerance, emotion regulation, and interpersonal effectiveness. These modifications are briefly noted.

Mindfulness Skills

In standard Dialectical Behavior Therapy, mindfulness skills target problems associated with identity confusion and emptiness whereas Radical Openness Dialectical Behavior Therapy mindfulness practices target problems associated with rigid adherence to rules, extreme needs for structure, and excessive desires to avoid making mistakes. Mindfulness practices focus on nonjudgmental acknowledgment of desires for compliance and rule adherence, while cultivating a compassionate, nonjudgmental stance valuing both an appreciation for rules and spontaneity.

Emotion Regulation Skills

In general, emotion regulation skills with overcontrolled individuals follows a standard Dialectical Behavior Therapy module with some important differences. First, overcontrolled individuals are less likely to exhibit extreme and/or public displays of emotionally dysregulated or impulsive behaviors. Accordingly, Radical Openness Dialectical Behavior Therapy emotion regulation skills target the tendencies of overcontrolled individuals to mask inner feelings. Instead, it emphasizes experiencing emotions and the expression of emotions. Another main difference between the two approaches is a focus on new skills to replace envy, resentment, revenge, and bitterness. These negative states result from the overlearned tendencies to compare oneself with others and to achieve more than others.

Distress Tolerance Skills

Unlike individuals with externalizing personality disorders who exhibit impulsiveness and crisis-oriented behaviors, there is little need for crisis survival skills among those with internalizing personality disorders. Rather, over-controlled individuals tend to be distress overtolerant. Accordingly, Radical Openness Dialectical Behavior Therapy focuses on only two of the standard distress tolerance skills: self-soothing and radical acceptance skills.

Interpersonal Effectiveness Skills

Most of the interpersonal skills taught in standard Dialectical Behavior Therapy are applicable to overcontrolled individuals. Nevertheless, overcontrolled individuals are urged to add Radical Openness skills to interpersonal effectiveness skills practices.

Resources

Linehan, M. (2015). *DBT skills training manual* (2nd ed.). New York, NY: Guilford.
Lynch, T. (in press). *Dialectical behaviour therapy for treatment resistant depression: Targeting emotional constriction.* New York, NY: Guilford.

Self-Management Skills

Self-management skills are needed to learn, maintain, and generalize new behaviors and to inhibit or extinguish undesirable behaviors and behavioral changes. In its widest sense, self-management means efforts to control, manage, or otherwise change one's own behavior, thoughts, or emotional responses to events. Thus, the skills of distress tolerance, emotion regulation, impulse control, and anger management can be thought of as self-management skills. More specifically, self-management skills refer to the behavior capabilities that an individual needs to acquire further skills. To the extent that individuals are deficient in self-management skills, their ability to acquire other skills is seriously compromised. Individuals often need some knowledge of the principles of behavior change to effectively learn self-management skills. For instance, an individual's belief that people change complex behavior patterns in a heroic show of willpower sets the stage for an accelerating cycle of failure and self-condemnation. The failure to master a goal becomes additional proof that explanations of failure, such as laziness, lack of motivation, or lack of willpower, are true. The clinician must confront and replace these notions of how individuals change. In short, principles of learning and behavioral control, as well as knowledge about how these principles apply in each individual's case, are important targets in teaching self-management skills. Learning these targeted concepts often involves changes in a individual's belief system. The intervention typically proceeds in the following manner.

First, the clinician assesses the individual's overall level of self-management, as well as specific subskills of goal setting, self-monitoring, environmental control, toleration of limited progress, and relapse prevention.

Second, the clinician formulates a plan for dealing with the noted skill deficit(s). If there are global deficits, it might require referral to a group focused on social skills training. Such groups are invaluable in providing social support while individuals are learning personal and interpersonal skills.

Third, skill training begins either in an individual- or group-treatment context. Usually the sequence involves modeling of a given skill, and then coaching to achieve increasing levels of mastery. Interventions that involve several modes of practice or enactment seem to be the most efficacious and time efficient. Video demonstration of the skills, role-play practice, and home-work exercises are integral features of such an approach. Assuming that an individual who has been referred to a skills training group is also in individual treatment, the clinician assesses and monitors progress.

Individuals need to learn how to formulate positive goals in place of nega-tive goals, to assess both positive and negative goals realistically, and to exam-ine their life patterns from the point of view of values clarification. Individuals typically believe that nothing short of perfection is an acceptable outcome. Behavior change goals are often sweeping in context and clearly exceed the skills the individuals may possess. Clinicians will need to teach individuals such skills as self-monitoring and environmental monitoring, setting up and evaluating baselines, and evaluating empirical data to determine relation-ships between antecedent and consequent events and their own responses. These skills are very similar to the hypothesis-testing skills taught in cognitive therapy.

The belief that an individual can overcome any set of environmental stim-uli is based on the assumption that it is possible to function independently of one's environments. Given this belief, it is not surprising that some individu-als have skill deficits when it comes to using their environments as a means of controlling their own behavior. Nevertheless, some individuals are more responsive to transitory environmental cues than others. As a result, the capa-bility to manage environmental surroundings effectively can be particularly crucial. Techniques such as stimulus narrowing, that is, reducing the number of distracting events in the immediate environment, and stimulus avoidance, that is, avoiding events that trigger problematic behaviors, can be targeted to counteract the belief that willpower alone is sufficient.

Some individuals respond to a relapse or small failure as an indication that they are total failures and may as well give up. Accordingly, they will develop a self-management plan and then unrealistically expect perfection in adhering to the plan. The issue and focus of relapse prevention is attitude change. It then becomes essential to teach individuals to plan realistically for relapse, to develop strategies for accepting the possibility of a slip, and to ameliorate the negative effects of relapse.

Because some individuals have limited tolerance for feeling bad, they have difficulties carrying out behavior change action plans that require persever-ance. Rather, they will often seek a quick fix that involves setting unreason-ably short time limits for relatively complex changes. In other words, they expect instantaneous progress. If it does not occur, they believe they have failed. Therefore, emphasizing the gradual nature of behavior change and tolerance of concomitant negative affect should be a major focus of clinician effort.

Fourth, the clinician works together with the individual to arrange for the individual to practice a given skill or skills outside the treatment context. This usually includes initiating conversations with strangers, making friends, making and going on dates. Assessment of the skill level is followed by additional modeling and coaching.

Resource

Linehan, M. (2015). *Skill training manual for treating borderline personality disorder* (2nd ed.). New York, NY: Guilford.

Sensitivity Reduction Training

Sensitivity reduction training is an intervention to neutralize and delimit an individual's vulnerability to criticism, misperception, and suspiciousness. Individuals who habitually misperceive and negatively distort social cues are prone to defensive and acting out behaviors. Instead, this intervention teaches individuals to more accurately attend to, process, and respond more effectively to social cues. This is a clinician-initiated intervention wherein the clinician collaborates with the individual to learn and practice more accurate use of social information. This intervention proceeds in the following fashion:

First, the clinician recognizes that these oversensitivity reactions involve errors and distortions in the course of the information processing. Information processing can be thought of in terms of four components: attending, information processing, responding, and feedback. Subsequently, this intervention is directed to these four components.

Second, the clinician assesses how the individual attends to the full range of social cues. This can be done by reviewing important social interactions of the individual, and critically assessing how the individual attends to pertinent social cues. For instance, an individual reports that as he enters a social gathering, a small group of people look at him and smile, then he hears a whispered comment after which everyone laughs. If the individual selectively attends only to the whispered comment and disregards the other two cues: smiling and laughter, he could misperceive the situation and respond defensively. If the individual is not identifying and attending to such pertinent cues, the clinician focuses training in this area.

Third, the clinician then assesses the accuracy of the individual's interpretation of this social information. Selective attention and misperception can be processed as threatening. Teaching the individual to interpret social cues more accurately is essential. This training can be accomplished with role playing, videotaped feedback, and instruction.

Fourth, the clinician assesses how the individual responds to these cues. Responding refers to the individual's response to the social cues of others ranging from spoken words, paralanguage, and overt actions. Responses can range from appropriate and prosocial to inappropriate and harmful. To the extent that the individual is able to accurately attend to and process social cues, the individual is more likely to appropriately respond to the cue. Training is directed at appropriate responding. Although the focus of training is often on verbal responding, at times the individual's tone of voice, facial expression, or hand gesturing needs to be changed to make it less menacing.

Fifth, the clinician assesses how the individual uses the consequences of his or her social behavior, and the extent to which it is appropriate or maladaptive. Negative feedback can be useful information and the individual needs to learn to use it constructively. Furthermore, with improvement in social behavior, positive consequences should accrue to the individual.

Resource

Turkat, I. (1990). *The personality disorders: A psychological approach to clinical management*. New York, NY: Pergamon Press.

Symptom Management Training

Symptom management training is an intervention strategy for controlling the distressing manifestations (i.e., symptoms) of psychiatric disorders. Although symptoms are of varying types and levels of intensity and duration, individuals tend to report symptoms without such differentiation, and unless the clinician clarifies the type and intensity/duration, referrals or needless changes in treatments, such as medication dosage or other medications added, can result in significant untoward effects on the treatment process. Personality-disordered individuals are more likely to experience low-grade, subclinical symptoms (i.e., persistent symptoms) than acute symptoms. Yet, they are likely to demand increased medication or changes in medication, not realizing that persistent symptoms are rarely responsive to medication. Accordingly, this intervention often requires the use of psychosocial and psychoeducational methods. Symptom management training involves learning such skills as self-monitoring, medication compliance, and relapse prevention. It can be taught in individual or group treatment settings. It is a clinician-initiated intervention that involves mutual collaboration to assess, teach-learn, and practice the requisite skills. This intervention proceeds in the following fashion.

First, the clinician assesses and evaluates the type and nature of symptoms experienced by the individual. Symptoms are of three types: (a) persistent symptoms (i.e., chronic, low-grade symptoms not ameliorated by medication), (b) warning symptoms (i.e., symptoms gradually increasing in intensity that precede an acute episode), and (c) acute symptoms (i.e., the full-blown inca-pacitating symptoms that often signal acute decompensation). The nature of symptoms includes both their intensity and duration.

Second, the clinician works with the individual to increase his or her awareness and understanding of the types and nature of symptoms and the skills necessary to effectively manage symptoms. The individual is taught the self-monitoring skill of identifying the type of symptom and intensity (i.e., rates and logs on a 5-point scale: 1 = *mild*, 5 = *very severe*), and duration (logs the amount of time in minutes and number of times the symptom types occur each day for 1 week).

Third, an intervention is planned and tailored to the particular type and expression of symptoms experienced by the individual. Accordingly, acute symptoms are usually treated with medication or medication combined with an individual or group psychosocial or psychoeducational treatment. Psycho-educational methods vary from learning activities and formats that include videotapes, role playing, and homework assignments. Because warning symp-toms can result from insufficient medication levels, it is useful to raise medi-cation levels or consider adding an additional medication. Because warning symptoms can result from stopping or decreasing medication, it is essential to inquire about medication noncompliance, which may necessitate checking with a caretaker or significant other. On the other hand, persistent symptoms seldom suggest insufficient medication levels or noncompliance. Thus, they do not require changing dosage or drug regimen, but rather psychoeducational methods such as distraction techniques. For example, the individuals with low-level but chronic dysphoria might achieve considerable relief by distract-ing themselves from the low energy and blue mood by listening to uplifting or energetic music or watching a funny video movie.

Fourth, the individual practices the interventions (i.e., rating and logging symptoms) and distraction techniques for a given time frame and reports the results at the next meeting with the clinician.

Resource

Liberman, R. (1988). *Social and independent living skills: Symptom management module: Trainers manual*. Los Angeles, CA: Rehabilitation Research.

Thought Stopping

Thought stopping is a self-control intervention to block and/or eliminate ruminative or intrusive thought patterns that are unproductive or anxiety-producing. It may also have the effect of increasing the individual's sense of control and reducing distress. This intervention is usually introduced and demonstrated by the clinician. It is then practiced and applied by the indi-vidual. As a result of applying this intervention the individual increases his sense of control. The intervention proceeds in the following fashion.

First, the clinician instructs the client on the similarities between normal and obsessive/intrusive thoughts. An agreement is reached to try to reduce the duration of the intrusive thoughts, thus making them more "normal" and increasing the client's sense of control.

Second, the clinician and client draw up a list of three obsessional thoughts and several specific triggering scenes. Then a list of up to three alternative thoughts (i.e., interesting or relaxing thoughts) is made. For example, a scene from a movie, lying on a sandy beach, or taking a walk through the woods. Each obsessional thought is rated for the discomfort it produces on a scale of 1 to 10 (1 = *lowest*, 10 = *highest*).

Third, the clinician demonstrates how to block obsessional thoughts and substitute an alternative thought. The clinician directs the individual to close his eyes and become relaxed with the instruction to raise a hand when the obsessional thought is first experienced. For example: "Sit back and relax and let your eyes close. I'll mention a specific triggering scene to you, and then describe you experiencing an obsessional thought. As soon as you begin to think the thought, raise your hand, even if I'm only describing the scene." The clinician then describes a typical triggering scene, and as soon as the individual raises a hand, the clinician says "Stop!" loudly. The clinician asks the client whether the obsessional thought was blocked and whether the individual was able to imagine the alternative scene in some detail. The discomfort arising from that obsessional thought is then rated on the 1–10 scale.

Fourth, the clinician then leads the client in practicing thought-stopping with different triggering scenes and alternative thoughts, and the discomfort ratings are recorded. Practice continues until the individual can sufficiently block and replace the obsessional thought.

Fifth, the procedure is modified so that following the clinician's description of the triggering scene and obsessive thought, the client says "Stop" and describes the alternative scene. Practice continues until the individual can sufficiently block and replace the obsessional thought.

Sixth, the clinician gives an intersession assignment (homework) to the client for 15 minutes of practice a day at times when the client is not distressed by intrusive thoughts. A log is kept with ratings of 1 to 10 made of the distress and vividness evoked by the intrusive thought.

Finally, after a week of practice the clinician prescribes the intervention to be used to dismiss mild to moderately distressing thoughts as they occur. The client is instructed that as his sense of control increases, the thoughts, when they occur, will become less distressing (on the 1–10 scale) until the individual experiences little or no concern about them.

Resource

McKay, M., Davis, M., & Fanning, P. (2012). *Thoughts and feelings: Taking control of your moods and your life* (4th ed.). Oakland, CA: New Harbinger Publications.

Summary

Character has been rediscovered as a basic component of personality and as a key factor in the effective treatment of the personality disorders. To the extent that an individual's temperament dimensions or styles are dysregulated, the individual will express distress or be distressing to others. Higher functioning individuals were socialized and learned self-management and relational skills to regulate such style dimensions as impulsivity, labile affects, and aggressivity during the course of normal child and adolescent development. A hallmark of the early development of personality-disordered individuals are deficits in some or many of these coping skills. Both structured psychosocial interventions and medication can be useful in regulating or modulating these style dimensions. This chapter has detailed 16 structured treatment intervention strategies that are useful in modulating affective, behavioral and relational, and cognitive styles.

Part II

Cognitive Behavior Therapy Strategies With Specific Personality Disorders

5 Avoidant Personality Disorder

Basically, individuals with avoidant personality disorder are aloof, ill at ease, socially awkward, and overly sensitive to criticism. Although they are desperate for interpersonal involvement, they avoid personal contact with others because of their heightened fear of social disapproval and rejection. While treatment of such individuals involves a number of unique therapeutic challenges, it can be highly effective and successful. This chapter describes a framework for effective treatment of this disorder from a cognitive behavioral perspective. It includes sections on assessment, case conceptualization, and treatment interventions. The section on assessment includes behavioral and cognitive factors, as well as a DSM-5 description and a prototypic description of this disorder. A prototype is a brief description that captures the essence of how a particular disorder commonly presents. Prototypic descriptions are useful and convenient and clinicians commonly rely on them rather than lists of behavioral criteria and core and instrumental beliefs (Westen, 2012). The section on case conceptualization provides both cognitive and behavioral formulations of this disorder. The longest section is on treatment. It emphasizes engagement, pattern analysis, pattern change, and pattern maintenance and termination strategies for effectively managing and treating this disorder. In addition to individual psychotherapeutic strategies and tactics, group, marital and family, medication, and integrative and combined treatment strategies are included. An extensive case example illustrates the treatment process.

Assessment

Behavioral

A behavioral assessment of this disorder emphasizes individual and interpersonal behaviors. Individuals with this disorder are characterized by social withdrawal, shyness, distrustfulness, and aloofness. They may also appear apprehensive and awkward. Their speech is both controlled and limited, and they are unlikely to initiate conversation with others, particularly strangers. Interpersonally, they are rejection sensitive and they tend to avoid activities and situations that involve relating to individuals they do not know and trust.

They fear being embarrassed, humiliated, negatively evaluated, and being awkward and showing signs of anxiety, uncertainty, or saying something inappropriate or foolish. Not surprisingly, they have few close friends and confidants. Although they are desperate for interpersonal involvement, they avoid personal contact with others because of their heightened fear of social disapproval and rejection sensitivity. Despite their desire for acceptance by others, they keep their distance from others and require unconditional approval before being willing to "open up." They gradually "test" others to determine who can be trusted to like them.

Cognitive

A cognitive assessment of this disorder emphasizes core beliefs, particularly those about their views of self and of others. Typically, they view themselves as incompetent in work and school settings as well as inept in social situations. They view others as likely to criticize, demean, or negatively evaluate them. Other core beliefs include the beliefs that they are worthless, unlovable, and unable to tolerate negative and unpleasant feelings. Related beliefs include avoiding unpleasant situations at all costs. Not surprisingly, such beliefs are reflected in their main strategy or pattern of avoiding situations in which they might be evaluated. They may refuse or avoid assuming new responsibilities or to seek job advancement for fear of failure and others' negative evaluation (Beck, 2015; Padesky & Beck, 2015).

DSM-5 Description

DSM-5 emphasizes specific behaviors for this disorder. Individuals who meet criteria for this diagnosis are characterized by an unremitting pattern of being socially inhibited, feeling inadequate, and overly sensitive to the negative evaluations of others. This is typically because they view themselves as socially inept, unappealing, or inferior to others. They consistently avoid work activities that require close interpersonal contact for fear of being criticized or rejected. They will not get involved with others unless they are certain of being accepted. Fearing they will be shamed or ridiculed, they are uncomfortable and act with restraint in intimate relationships. Similarly, they experience feelings of inadequacy and inhibition in new interpersonal situations. Not surprising, they refuse to take personal risks or engage in activities that may prove embarrassing (American Psychiatric Association, 2013).

Prototypic Description

These individuals are frightened and interpersonally awkward. They are also extremely sensitive to criticism and rejection. Just the idea of meeting someone new engenders fear of being humiliated or embarrassed. So, it is much easier to avoid any new work or social relationship that could threaten their personal sense of security and safety. Still, they crave connection with others that they have come to trust. Accordingly, they may have a couple of friends or a relative with whom they can relax and feel safe (Frances, 2013).

Case Conceptualization

According to Beck (2015), individuals with avoidant personality are fearful of initiating relationships as well as fearful of responding to other's attempts to relate to them because of their overriding belief that they will be rejected. For them, such rejection is unbearable so they engage in social avoidance. Furthermore, they engage in cognitive and emotional avoidance by not thinking about things which could cause them to feel dysphoric. Because of their low tolerance for dysphoria, they further distract themselves from their negative cognitions. Underlying these avoidance patterns are maladaptive schemas or long standing dysfunctional beliefs about self and others. Schemas about self include themes of being different, inadequate, defective, and unlikable. Schemas about others involve themes of uncaring and rejection.

These individuals are likely to predict and interpret the rejection as caused solely by their personal deficiencies. This prediction of rejection results in dysphoria. Finally, avoidant individuals do not have internal criteria to judge themselves in a positive manner. Thus, they must rely on their perception. They tend to misread a neutral or positive reaction as negative which further compounds their rejection-sensitivity and social emotional and cognitive avoidance. In short, they hold negative schemas which lead them to avoid solutions where they could interact with others. They also avoid tasks which could engender uncomfortable feelings, and avoid thinking about matters which produce dysphoria. Because of their low tolerance for discomfort, they utilize distractions, excuse making, and rationalizations when they begin to feel sad or anxious (Padesky & Beck, 2015).

Turkat (1990) describes this disorder as primarily anxiety-based, and characterized by timidity and anxiety concerning evaluation, rejection, and/or humiliation. He notes that the disorder is very responsive to behavioral interventions, particularly anxiety management desensitization methods where the hierarchy is based on fear of rejection, criticism, and/or evaluation.

Treatment

Engagement Strategies

Early Session Behavior

In the initial session, these individuals are likely to be somewhat guarded and disengaged. Initially, their communication style tends to be monotonic and monosyllabic, and perhaps even circumstantial. Some will appear suspicious or quite anxious, but all are hypersensitive to rejection and criticism. Accordingly, they will observe the clinician closely for any indication of acceptance or rejection. Such reluctance and guardedness should be approached with empathy and reassurance. The clinician would do well to avoid confrontation, which these individuals will interpret as criticism. Rather, the clinician's judicious use of empathic responding encourages sharing of past pain and anticipatory fears. When these individuals feel that clinicians understand their hypersensitivity and will protect them, they become considerably more willing to trust and cooperate with treatment. After feeling safe and accepted, the atmosphere of the interview changes dramatically. When sufficient rapport has been established, they are more comfortable in describing their fears of being embarrassed and criticized, as well as their sensitivity to being misunderstood. They may experience these fears of being embarrassed as silly and express it. However, to the extent to which clinicians retreat from this empathic and accepting stance, these individuals are likely to feel ridiculed and withdraw again (Othmer & Othmer, 2002).

Facilitating Collaboration

Although the process of achieving collaboration with the avoidant individual tends to be both difficult and protracted, it is well worth the effort. Basic to the difficulty in achieving collaboration is the avoidant individual's tendency to "test" the clinician and the treatment process and the tendency toward premature termination. Because of their underlying sensitivity to criticism and their mistrust of people, these individuals have become masters of testing their psychological environment to ascertain which individuals will be positive or at least neutral toward them, and which individuals are likely to criticize, tease, or emotionally challenge them. Sometimes there may be a very small number of persons—usually a family member and a friend or colleague—in whom they feel somewhat comfortable to be with and trust to some degree.

However, they tend to be rather uncomfortable and distrusting of most individuals, including new clinicians. Subsequently, they will test new clinicians in early sessions by changing appointment dates and times, canceling at the last minute, coming late for sessions, or failing to do homework. The testing continues until they become convinced that the clinician's initial noncritical and nonjudgmental behavior is more than social veneer that falls away when challenged. Beneath this testing is the belief that people really are basically uncaring and critical. To the extent to which the clinician is able to remain supportive, caring, and uncritical in the initial sessions in the face of this testing, the avoidant becomes more amenable to establishing a tentative bond and trust with the clinician. Only then does collaboration become possible. On the other hand, to the extent that the clinician "fails" these tests, the clinician should not be surprised about premature termination. If there is even the slightest hint that an individual is rejection-sensitive or mistrustful, the clinician would do well to anticipate that the individual will engage in testing behaviors and respond accordingly, particularly with unconditional regard (Sperry, 2003).

Transference and Countertransference

The most common transference of the avoidant individual is testing the clinician's capacity to be nonjudgmental and caring. As noted in the section above, this transference is very common in initial sessions. Accepting and sometimes interpreting—particularly through a predictive intepretation—the individual's testing behavior can be useful. Once the clinician passes the various tests of being caring and nonjudgmental, the avoidant individual tends to become increasingly trusting of the clinician. Needless to say, the clinician's stance of unconditional regard is so attractive to these individuals that the clincian may be perceived by them as their confidant and most trusted friend. Accordingly, the clinician's task is to resist the exclusivity of this role, and work toward broadening the individual's social support system. Later in the treatment process, overdependence on the clinician is commonly noted. The avoidant individual may also endeavor to have the clinician assume responsibility for many or all of their personal decisions. The clinician's challenge is to gently but firmly set limits on the individual's dependency (Gabbard, 2005).

Common countertransferences are the clinician's feelings of frustration at the individual's testing behavior. There is also a brittle quality to these individuals that may arouse the clinician's rescue fantasies. In the era of managed care, it is not uncommon for these countertransferences to be provoked in situations when clinical protocols emphasize individual engagement and/or require setting treatment goals in the very first session. In these situations, the individual's brittleness and proclivity to premature termination clearly must come before the protocol. As the avoidant individual becomes more involved in the collaborative treatment process, the clinician may fall prey to unrealistic expectations of the individual with regard to increased social involvement (Gabbard, 2005). The clinician may erroneously assume that because the individual has been able to establish such a trusting relationship with the clinician, that it can be replicated with others. Monitoring these feelings and urges rather than acting on them is necessary for effective treatment.

Pattern Analysis Strategies

Pattern analysis with avoidant personality disordered individuals involves an accurate diagnostic and clinical evaluation of schemas, styles, and triggering stressors as well as level of functioning and readiness for therapeutic change. Knowledge of the optimal DSM-5 criterion along with the maladaptive pattern of the avoidant personality disordered individual is not only useful in specifying diagnosis but also in planning treatment that is tailored to the avoidant individual's unique style, needs, and circumstances. The optimal criterion specified for the avoidant personality disorder is avoidance of occupational activities that involve significant interpersonal contact because of fear of criticism, disapproval, or rejection (Allnutt & Links, 1996). Both planned treatment goals and interventions should reflect this theme of fear of rejection and anticipatory avoidance.

Pattern refers to the predictable and consistent style and manner in which avoidant individuals think, feel, act, cope, and defend themselves. Pattern analysis involves both the triggers and response—the "what"—as well as an explanatory statement—the "why"—about the pattern of a given avoidant individual. Obviously, such a clinical formulation specifies the particular schemas and temperamental styles unique to a given individual rather than the more general clinical formulation that will be noted here.

Triggers

Generally speaking, the "triggers" or "triggering" situations for avoidant individuals are stressors related to close relationships and public appearance (Othmer & Othmer, 2002). This means that when avoidant-disordered individuals are engaging in behaviors, discussing, or even thinking about the demands of relationships or being in public, they become distressed and their disordered or maladaptive pattern is likely to be triggered and their characteristic symptomatic affects, behaviors, and cognitions will be experienced or exhibited. Rather than face the demands of others and risking humiliation and rejection, avoidant individuals prefer to place themselves in safe, rejection-free environments. Usually, this means being alone or in a low-demand social environment.

Schemas

The underlying schemas in the avoidant personality involve a self-view of social inadequacy and unlikability, and a view of the world as unfair, critical, and demeaning alongside a demand that others like and accept the avoidant individual (Beck, Davis, & Freeman, 2015; Sperry & Mosak, 1996). Not surprisingly, the avoidant's dysfunctional strategy is to avoid valuative situations as well as unpleasant feelings or thoughts. Common maladaptive schemas observed in avoidant personality disordered individuals include the defectiveness/shame schema and the undesirability/alienation schema. The defectiveness/shame schema refers to the core set of beliefs that one is inwardly defective and flawed, and thus basically unlovable and unacceptable. The undesirability/alienation schema refers to the core set of beliefs that one is outwardly different from others or is undesirable to others (Bricker, Young, & Flanagan, 1993).

Style/Temperament

There are four unique style dimensions in the ABCDEF Profile that characterize individuals with this pesonality disorder: Affective, Behavioral-interpersonal,

Cognitive, and Distress tolerance. Avoidant personality disordered individuals have affective styles characterized as shy, tense, apprehensive, and highly vulnerable to rejection and humiliation. Their behavioral and interpersonal style is characterized by social withdrawal, shyness, and under-assertive communication. Their cognitive style is one of hypervigilance and self-doubt as they scan their emotional environment searching for clues of either unconditional acceptance or potential rejection (Sperry, 2003). They also tend to be distress overtolerant meaning they can tolerate high distress that results in adverse long-term consesquences (Lynch & Mizon, 2011). Overall, their pattern reflects an internalizing disorder.

Pattern Change Strategies

Generally speaking, the overall goals of treatment with avoidant personality disordered individuals are to increase their capacity to tolerate feedback from others and become more selectively trusting of others. That means that instead of automatically assuming that others intend to criticize, reject, or humiliate them, or reflexively "testing" the trustworthiness of others, avoidant individuals will be able to take some measured risks in relating to others. This might mean assertively communicating their needs and wants, or it might mean taking the risk of requesting some feedback from others who previously have been supportive of them.

Avoidant individuals already know how to relate to a small and select number of individuals, often relatives. If the clinician simply becomes one of them, the individual's basic pattern of avoidance may remain unchanged. It is only when these individuals learn to recognize the impact of their pattern on others and take risks in new relationships that they can change.

Although individual therapy can help avoidant individuals recognize and analyze their pattern of avoidance and withdrawal, couples therapy and group therapy permit both clinician and individual to observe the impact of this pattern on others, and for the individual to risk new behaviors. If the individual is married or in a long-term relationship, triangular patterns are often present. For instance, the avoidant individual may be married to a spouse who travels extensively and makes few if any emotional demands on their avoidant partner, providing the avoidant partner the opportunity for a secret extramarital affair. This triangular pattern provides some degree of intimacy as well as protection from public humiliation, while also insuring interpersonal distance.

Schema Change

The schemas of avoidant individuals include themes of defectiveness, inadequacy, and unlikability. These schemas are supported by injunctive beliefs such as "don't show your feelings," "don't get close to others," "don't get intimate," and "don't be disloyal to your family" (Beck, Freeman, & Associates, 1990). Schema change from a cognitive therapy perspective has the clinician and individual working collaboratively to understand the developmental roots of the maladaptive schemas. Then these schemas are tested through predictive experiments, guided observation, and reenactment of early schema-related incidents. Finally, individuals are directed to begin to notice and remember counter-schema data about themselves and their social experiences.

CBASP Strategies

While Cognitive Behavioral Analysis System of Psychotherapy (CBASP) was originally developed by McCullough (2000; McCullough, Schramm, & Penberthy, 2015) for the treatment of chronic depression, it has been extended to the treatment of avoidant personality disorder (Driscoll, Cukrowicz, Reardon, & Joiner, 2004). The basic premise of CBASP is that clinicians can help individuals to discover why they did not obtain a desired outcome by evaluating their problematic thoughts and behaviors. The main intervention of this approach is Situational Analysis, which has been shown to be clinically effective in identifying and correcting maladaptive pattens of thinking and behavior characteristic of APD (Driscoll et al., 2004). Situational Analysis is a process that is recorded by the client on the Coping Survey Questionnaire usually before a session and then reviewed with the therapist during the session. It helps articulate several elements of a problematic situation and the client's interpretations and behaviors.

Generally speaking, clients with avoidant personality disorder are considered to be excellent candidates for CBASP. Nevertheless, it has been noted that they tend to underestimate and underreport positive social experiences while discounting their influence in successful social situations. Because of their basic social avoidance, in-session roleplaying and in vivo exposure homework assignments are a central therapeutic strategy in early sessions. Because they are often pessimistic, perfectionistic, hypersensitive to rejection and hypervigilant to threat cues, these clients are prone to all-or-nothing thinking, magnification, overgeneralization, and mind reading. Accordingly, clinicians should anticipate that these cognitive distortions will be regularly encountered when assisting these clients in evaluating and revising inaccurate interpretations during the remediation phase of treatment (Driscoll et al., 2004).

In addition, cognitive behavior group therapy is recommended as an adjunct to individual CBASP for the purpose of enhancing client motivation, self-determination, and acceptance. Group sessions that are sufficiently structured can increase client social competence while reducing social anxiety. Such sessions typically involve in-session exposure exercises, progressive in vivo exposure assignments, as well as traditional cognitive restructuring exercises. In these group sessions clients are asked to identify their desired outcomes for in-session role plays and in vivo homework situations. Clinical experience shows that having these clients specify how modifying distorted interpretations and changing behaviors will help them achieve their desired outcomes enhances their self-determination, mindfulness, and acceptance in anxiety-provoking situations. The interested reader will find an extended transcription of the use of CBASP with such individuals (Driscoll et al., 2004).

Style-Skill Change

Because avoidant individuals avoid thinking about matters that cause unpleasant emotions they may report that their minds "go blank," or they may shift topics when they experience more than mild emotions during sessions. Increasing emotional tolerance is an early treatment goal. This can be accomplished by affect regulation training in which individuals are helped to become aware of and "stay with" their distressing thoughts and fantasies. Repeated experiences of "staying with" strange emotions engender emotional tolerance and desensitize their hypersensitivity while at the same time modifying maladaptive beliefs about experiencing uncomfortable emotions.

Avoidant individuals tend to exhibit a cognitive style of hypervigilance that results in cognitive avoidance, just as they avoid unpleasant thoughts. These unpleasant thoughts include both those from early childhood and current concerns, such as job and household responsibilities, and especially treatment-related issues like intersession assignment and activities. They may even report that they are unaware of any thoughts during anxiety producing situations, particularly interpersonal situations. Instead they describe their internal experiences in terms of fleeting, negatively tinged sensations or images. In such instances, the clinician should encourage the individuals to provide verbatim accounts of what was said and done. Prompting this endeavor will assist the individual in identifying such cognition. In time, the individual will become more able and willing to "stay with" experiences rather than "shutting down." Sensitivity reduction training can also be useful in desensitizing hypervigilance.

Avoidant individuals have social skill deficits because of their relational style and their impoverished social experience. These can range from a few circumscribed social deficits to multiple deficits encompassing most social interactions. Alden (1992) listed several types of deficits: (a) behavioral avoidance, wherein individuals turn down invitations, cancel appointments, or avoid answering the phone; (b) inhibition, whereby these individuals avoid eye contact, initiate few conversations, and talk less than others; (c) surface agreement and compliance, wherein they are likely to voice agreement and comply with the requests of others even when they don't endorse the plan or intend to follow through; (d) assumption of a moderate position, meaning they avoid taking a stand or expressing their own opinion in issues; (e) and absence of self-disclosure, wherein, because of their belief that they are defective, they are extremely anxious about revealing personal information and do not reciprocate the self-disclosures of others.

Assertive communication training can be used to teach individuals to think and speak more assertively and with a "non-avoidant voice." Interpersonal skills training can be useful in reversing some of these skill deficits, as well as modifying their shy, inhibited style. In the psychotherapeutic setting, these individuals may need to be encouraged to act "as if" they are confident, assertive, and likable.

Medication Strategies

Currently, there are no psychotropic medications specifically indicated for treating the Avoidant Personality Disorder (Silk & Feurino, 2012). Nevertheless, medications are used that target specific troubling symptoms associated with the disorder, such as depression, anxiety, or sleep problems. Generally, these medications are used as an adjunct to psychotherapy and skills training. Because troubling symptoms often respond to medications sooner than most psychological interventions, medications are usually prescribed at the onset of treatment (Sperry, 1995b). Unfortunately, there is little research evidence to provide guidelines for the use of such medications (Silk & Feurino, 2012).

However, because of the comorbidity of this disorder to Social Anxiety Disorder, it was speculated that this personality disorder might respond well to medications with anxiety reducing effects such as selective serotonin reuptake inhibitors (SSRIs). A randomized controlled trial showed that individuals with avoidant personality disorder do respond to low doses of sertraline (Zoloft), an SSRI medication (Silk & Feurino, 2012).

Group Treatment Strategies

Avoidant personality disordered individuals typically fear group therapy in the same way they fear other novel and socially demanding situations. As a result of taking measured risks of self-disclosure and receiving feedback from other group members, avoidant individuals can greatly modify their social sensitivity. For this reason, group therapy is particularly effective for avoidant individuals who can be persuaded to undergo this mode of treatment. Empathetic group therapy can assist these individuals in overcoming social anxieties and developing interpersonal trust and rapport.

Because avoidant individuals tend to avoid activities that involve significant interpersonal contact for fear of being exposed or ridiculed, it should not be surprising that it takes longer for them to adapt to a group setting and actively participate in treatment. Accordingly, combining cognitive therapy and social skills training in a group-therapy context can be quite effective in identifying underlying fears, increasing awareness of the anxiety related to fears, and shifting attentional focus from fear-related thinking to behavioral action. The group therapist's role in pacing the avoidant individual's disclosure and engagement within the group can be very important. Structured activities can help the avoidant individuals to organize how they think and act so they are more efficient both inside and outside the therapy context. For example, interpersonal skills training that focuses on the process of friendship formation is particularly well-suited for group treatment contexts (Sperry, 2003).

Marital and Family Therapy Strategies

Although there is value in recognizing how their current dysfunctional patterns were developed, the real measure of treatment success with avoidant individuals is improvement in interpersonal functioning. Because avoidant individuals may provide clinicians with vague descriptions of their interpersonal experiences, it may be necessary to query relatives and significant others to fill in the important gaps of information. Family treatment may be indicated to establish a family structure that allows more room for interpersonal exploration outside the tightly closed family circle. Furthermore, couples therapy is indicated for avoidant individuals in marriages or long-term relationships where intimacy problems are prominent, that is, where interpersonal distance characterizes the avoidant partner's relational style and is the source of conflict (Sperry, 2003).

Combined and Integrative Treatment Strategies

Clinical experience suggests that avoidant individuals are often unable to focus on the individual–clinician relationship to the degree necessary to use traditional psychodynamic approaches. Likewise, these individuals may have difficulty fully using cognitive-behavioral interventions in the interpersonal context of therapy. Accordingly, an integrative treatment strategy may be more appropriate. Alden (1992) described an integration of the cognitive and the psychodynamic-interpersonal approaches that has been developed specifically for the treatment of avoidant personality dynamics. This approach focuses on modifying the cognitive-interpersonal patterns of the avoidant personality, which is characterized by dysfunctional beliefs of being different or defective and that these defects and feelings are obvious to others who will respond with disgust, disapproval, or dismissal.

Alden (1992) described four steps in the integrative approach. The first step is recognition of treatment process issues. The clinician must quickly recognize that these individuals tend to withhold or understate information that is clinically relevant. It should be anticipated that these individuals will respond to direct questions with "I don't know" or "I'm not sure" answers. In the early phase of treatment, such noncommital and evasive responses characterizes their thought processes as well as prevents them from encoding details about social encounters. Rather then interpreting "resistance" or focusing on global and vague interpersonal beliefs and behavior as treatment targets, the clinician can simply recognize that this communication style reflects their inability to process positive information, maintain attentiveness, and change their firmly established negative beliefs and schemas.

Treatment then focuses on increasing awareness of cognitive-interpersonal patterns. There are four components to an interpersonal pattern: beliefs and expectancy of the other person; the behavior that arises from these beliefs; the other person's reaction; and the conclusion drawn from the experience. The individual's task is to engage in a process of self-observation and analysis of their relational patterns, whereas the clinician's task is to draw attention to the beliefs that underlie the individual's self-protective behaviors.

Next, as they come to recognize and to understand their cognitive-interpersonal patterns and styles, the clinician can increase their motivation to try new behavior by helping them recognize that old and new views of self are in conflict, and that such conflict can be reconciled. Assisting individuals to integrate their current beliefs with their earlier interpersonal experiences helps them understand that their social fears and expectations resulted from both their experience of being parented and their temperament. As they continue to recognize and understand their cognitive-interpersonal patterns, these individuals begin to try different strategies, either on their own or with the clinician's prompting. This integrative approach also involves behavioral experimentation and cognitive evaluation. Friendship formation and assertive communication are the two basic interpersonal skills that avoidant individuals must increase. Role playing and directed assignments are particularly useful in developing assertive communication skills (Sperry, 2003).

A basic premise of this book is that although a single treatment modality like psychotherapy may well be effective for the highest functioning personality disordered individual, that modality is less effective for moderate functioning and largely ineffective for more severely dysfunctional individuals. For the most part, lower functioning individuals tend to be more responsive to combined treatment modalities. Even though avoidant individuals initially are reluctant to engage in group therapy, moderate and lower functioning avoidant individuals tend to make considerable progress when involved in both individual and group therapy concurrently. When this is not possible, time-limited skill-oriented group training sessions or a support group may be sufficient. Because their pattern of avoidance and social inhibition makes entry into and continuation with therapeutic groups distressing, individual sessions can be focused on transitioning the individual into the group. Finally, medication may be necessary in the early stages of treatment, and can be particularly useful in reducing distress and self-protective behavior during the transition into concurrent group treatment.

Pattern Maintenance and Termination Strategies

Termination Issues

Termination can be particularly problematic for avoidant individuals. Although these individuals were prone to premature termination in the initial phase of treatment, once they become engaged in the treatment process they often find it difficult to face planned termination. For this reason, it is essential that the treatment plan include provision for weaning therapy in the final phase. Avoidant individuals typically need prompting and encouragement to test out their fears about reducing the frequency of sessions. Occasionally, some avoidant individuals are ready and willing to terminate but may fear hurting the clinician's feelings by suggesting or readily agreeing that they are ready for termination.

Spacing out sessions allows individuals to deal with and discuss their fear, particularly regarding rejection. It also allows them the opportunity to engage in new social and interpersonal experiences between sessions and deal with the risks attendant to such experiences. Perhaps if they were on medication and involved in weekly individual or group therapy, they might now have scheduled medication monitoring appointments at 3- to 6-month intervals already. If they were not receiving, or have already been weaned from, medication, they might have booster sessions scheduled at 3-, 6-, or 12-month intervals.

Finally, it is helpful for clinicians and avoidant individuals to collaboratively develop a plan of self-therapy and self-management following termination. It is recommended that these individuals set aside an hour a week to engage in activities that continue the progress made in formal treatment. They could look for any situations they might have avoided that week and analyze obstacles and thoughts that interfered. Or they might look ahead at the coming week and predict which situations could be troublesome, and plan ways to cope with possible avoidance behaviors. The goal of such effort is, of course, to maintain treatment gains and maintain the newly acquired pattern.

Relapse Prevention Strategies

Another essential aspect of the treatment plan and process is relapse prevention. Because avoidant individuals can easily revert to their previous avoidant pattern, it is necessary to predict and plan for relapse. The final phase of treatment should largely focus on relapse prevention. An important goal of relapse prevention is predicting likely difficulties in the time period immediately following termination. The individual needs to be able to analyze specific external situations such as new individuals, unfamiliar places, as well as internal states such as specific avoidant beliefs and fears, and other vulnerabilities that increase the likelihood of them responding with avoidant behavior in the face of predictable triggers. Once predicted, individuals can develop a contingency plan to deal with these stressors. Clinicians may find it useful to have avoidant individuals think and talk through the following questions: What can I do if I find myself resorting to avoidant patterns? What should I do if I start believing my old avoidant beliefs more than my new beliefs? What should I do if I relapse?

A belief that is particularly troubling for avoidant individuals is, "If others really knew me, they would reject me." This belief is typically activated when avoidant individuals begin developing new relationships or when they begin to self-disclose at a deeper level with individuals they already know. In such instances, it can be helpful for individuals to view these fears of revealing themselves with a trusted person to trace what actually happened when they were eventually able to self-disclose. Finally, a relapse prevention plan will specify outcome goals and activities for the post-termination period: Usually, these goals involve establishing new friendships, deepening existing relationships, acting more assertively, tackling previously avoided social tasks, and trying new experiences such as volunteering or attending a workshop alone.

Case of Geri, Continued

This is a continuation of the case from Chapter 2. Briefly, Geri is a never-married African American female administrative assistant who presented with a 3-week history of sad mood, loss of appetite, insomnia, and increasing social isolation. Her symptoms began soon after her supervisor told her that she was being considered for a promotion and a transfer from her small and safe work group to a larger, diverse department at another location. As a child, she reports isolating and avoiding others when she was criticized and teased by family members and peers. She is highly acculturated, and believes that her depression is a result of work stress and a "chemical imbalance" in her brain.

Comprehensive Assessment and Diagnosis. A comprehensive diagnostic and functional assessment was completed. Her history and mental status exam are consistent with criteria for a DSM-5 diagnosis of Major Depressive Disorder, Single Episode, as well as criteria for Avoidant Personality Disorder. Figure 5.1 portrays her ABCDEF Profile.

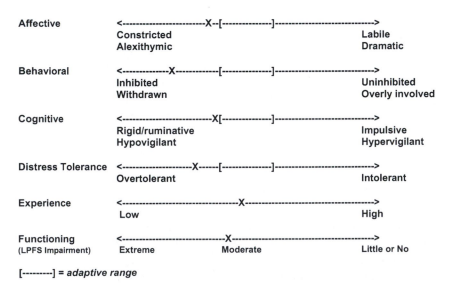

Figure 5.1 ABCDEF Profile for Avoidant Personality Disorder: Case of Geri

Engagement Process

She had missed the first appointment for the initial evaluation and had come late for the second with the explanation that she could not find the clinic. She indicated she had come only at the insistence of the director of human resources and didn't believe she needed treatment. Self-disclosure was clearly difficult for her. She did, however, view her job transfer as a significant loss, and she thought that it might have triggered her depressive symptoms and isolative behavior. There was no indication that she was a danger to herself, and it appeared that outpatient treatment was possible. Because it was anticipated that she would "test" and provoke the clinician into criticizing her for changing or canceling appointments or coming late, and that setting up a follow-up appointment would probably be difficult, the clinician made a predictive interpretation to that effect near the end of the first session. Needless to say, the appointment was made with ease, and Geri did arrive at her next appointment on time.

Pattern Analysis

No personal or family psychiatric or alcohol and substance abuse history was reported; however, she described intense feelings of humiliation and rejection following the birth of a younger brother, after having been very much spoiled by her parents. She came to believe that the opinions of others were all that counted. Yet, she was teased and ridiculed by her peers for her personal appearance, especially her obesity. There were also strong parental injunctions against discussing important matters with "outsiders." It appears that she distances and isolates herself from others, anticipating and fearing their disapproval and criticism. She views others as critical and harsh and is convinced she is viewed by others as inadequate. Therefore, she is slow to warm up and trust others, and "tests" others' trustability by being late for, canceling, or missing agreed on engagements. She had also spent much of her free time reading romance novels, and watching TV rather than going out. Lack of social skills in relating to new or less-known individuals and a limited social network further contributed to an isolated lifestyle and reinforced her beliefs about self, the world, and others. With the exception of social relations, she has functioned above average in all life tasks. She agrees she is severely depressed and wants to cooperate with combined treatment involving medication started and monitored on an outpatient basis along with time-limited psychotherapy. She was not particularly psychologically minded and had significant skill deficits in assertive communication, trust, and relational skills. Nevertheless, she continues to be abstinent for 2 years after completing a smoking cessation program. Her support system includes some contact with an older female friend and a pet collie.

Developmental history data suggested that Geri had internalized the schemas of defectiveness/shame and social undesirablitity/alienation, which can be associated with the avoidant personality. Her apprehensive affects, hypervigilance, shyness, and deficits in assertiveness and other interpersonal skills were also indicative of the avoidant personality.

Concise Case Conceptualization. Geri's increased social isolation and depressive symptoms (*presentation*) seem to be her reaction to the news of an impending job transfer and promotion (*precipitant*). Throughout her life, she found it safer to avoid others when possible and conditionally relate to them at other times (*pattern*). This is an internalizing pattern of "moderate impairment" on the Level of Personality Functioning Scale. Her pattern can be understand in light of demanding, critical, and emotionally unavailable parents, strong parental injunctions against making personal and family disclosure to others, the teasing and criticism of peers, and schemas of defectiveness and social isolation. As a result, she lacks key social skills and has a limited social network. Her family history of depression may biologically predispose her to sadness and social isolation, as did the under development of relational skills (*predisposition*). This pattern is maintained by her shyness and limited social skills, and the fact that she lives alone and finds it safer to socially isolate (*perpetuants*). A more adaptive pattern is for her to feel safe and safely connect with others. Treatment goals were to reduce her depressive symptoms and increase social connections which would reflect a more adaptive pattern (*treatment goals*).

Pattern Change

The treatment plan for Geri was developed based on her presentation as well as her pattern and style factors. Combined treatment with an antidepressant and psychotherapy focused on ameliorating symptoms, returning to work and establishing a supportive social network, and increasing interpersonal skills were the initial treatment outcome goals established. The treatment and strategic goals were developed to facilitate therapeutic outcomes by maximizing therapeutic leverage while minimizing the influence of previous perpetuants and other forms of resistance to change.

Treatment consisted of a trial of antidepressant that was sedating and which it was hoped would reverse her insomnia as well as her depression. Twenty-minute weekly outpatient sessions with the psychiatrist focused on symptom reduction and returning to work. This meant that some collaboration with her supervisor about work and peer support was initiated. The supervisor agreed that Geri needed a familiar, trusting social support, and was able to assign one of Geri's coworkers to the same office to which she had been moved. An initial treatment agreement was established for six 45-minute sessions combining medication and interpersonal therapy. They also discussed that skill-oriented group therapy was probably the treatment of choice for her to increase trustability and decrease her social isolation. Because her pattern of avoidance would make entry into and continuation with the group difficult, the plan was for the individual sessions to serve as a transition into group, after which shorter individual sessions would focus on medication management, probably on a monthly and then bimonthly basis.

Knowing her pattern, the clinician anticipated that she would test the clinician and group therapist's trustability and criticalness. Throughout treatment both clinicians continued to be mindful of the therapeutic leverage—her strengths and previous success with smoking cessation—as well as the perpetuants that would likely hamper treatment.

The initial treatment plan for her involved the combined modalities of medication management and a short course in interpersonal psychotherapy for depression with gradual transition into a time-limited group therapy focused on interpersonal skill development. As her depressive symptoms ameliorated and a maintenance medication schedule was established, the clinician began preparing her for transition into the group. Because of Geri's fear and ambivalence of the group process, the clinician suggested and she agreed that it might be helpful to meet with the therapist who leads the interpersonal skills group she was slated to join. During their fifth session, the group therapist was briefly introduced to Geri and discussion of a three-way treatment agreement unsued. The three agreed that Geri would continue in individual weekly appointments concurrent with weekly group sessions. And assuming things were proceeding well enough, sessions with the prescribing clinician would be reduced to monthly medication checks.

A subsequent two-way discussion between group therapist and clinician concluded that there was little likelihood that projective identification and splitting would be issues with her. Instead, difficulty maintaining active group participation and follow-up on "homework" between group sessions were predicted. The clinician agreed to encourage and support the individual's group involvement in his concurrent individual sessions with her. Furthermore, the group therapist and clinician planned on conferring after the third group session regarding the transition from weekly to monthly sessions with the clinician.

Pattern Maintenance and Termination

Treatment proceeded with few surprises. Her depressive symptoms were ameliorated within 5 weeks and she was continued on a maintenance dose for a period of 1 year. Medication monitoring sessions were reduced to monthly visits for the first 4 months and then bimonthly afterward. Progress in group sessions included increased confidence in social situations, especially in her job setting. After 6 months of weekly group sessions she felt ready to terminate and continued with bimonthly sessions with the prescribing clinician. She still maintains some interpersonal reserve but she is able to socialize regularly with two other female coworkers. Her job performance gradually returned to baseline.

Case of Jason, Continued

This is a continuing case from Chapter 3. Jason is a college student presenting for therapy because social anxiety was inhibiting his life in various ways.

Although he can participate in most solitary and family activities, he experiences considerable anxiety in situations in which he has to interact with others. This includes being in class, going to the grocery store, having to speak in class, etc. This has been somewhat problematic since age 12 but has increased since he is away from home and in college where activities that he previously did not have to attend to, i.e., going shopping or speaking in class were not problems since his mother did most of the shopping and home schooled him. His DSM-5 diagnoses were Avoidant Personality Disorder with Social Anxiety Disorder.

The transcription below is of the follow-up session to the transcription in Chapter 3. It demonstrates his increasing ability to engage in consequential thinking and learning from experience. The result is progress toward treatment goals of increasing social connectedness and reduction of anxiety symptoms. The treatment approach utilized is a form of CBT that focuses on replacing hurtful (maladaptive) thoughts and behaviors rather than restructuring cognitions in more conventional CBT.

Therapist: Hi Jason, welcome, come in and have a seat. (Pause). So, how has your week been?

Jason: Well, it's been okay, I guess. I went to the grocery store again on Friday.

Therapist: Good. And how did that go?

Jason: Well, I still felt anxious for being there alone, and I pretty much grabbed all of the stuff I needed and then headed straight for the checkout line.

Therapist: Did you make eye contact or talk to anyone while you were there?

Jason: Yeah, when I was picking out a few apples there was a lady restocking the fruit and she smiled at me.

Therapist: And what did you do?

Jason: I gave her a quick smile and then I looked down.

Therapist: And what was your interpretation of that situation?

Jason: That it was crazy that she was smiling at me, I mean, for a minute I couldn't figure out if she was smiling at me or at someone behind me.

Therapist: What does that mean to you?

Jason: That maybe she had confused me with someone else or maybe she was just smiling because that was part of her job or maybe she was smiling because she thought I looked like a loser at the grocery store all by myself.

Therapist: And so these thoughts that were racing through your head at this time sound like they were really stressful to you. What was your SUDS level like right then?

Jason: I would say probably around 80 or so. I was really sweaty and I couldn't believe she was actually smiling at me.

Therapist: And how about after you smiled back and then walked away?

Jason: It went down a lot. I was proud of myself for smiling back at her and so I felt a little better about being there alone.

Therapist:	That's wonderful. So by simply smiling back you eased your anxiety a little. How did it go in the checkout line?
Jason:	Better this week, I guess. I looked at the checkout girl and said "Hi." But this time I didn't look down right away. Instead I looked at the computer screen with my grocery total on it. She said "Hi. How are you today?" and smiled at me, and then I smiled back again! Right after that I looked down.
Therapist:	And what was going through your mind at that moment?
Jason:	I was like, whoa. She is actually looking at me right now and I have to think of something to do right away so I don't look like an idiot, fumbling around and stuttering like last time. I couldn't think of anything to say so I just smiled.
Therapist:	And how was your SUDS level?
Jason:	I would probably say around an 85 but when I walked out to the parking lot I was happy that I smiled and said "Hi." I felt better about having gone there, like maybe I had done a little better this week.
Therapist:	That is awesome! So you still experienced stress this time at the grocery store but when you kept your head up and smiled back at people, you felt better about it afterward. So this might fit in with our revised DO we agreed on last week, right? That you would be able to greet and make eye contact with someone while you were there and tolerate the stress it would bring you?
Jason:	Yeah, you're right. And then I felt better about it afterwards.
Therapist:	Do you think you could go back and do it again?
Jason:	Definitely.
Therapist:	That's great! It seems like you really made a lot of progress at the grocery store. Good job! Would you like to go over the homework we have for this week?
Jason:	Sure. But, this one wasn't so good.
Therapist:	That's okay, it will help us for next time. This was when you were going to try and ask someone to go and see a movie with you, remember? Can you tell me about it?
Jason:	Well, I wanted to ask this girl I sit next to in my biology class if she wanted to go and see this indie film I had heard was playing on campus on Thursday. We were getting ready to leave at the end of the lecture and I grabbed my stuff and tried to talk to her, but it didn't work out very well.
Therapist:	Okay, well, what were your interpretations or thoughts in that situation?
Jason:	That she would think I was trying to stalk her or that I was some kind of freak. I was terrified that I would say the wrong thing or not say anything at all and then class would be over. Mostly I thought that I was not normal because I couldn't find the words to ask her.
Therapist:	So your interpretation was that you were not normal because you couldn't think of anything to say. That seems like a good interpretation for us to look at. What was your SUDS level for this thought?

Jason:	Almost a 90. . . . I was petrified.
Therapist:	Okay, well, what about your behaviors?
Jason:	Well, like I said, I grabbed all my stuff trying to find the words and I tried to look at her, which didn't last very long and then all I could say was "um, hey, do you like indies?" And she must not have heard me or something or I didn't say it very loud because she gave me a funny look and goes, "huh?" and then I looked down and said "nothing." I grabbed my bag and took off down the lecture hall to the doors.
Therapist:	So your behaviors in this situation were to speak softly, look down, grab your bags, and leave.
Jason:	Yeah. Pretty much how I thought it would go.
Therapist:	Well, we can review this in a minute. What was your desired outcome?
Jason:	To ask her if she wanted to see the independent film they were playing on campus.
Therapist:	And what was the actual outcome?
Jason:	I didn't even ask her and I ran off. And my SUDS was at a 90 for about 15 minutes until I got back to my dorm room and could shut the door and calm down.
Therapist:	So, did you achieve your desired outcome then?
Jason:	No, of course not. I was so sweaty I had to take a shower and I stayed in my room all night on the computer.
Therapist:	Okay, well, then, let's go on to the next phase so we can see what might have made things different in the end. First, let's look at your interpretations and see which ones were helpful or hurtful to you in getting your desired outcome of asking someone to go see a movie. Your first interpretation was that "you were not normal because you couldn't think of anything to say in that moment." Do you think that this interpretation was helpful or hurtful in this situation?
Jason:	Hurtful.
Therapist:	How was it hurtful?
Jason:	Because it made me feel even more anxious and like I was going to fail again and then she would think I was weird and it would always be uncomfortable having to sit there in class with her after that.
Therapist:	Can you think of any thoughts that might have been more helpful instead?
Jason:	Um, well, that I am normal. Or at least I am not a freak.
Therapist:	Good, good. Now how would that have helped you?
Jason:	Well, I wouldn't have freaked out so much right before and maybe I would have been able to actually think of something to say since I wasn't so scared. I guess I would have been more likely to find something good to say and say it louder.
Therapist:	So telling yourself, "I am normal and I am not weird for asking her if she likes indie films or for being anxious about it" would have made it easier for you to ask her.

Jason:	Yeah, I think so.
Therapist:	Well, you did ask her, even though she didn't hear you right away. Perhaps it was your anxiety that really bothered you and got you upset in this situation?
Jason:	Yeah, definitely.
Therapist:	Well, do you think your replacement thought would have made you less upset or stressed, or maybe help you accept those feelings?
Jason:	Probably.
Therapist:	So your first interpretation that you were not normal because you couldn't think of anything to say was hurtful because it actually made you anxious, which makes thinking of words difficult for anyone. If you replaced that thought with the one that says, "I am normal and it is okay to be anxious when asking someone to see a movie," you would have been more likely to be at a SUDS level that would allow you to think more clearly and find something to say, and then ask her. Is this right?
Jason:	Yeah.
Therapist:	Okay, well, let's move on to your behaviors. The first one was to grab your stuff right away. Was this helpful or hurtful in terms of getting your desired outcome?
Jason:	Hurtful. . . . Probably because it looks like I just want to rush off.
Therapist:	So what might have been a better behavior?
Jason:	To take my time, and slowly gather up my books while I was thinking of how to ask her.
Therapist:	That's good, that would have given you a little more time to not be anxious and think of the words. What about speaking softly, did this help you or hurt you in terms of getting your desired outcome?
Jason:	Hurt, because she didn't hear me and then she gave me a funny look and I freaked out.
Therapist:	What might have been a better behavior?
Jason:	To speak louder and look at her so she could understand what I was saying.
Therapist:	Great, you are really good at this part. Then perhaps she might have said, "yes, I like those movies," and you could then have asked her to go with you to see it. This would have prevented her from asking "huh?" which made you even more anxious and led you to say "nothing" and leave.
Jason:	Yeah, I see.
Therapist:	So, in this situation, if you would have thought to yourself, "I am normal and it is okay to be anxious when you ask someone to see a movie," instead of, "I am not normal because I can't think of anything to say," and if you would have spoken louder and not grabbed up all your stuff and rushed off you would have been more likely to get your desired outcome of asking someone to see a movie with you. Is that accurate?

Jason:	Sure, definitely.
Therapist:	Would you like to practice what this situation might look like if it happens again, this time with the new interpretations and behaviors? (Yes). I could be the girl in your class and you could practice asking me.
Jason:	I'll try.
Therapist:	Good, I think you can do it. Let's pretend we are sitting in class and it is almost time to leave. Everyone starts to pack up their belongings and you start to slowly put your books away. What are you thinking to yourself?
Jason:	That I am normal and it is okay to be anxious about asking someone to see a movie.
Therapist:	Good, and what are you doing?
Jason:	I am slowly putting away my books and then I look up and say, "hey, do you like indie films?
Therapist:	"Yeah, they're cool. Why?"
Jason:	"Well, because they're showing one in the old theater tonight about that news reporter in Iraq. Do you want to go see it with me?"
Therapist:	"Sure, what time is it?"
Jason:	"7:30. I could meet you out front if you like."
Therapist:	"That would be cool. Thanks."
Jason:	Okay. I see what you mean. I could carry on a whole conversation then. What if she says no?
Therapist:	Well, your desired outcome is to just get up the courage to ask someone to see a movie. There is a chance that that person might say no, but your plan is to ask. I think the more practice you get at asking people, the more chances there are for them to say yes, don't you agree?
Jason:	Yeah, I mean, if she said yes, then what would I say to her at the movie?
Therapist:	Well, this is something we can always work on in the future. I think you did great work today. Do you want to make for homework to try and ask someone to see a movie again? You don't have to ask the same girl, maybe try it with someone you know in your dorm?
Jason:	Yeah, that sounds like a good idea.
Therapist:	Okay, well, I will see you next week then. Bye.

Summary

Effective treatment of the avoidant personality disorder requires that these individuals become sufficiently committed to a treatment process that is tailored and focused on modifying their maladaptive avoidant pattern. Because these individuals tend to have considerable difficulty engaging in and profiting from traditional psychotherapy, an integrative-combined approach, which

Table 5.1 Treatment Strategies for Avoidant Personality Disorder

ENGAGEMENT	Engage in "testing" behavior (cancel appointment/reschedule, etc.). Premature termination is likely to the extent they feel criticized or hurt. **Tx:** Anticipate and accept "testing" of therapist's trustworthiness
Transference	Limited self-disclosure and "holding things in." Distrust and rejection sensitivity and subsequent "testing" behavior. Tendency for overdependence and desire for therapist to be their friend. **Tx:** Interpret "testing" behavior; set limits on dependency
Countertransference	Tendency to be more protective and caring toward, and limit corrective feedback. Wish to repair some deficiencies or failures in relationships with parents or significant others. May feel sad in sessions, or angry at those who do not give them what they need. Also, tend to feel pleased or satisfied, and hopeful about treatment progress/pattern. **Tx:** Monitor countertransference
PATTERN ANALYSIS	**Triggers:** Close relationships and public appearance.
PATTERN CHANGE	***Treatment Goals:*** Better tolerate corrective feedback; Become more selectively trusting of others.
Schemas	Defectiveness/shame; Social undesirability/alienation **Tx:** Schema change strategy and/or Interpretation strategy
Styles/Skills	
a. *Affective Style*	Hypersensitive and apprehensive **Tx:** Affect regulation
b. *Behavioral/Interpersonal Style*	Avoidance/withdrawal behavior; Shyness and under-assertiveness **Tx:** Interpersonal skills training & Assertive communication training
c. *Cognitive Style*	Somewhat to very hypervigilant **Tx:** Sensitivity reduction training
d. *Distress Tolerance*	Distress overtolerant **Tx:** RO-DBT-Distress Tolerance training
MAINTENANCE/ TERMINATION	Homework avoidance; Anxiety and ambivalence about termination **Tx:** Process avoidance in terms of schemas/automatic thoughts; use daily log/diary; Space out sessions; Booster sessions

focuses on characterological, temperament, and skill dimensions, is usually essential for effective treatment outcomes. The case example illustrates the common challenges that these individuals present, and the kind of clinician flexibility and competence as well as treatment resources required. Table 5.1 summarizes the treatment intervention strategies most likely to be effective with this disorder.

6 Borderline Personality Disorder

Basically, individuals with borderline personality disorder are impulsive, emotionally labile, and relationally unstable. While treatment of such individuals involves a number of unique therapeutic challenges, it can be highly effective and successful. This chapter describes a framework for effective treatment of this disorder from a cognitive behavioral perspective. It includes sections on assessment, case conceptualization, and treatment interventions. The section on assessment includes behavioral and cognitive factors, as well as a DSM-5 description and a prototypic description of this disorder. A prototype is a brief description that captures the essence of how a particular disorder commonly presents. Prototypic descriptions are useful and convenient and clinicians commonly rely on them rather than lists of behavioral criteria and core and instrumental beliefs (Westen, 2012). The section on case conceptualization provides both cognitive and behavioral formulations of this disorder. The longest section is on treatment. It emphasizes engagement, pattern analysis, pattern change, and pattern maintenance and termination strategies for effectively managing and treating this disorder. In addition to individual psychotherapeutic strategies and tactics, group, marital and family, medication, and integrative and combined treatment strategies are included. An extensive case example illustrates the treatment process.

Assessment

Behavioral

A behavioral assessment of this disorder emphasizes individual and interpersonal behaviors. Individuals with this disorder are characterized by a diverse array of behaviors ranging from anxiety, anger, and mood lability, to disturbances of consciousness such as depersonalization and dissociation, and even brief psychotic episodes. Chronic loneliness, a sense of emptiness, boredom, identity confusion are commonly observed, as well as impulsive behavior that can include self-injury or self-mutilation. Their occupational accomplishments are often less than their intelligence and ability warrant. Their personal lives are characteristically unfocused and unstable and are marked by frequent disappointments and rejections. They often have irregular circadian rhythms, especially of the sleep-wake cycle. Accordingly, chronic insomnia is a common complaint. Interpersonally, they tend to be emotionally labile and exhibit a pattern of intense and chaotic relationships. They fluctuate quickly between idealizing and clinging to an individual and then devaluing and opposing that same individual. They are exquisitely rejection-sensitive, and experience feelings of depression and fears of abandonment following the slightest relational conflict (Sperry, 2003).

Cognitive

A cognitive assessment of this disorder emphasizes core beliefs, particularly those about their views of self and of others. Typically, they view themselves as defective, vulnerable, and neglected. They view others as potentially danger-ous and unpredictable. Although they would like to believe that others can be caring and nurturing, they find them to be untrustworthy and may be hurtful or rejecting. Related beliefs include trusting others leads to abuse or abandon-ment, and being along means being unable to cope. They are also convinced that they must demand what they need and fight back. Not surprisingly, such beliefs are reflected in their main strategy or pattern of being subservient to others while punishing them, alternating protest with inhibition, and reduc-ing tension by engaging in self-harmful behaviors (Arntz, 2015; Beck, 2015).

DSM-5 Description

Individuals with this personality disorder are characterized by an unremitting pattern of unstable relationships, emotional reactions, identity, and impul-sivity. They engage in frantic efforts to avoid abandonment, whether it is real or imagined. Their interpersonal relationships are intense, unstable, and alternate between the extremes of idealization and devaluation. They have chronic identity issues and an unstable sense of self. Their impulsivity can result in self-damaging actions such as reckless driving or drug use, binge eat-ing, or high-risk sex. These individuals engage in recurrent suicidal threats, gestures, acting out or self-mutilating behavior. They can exhibit markedly reactive moods, chronic feelings of emptiness, emotional outbursts, and dif-ficulty controlling their anger. They may also experience brief, stress-related paranoid thinking or severe episodes of dissociation (American Psychiatric Association, 2013).

Prototypic Description

These individuals have intense and frustrating relationships which begin with high hopes but predictably degenerate into conflict and disappoint-ments. Because they are terrified of being abandoned, they drive others away with unrealistic demands, relentless anger, and self-fulfilling expectations of abandonment. Real or imagined losses can lead to suicide attempts or self-mutilation. The result is repeated destructive relationships and a fragile sense of self. They may engage in impulsive sexual and aggressive behaviors. Suicide rates are high for such individuals. However, those who survive may find some sense of balance and serenity in midlife (Frances, 2013).

Case Conceptualization

From a Cognitive Therapy perspective, three basic assumptions are noted in those with borderline personality disorders: "I am powerless and vulnerable"; "I am inherently unacceptable"; and "the world is dangerous and malevolent" (Arntz, 2015; Pretzer, 1990). Because of their inherent belief they are helpless in a hostile world without a source of security they vacillate between autonomy and dependence without being able to rely on either. In addition, borderlines tend to display "dichotomous thinking," the tendency to evaluate experiences in mutual exclusive categories, all good or all bad, success or failure, trustworthy or deceitful. The combination of dichotomous thinking and basic assumptions are the basis of borderline emotion and behavior, including acting out and self-destructive behaviors.

Young, Klosko, and Weishaar (2003) believe that "early maladaptive schemas" develop during childhood and result in maladaptive behavior patterns which reinforce these schemas. Schemas such as abandonment/loss: "I'll be alone forever. No one would love me or want to be close to me if they really got to know me"; and emotional deprivation: "No one is ever there to meet my needs, to be strong for me, to care for me." These schemas are believed to be common in those with this disorder.

Linehan (1993) describes a behavioral formulation of borderline pathology. Central to this formulation is an "invalidating environment" in which parents repeatedly criticize, minimize, and punish the child's emotional expression. This engenders the belief that strong emotions are dangerous and must be avoided. The resulting dysfunction in emotional regulation is linked to dramatic overreaction and impulsivity. Subsequently, borderline individuals develop little or no skill in emotion regulation. The combination of intense emotional responses, inadequate emotional regulation skills, impulsive behavior, and a disparaging self-attitude presages unrelenting crisis for which they are unable to effectively cope, and overreliance on others. From a different behavioral perspective, Turkat (1990) contends that problem-solving deficits are the basis for borderline pathology.

There is also a neuroscience conceptualization of this disorder and its treatment. As noted in Chapter 4, recent research suggests that the symptoms of this disorder are the result of failures of prefrontal circuits to appropriately regulate the limbic system. Presumably, this malfunction begins early in life and is influenced by genetic factors, adverse experiences, and other environmental factors. As already noted, Linehan (1993, 2015) contends that parental invalidation is such a factor. The end result of these influences is disrupted brain development, and problems in the neural circuits that facilitate top-down control of the limbic system including the amygdala and hippocampus (Hooley, Cole, & Gironde, 2012). The result of neural circuit failure are symptoms of emotional dysregulation, behavioral and cognitive disinhibition, and distress intolerance.

In terms of treatment informed by this neuroscience perspective, there are two possible treatment strategies employed with this disorder. The top-down strategy utilizes various psychotherapeutic interventions in an effort to modify these cortical influences on limbic circuits. These include conventional CBT in which cognitive restructuring attempts to challenge maladaptive beliefs and schemas. In contrast, the bottom-up strategy involves the use of skill training and/or medication to modulate the individual's externalizing pattern and symptoms by normalizing the activity of limbic circuits (Hooley et al., 2012). Psychotropic medication is another bottom-up strategy to normalize these circuits. There is mounting evidence that the group skill training interventions used in Dialectical Behavior Therapy are more effective in regulating or modulating these circuits than conventional psychotherapy. Skill training may actually be more effective than medication as a bottom-up strategy (Fawcett, 2002).

Treatment

Engagement Strategies

Early Session Behavior

Interviewing individuals with borderline personality features presents clinicians with a special challenge due to the instability and ambivalence of this personality. Lability or instability is present not only in their moods and cognitions, but also in their rapport with the clinician. Instability involving rapport can be handled by empathically focusing on it. This can be accomplished by focusing the discussion, tracking the discussion, and curbing outbursts and diversions. With this individual, open-ended questioning is preferable to closed-ended and pointed questioning. Furthermore, instability can be handled by focusing on its pathological part that needs to be explored. Because instability affects rapport, the clinician should continually acknowledge its presence and effect. As a result of these strategies, borderline individuals become less defensive and more willing to disclose, which leads to increased rapport (Othmer & Othmer, 2002).

In a manner similar to the way in which they relate to others, borderline individuals will also direct their angry and rageful affects toward clinicians. Experienced clinicians expect borderline individuals to relate in this manner at the outset of treatment. Nevertheless, this manner of relating does heighten tension in the therapeutic relationship. Managing this tension and providing the resources to keep the therapeutic relationship at an active working level is a constant challenge in the treatment of these individuals (Sperry, 2006).

Dealing with ambivalence requires confronting their contradictory statements while simultaneously displaying an understanding of their ambivalent feelings. They may enthusiastically describe a new relationship one moment and then devalue it in the next when they recall something unpleasant about that relationship. Generally speaking, therapeutic confrontation can effectively neutralize their splitting and projective identification, just as it moderates overidealization and devaluation. Therapeutic confrontation also helps them realize that their ambivalence is the result of a perceived lack of support and understanding from the other person. Finally, therapeutic confrontation permits them to realize—however painful—the extent to which they have allowed others to profoundly influence their sense of well-being (Waldinger, 1987).

Therapeutic confrontation is probably not indicated when there is evidence of childhood sexual and physical abuse in the borderline individual, at least in the early phases of treatment. There is developing literature on how treatment is modified when such abuse issues are present (Gunderson & Chu, 1993). In fact, some would contend that interpretation of aggressive themes and transference interpretations must be made carefully, if at all, and that the clinician must validate the role of bad parenting in the individual's past as a motivating force for that aggression (Buie & Adler, 1983).

Family members are often incorporated into the treatment process with the expectation that the borderline's self-harmful behavior can be reduced or compliance with medication or other aspects of treatment will be improved. Clinicians should anticipate the emotional response of family members toward the borderline individual whenever they are involved in the treatment process, particularly family treatment sessions. At times, family members may be intrusive and overcontrolling, while rejecting and hostile at other times. This vacillating pattern can significantly complicate the treatment process making family sessions difficult if not impossible. Unless this pattern is therapeutically confronted, family communications will not improve. Nor, is it likely that compliance will increase or that self-harmful behavior be reduced. More on involving family members in treatment is described in a subsequent section (see Marital and Family Strategies).

Facilitating Collaboration

By definition, personality-disordered individuals find it difficult to cooperate and collaborate, much less take responsibility for their own behavior (Cloninger, 2000). This is particularly true for borderline individuals who typically enter treatment for the express purpose of feeling better rather than making changes in their lives. They want to have their abandonment feelings disappear, their worries soothed, and their problems of daily living resolved. Their secret desire is that someone all powerful and all nurturing will "make up" for their heretofore chaotic and rejection-ravaged life. In short, they believe that it is someone else's responsibility to make everything better for them. It is certainly not their responsibility because they did not create their problem-strewn lives. In the therapeutic setting that "someone" is the clinician.

Limit setting and treatment contracting are two other powerful strate-gies for achieving engagement. Usually, these strategies are used with lower functioning borderline individuals who are parasuicidal or act out in various other ways (Linehan, 1993). Establishing a written contract to avert suicidal behaviors is one of the most common uses. Contracts can be used to facilitate treatment adherence such as attendance for after-care programs, reducing fighting or compulsive behaviors, or increasing medication compliance.

Clinicians should consider the "no treatment option" whenever evaluat-ing treatment requests involving a borderline-disordered individual. In this option, borderline individuals with a long history of treatment failure are not automatically offered psychotherapy or even medication management when it is requested or demanded (Frances, Clarkin, & Perry, 1984). Because of the high likelihood of repeating their failure pattern again and when no noticeable change in readiness for treatment is assessed, the clinician has two options. The first is the offer to reevaluate the individual at a later time when the individual is more ready for treatment. The second is the offer of an extended treatment evaluation of three to four sessions during which the clinician evaluates the individual's readiness for treatment based on their response to prescribed intersession tasks. Compliance with the tasks demonstrates some measure of willingness for collaboration and self-responsibility, and leads to an extension of the treatment contract for an additional set of sessions. This strategy reinforces the individual's success with treatment sessions, rather than reinforcing the individual's failure as in previous treatment episodes. Examples of intersession tasks include keeping a log of symptoms or target behaviors, or accomplishing specific tasks like attending two 12-step meetings and finding a 12-step sponsor within a given time frame.

Another common engagement strategy is establishment of a holding envi-ronment, which can refer to the clinician's containment function or to a treatment philosophy in an inpatient or partial hospitalization program. The holding or containing function refers to the clinician's capacity to receive and "hold" the individual's projections without absorbing them or acting on them. Furthermore, the clinician is able to mediate these projections back to indi-viduals so that they may integrate these parts of themselves that previously were not tolerable, such as anger and rage. Kernberg (1984) described how a holding environment can serve as the operational philosophy in an inpatient unit or partial hospital program for the treatment of borderline personality disordered individuals.

Transference and Countertransference

Given that interpersonal relationships tend to be inordinately troublesome for borderline individuals, matters involving transference and countertrans-ference should be of considerable concern to the clinician. Transference in borderline individuals runs the gamut from helplessness and merger fantasy to scornfulness. Dependency transferences may be the most common. In the dependency transference, the borderline individual relies on the clinician to make decisions and otherwise take responsibility for their well-being. As noted earlier, this underlying attitude considerably limits treatment progress.

Common clinician countertransferences include anger, guilt, antagonism, fear, rejection, feelings of manipulation, and rescue fantasies. Clinicians can easily become angry because of the borderline's demandingness, overdependence, or acting-out behavior. Obviously, clinicians need to monitor their thoughts and reactions to these individuals who are incredibly sensitized to the paralanguage of others. For instance, the clinician can respond to the borderline individual's hostility by saying, "I'm getting the impression you're trying to make me angry at you instead of letting me help you. Let's see if *we* can understand what's happening." Because of the borderline's rejection sensitivity and tendency to feel blamed, it is therapeutically valuable to emphasize the interpersonal nature of the verbal interaction. In addition, clinicians may have to set limits on the individual's hostility so as to hold their own countertransference in check: "I'm not sure *we're* going to accomplish anything if you continue screaming. It's important that you work on controlling your anger so you can express it in a less provocative way."

Pattern Analysis Strategies

Pattern analysis with borderline-disordered individuals involves an accurate diagnostic and clinical evaluation of schemas, styles, and triggering stressors as well as their level of functioning and readiness for therapeutic change. Knowledge of the optimal DSM-5 diagnostic criterion along with the maladaptive pattern of the borderline personality disordered individual is not only useful in specifying diagnosis but also in planning treatment that is tailored to the individual's unique style, needs, and circumstances. The optimal criterion specified for the borderline personality disorder is frantic efforts to avoid real or imagined abandonment (Allnutt & Links, 1996). Borderline personality disordered individuals often respond to abandonment with angry outbursts as well as splitting and projective identification. Self-destructive impulsive behaviors, such as wrist-slashing, overdosing, promiscuity and substance abuse, are common. Fear of abandonment also amplifies ambivalence about relationships, which further interferes with establishing and maintaining stable, enduring relationships. This means that treatment planning must be of necessity to target these overmodulations of affective style, behavioral style, and cognitive style for intervention.

Pattern refers to the predictable and consistent style and manner in which an individual thinks, feels, acts, copes, and defends the self. Pattern analysis involves both the triggers and response—the "what"—as well as a clinical formulation or explanatory statement—the "why"—about the pattern of a given borderline individual. Obviously, such a clinical formulation specifies the particular schemas and temperamental styles unique to a given individual rather than the more general clinical formulation that will be noted here.

Triggers

Generally speaking, the "triggers" or "triggering" situations for borderline individuals are stressors related to close personal relationships and personal goals. This means that when borderline-disordered individuals are engaging in behaviors, discussing, or even thinking about certain relationships or achieving certain personal goals and become distressed, their disordered or maladaptive pattern is likely to be triggered and their characteristic symptomatic affects, behaviors, and cognitions are likely to be experienced or exhibited. Borderline individuals perceive these triggers in typical ambivalent fashion. For instance, the stress of a close relationship may trigger the thought, "People are great, no they are not," while the stress of a personal goal triggers the thought: "Goals are good, no they are not" (Othmer & Othmer, 2002). Whether the individual's full maladaptive pattern, particularly acting-out behavior, ensues, is dependent on various situational factors.

Schemas

Generally speaking, the underlying schemas of borderline-disordered individuals involve a self-view of uncertainty about self-identity, gender, career, and their very worth. Their worldview is equally uncertain as they are ambivalent about others' loyalty to them, the stability of the world, and the likelihood that they can make a commitment to anything or anyone (Sperry & Mosak, 1996). Among the most frequently encountered schemas in borderline individuals are unlovability/defectiveness, abandonment/loss, and dependency/incompetence (Layden, Newman, Freeman, & Morse, 1993; Young, 1994). The unlovability/defectiveness schema refers to the core belief that one is internally flawed, and if others recognize this they will withdraw from the relationship. The abandonment/loss schema is central to this personality disorder and refers to the expectation that one will imminently lose any and every close relationship. The dependency/incompetence schema refers to the core belief that one is incapable of handling daily responsibilities competently and independently, and so must rely on others to make decisions and initiate new tasks.

Style/Temperament

There are four unique style dimensions in the ABCDEF Profile that characterize individuals with this personality disorder: Affective, Behavioral-interpersonal, Cognitive, and Distress tolerance. Needless to say, these styles exacerbate and are exacerbated by their schemas. Borderline individuals are prone to overmodulated thinking, such as splitting and projective identification. They are also characteristically impulsive, and their affects, particularly moods, tend to be overmodulated and distress intolerant (Linehan, 2015; Mara, 2005).

This impulsive style can further exacerbate their proclivity to self-destructive behavior, including self-mutilation. Relationally, because of their history of impulsivity and overmodulated affects, these individuals tend to exhibit limited interpersonal skills, which further exacerbates their schemas of abandonment, unlovability, and incompetence.

Pattern Change Strategies

Generally speaking, the overall goal of treatment is to achieve some measure of stability and cohesiveness. Accomplishing this goal requires a fourfold strategy: (a) reduce symptoms of the a co-occurring clinical disorder; (b) remodulate problematic temperament/style features such as impulsivity, distress intolerance, and parasuicidality; (c) increase the individual's levels of life functioning; and (d) modify character/schema features. This section describes six different strategies for pattern change: style modulation, medication, schema modification, group treatment modalities, marital and family therapy modalities, and combined/integrative modalities.

Schema Therapy

In Schema Therapy, BPD individuals are viewed as vulnerable children who were lonely and mistreated and behave inappropriately as adults because they are desperate. Lacking a healthy adult role model they could internalize in their early years, they lack the internal resources to sustain themselves when they are alone as adults. To compound matters, as adults the only people they may be able to turn to are those who would hurt and abuse them. Accordingly, BPD clients seem to need much more than their therapist can or should attempt to provide. While these clients often expect the therapist to become their parent, Young, Klosko, and Weishaar (2003) advocate providing "limited parenting" as a realistic and therapeutic alternative to that expectation.

Clients with BPD present a unique challenge to therapists who endeavor to focus treatment around schema change. The main challenge is that these clients can rapidly shift from one extreme emotional state to another. Schemas which are presumed to be reflect traits rather than states, cannot explain this rapid shifting. Efforts to assess schemas in these clients can be confusing since they seem to have so many maladaptive schemas. For instance, it is not unusual for BPD clients to endorse nearly all the maladaptive schemas on the Young Schema Questionnaire (Young & Brown, 2001). As noted in Chapter 3, Young and his colleagues adopted the construct of schema mode to represent this rapid shifting. A schema model involves "those schemas or coping responses–adaptive or maladaptive—that are currently active for an individual" (Klosko & Young, 2004, p. 276).

Schema therapy with BPD is an intensive and extensive treatment process. It consists of three stages:

1. The bonding and emotional regulation stage in which the goals are to facilitate the re-parenting bond and negotiate limits, as well as contain and regulate their affects.

2. The schema model change stage, in which the goals are to build the client's health adult mode, emphasizes caring for the Abandoned Child, expunging the Punitive Parent, and teaching the Angry and Impulsive Child appropriate ways to express emotions and needs.
3. The autonomy stage in which the goal is to foster healthy relationships outside of therapy and generalize from the therapy relationship to appropriate significant others outside the treatment context (Klosko & Young, 2004).

Each stage of treatment consists of experiential, cognitive, and behavioral interventions. For example, stage 1 interventions include such DBT skills as mindfulness meditation which fosters calming and affect regulation (Linehan, 2015), assertiveness training, and more cognitive focused techniques such as flash cards and the schema diary which are utilized between sessions. Flash cards are small cards which clients carry around and read when upset. The therapist and client work to compose a message on different cards for different trigger situations. The schema diary is a log kept by clients which help them think through a problem and generate a healthy response (Young et al., 2003).

Dialectical Behavior Therapy

Linehan and colleagues view BPD as reflecting a pervasive pattern of affective, behavioral and cognitive instability and dysregulation (Linehan, 2015). The defining feature of DBT is its emphasis on dialectics, the reconciliation of opposites. The basic dialectic for therapists working with DBT is accepting the clients' behaviors, thoughts and affects in the moment while simultaneously encouraging them to change. Accordingly, DBT treatment requires "moment to moment changes in the use of supportive acceptance versus confrontation and change strategies. This emphasis on acceptance as a balance to change flows directly from the integrative of a perspective drawn from Eastern (Zen) practice with Western Psychological practice" (Linehan, 1993, p. 19).

Linehan (1993, 2015) specified four primary modes of treatment in DBT: individual therapy; group-based skills training, telephone contact, and therapist consultation. Group therapy and other modes of treatment may be added at the discretion of the therapist.

The individual therapist is the primary therapist and the main work of therapy is carried out in the individual therapy sessions. Individual therapy is conceptualized as having three stages: beginning, middle, and end (Marra, 2005). Essential components of individual therapy from a DBT perspective include: dialectical analysis and coaching clients to think dialectically about their own situation; validation of the client's feelings, thoughts and experiences; balancing emotion-focused and solution-focused coping; prompting improved shifting of attention from internal to external cues; teaching new psychological coping skills, and non-pejorative interpretation of the client's behavior and affect.

This stage focuses on reducing parasuicidal and suicidal behaviors, therapy-interfering behaviors, and behaviors that comprise quality of life. It also focuses on developing the necessary skills to resolve these problems. Emphasized are mindfulness skills, interpersonal effectiveness skills, emotion modulation skills, and distress tolerance skills. Each of these skills targets key style/temperament over modulations. However it is possible to accomplish skill training in the context of individual therapy with select clients (Marra, 2005).

Telephone contact with the therapist after hours is offered not as psychotherapy but rather to help and support clients to find alternatives to self-injury and for relationship repair when the client believes she damaged her relationship with her therapist and wants to rectify it prior to the next session.

DBT therapists are encouraged to participate regularly in therapist consultation groups. These groups provide both emotional support for therapists dealing with difficult clients as well as ongoing training in DBT methods.

Following an initial period of pre-treatment involving assessment, commitment and orientation to therapy, DBT consists of three stages of treatment.

1. This stage focuses on reducing parasuicidal and suicidal behaviors, therapy-interfering behaviors, and behaviors that compromise quality of life. It also focuses on developing the necessary skills to resolve these problems. Skills training is usually carried out in a group context, ideally by someone other than the individual therapist. In the skills-training groups clients are taught skills considered relevant to the particular problems of personality-disordered individuals. There are four groups of skills: core mindfulness skills, interpersonal effectiveness skills, emotion modulation skills, and distress tolerance skills.

2. This stage deals primarily with difficult problems of living, including treatment of post-traumatic stress related issues when present. Much of this work is done in individual sessions.

3. The focus of this stage is on self-esteem and individual treatment goals.

The targeted behaviors of each stage are brought under control before moving on to the next phase. In particular, post-traumatic stress related problems such as those related to childhood sexual abuse are not dealt with directly until stage 1 has been successfully completed. Therapy at each stage is focused on the specific targets for that stage which are arranged in a definite hierarchy of relative importance. These include: decreasing suicidal behaviors, decreasing therapy-interfering behaviors, decreasing behaviors that interfere with the quality of life, increasing behavioral skills, decreasing behaviors related to post-traumatic stress, improving self-esteem, and individual targets negotiated with the client.

The core strategies in DBT are 'validation' and 'problem solving'. Attempts to facilitate change are surrounded by interventions that validate clients' behavior and responses in relation to the client's current life situation, and that demonstrate an understanding of their difficulties and suffering. Problem solving focuses on the establishment of necessary skills. Other treatment modalities include contingency management, cognitive therapy, exposure-based therapies, and medication. Because parasuicidal, suicidal and other forms of acting-out behaviors are common with BPD individuals, contingency management is commonly employed in each stage of treatment.

The provision of DBT therapy is easier to accomplish in an inpatient, partial hospitalization or residential treatment setting than in private practice. The reason is that, as described by Linehan (1993), DBT is best implemented with a treatment team in which one therapist provides psychosocial skills training, another provides individual therapy, others provide a consultation function, and the therapists have access to a therapist consultation group for support.

Marra (2005) has offered suggestions for adapting DBT treatment in private practice settings. While he recommends that skills training be provided by another therapist, he offers guidelines when that is not possible. Nevertheless, he encourages therapists in private practice who want to use DBT to have regular contact with a psychotherapy consultant as a substitute for involvement in a therapist consultation group. The purpose of such consultation is to clarify diagnosis, treatment plans and specific interventions with another professional who can offer a fresh perspective, confront the therapist's interpretation of data and situations, and warn of potential boundary violations.

CBASP Strategies

While Cognitive Behavioral Analysis System of Psychotherapy (CBASP) was originally developed by McCullough (2000; McCullough, Schramm & Penberthy, 2015) for the treatment of chronic depression, it has been extended to treatment of BPD. Based on his experience working with BPD clients, McCullough (2002) is not convinced that CBASP itself can be effective with severe borderline personality disorder, especially with comorbid chronic depression. Others believe that CBASP can be used as the main treatment for BPD (Driscoll, Cukrowicz, Reardon, & Joiner, 2004). In my experience, CBASP may be the principal treatment for those with this disorder who are high functioning. However, for those who are lower functioning, skill training is often essential to achieve modulation or better self-control over affective, behavioral, cognitive dysregulation and distress intolerance. Then CBASP can target issues in learning from experience (Sperry, 2005).

The basic premise of CBASP is that the therapist can help clients to discover why they did not obtain a desired outcome by evaluating their problematic thoughts and behaviors. One of the main interventions of this approach is Situational Analysis which has been shown to be clinically effective in identifying and correcting maladaptive patterns of thinking and behavior characteristic of BPD. Situational Analysis is a process that is recorded by the client on the Coping Survey Questionnaire usually before a session and then reviewed with the therapist during the session. It helps articulate the elements of a problematic situation and the individual's interpretations and behaviors.

Clinicians using CBASP note that BPD individuals often have interpretations of interpersonal encounters that reflect early maladaptive schemas of loss, guilt and mistrust (Driscoll, Cukrowicz, Reardon, & Joiner, 2004). Accordingly, when using CBASP, clinicians should attend to these schema-related interpretations, and challenge whether they helped or hindered the individual's progress in achieving a desired outcome. This form of challenging tends to be experienced by individuals as less judgmental and thus less likely to elicit negative reactions as compared to more direct challenges of schema-related cognitions and beliefs. Similar to the DBT approach, the CBASP approach to challenging interpretations can validate individuals' experience of expressing their thinking during the problematic situation, as well as encourage them to consider revising their disruptive interpretations.

The CBASP strategy can also be quite useful in analyzing crises that occur between sessions. In these circumstances, the clinician focuses attention on the interpretations the individual had during the crises and the specific behaviors involved. This strategy helps individuals understand how various behaviors and interpretations can escalate a crisis. It also identifies targets for change. It is suggested that when dealing with more dysregulated BPD individuals, the clinician should probably focus more attention on overt behaviors initially, whereas more focus on interpretations is possible with less dysregulated individuals earlier in the treatment process (Driscoll, Cukrowicz, Reardon, & Joiner, 2004).

Another application of CBASP is helping BPD individuals understand conflicts that occur with clinicians during a treatment session. In these circumstances, the goal is to highlight the disruptive interpretations, behaviors, and desired outcomes during the conflict with the clinician. Because this process requires individuals to deal with strong emotions arising from the conflict, it is recommended for use in later phases of treatment. The interested reader is directed to a transcription of a session in which CBASP is utilized (Driscoll, Cukrowicz, Reardon, & Joiner, 2004).

Style Change Strategies

For all practical purposes, style modulation strategies include medication and social skills training. Either alone or in combination with rational psychopharmacotherapy, social skills training is an effective strategy for remodulating disordered style dimensions. The goal of this strategy is to achieve sufficient affective, behavioral, and cognitive stability so that the individual will sufficiently be ready and amenable to work on more traditional therapeutic issues.

Needless to say, many borderline-disordered individuals have unmodulated styles because they never adequately learned sufficient self-control skills during their formative years. Thus, it becomes necessary for them to reverse these specific skill deficits in the context of treatment. Either within an individual or group treatment context, these skills are learned and practiced. Six different types of skill training are particularly useful for the kind of unmodulated styles most commonly seen in borderline individuals. Emotion awareness training and emotional regulation training target overmodulated affects. Impulse control training targets impulse dyscontrol. Self-management training is particularly useful in reducing self-destructive behaviors such as self-mutilation and the multiple forms of parasuicidality. Interpersonal skill training is targeted for a wide range of interpersonal skill deficits including effective communication and making and keeping friends. Cognitive awareness training targets the propensity for splitting and projective identification. Finally, distress tolerance training targets distressing thoughts that the individual can no longer cope with further stressors without incurring disastrous consequences.

Not surprisingly, the course of treatment with borderline individuals—particularly those who are lower functioning—can easily become crisis oriented because of their chaotic pattern. Not only can level of readiness change from session to session, but continuity of therapeutic focus can seldom be maintained from session to session, particularly in the early stages of treatment. For this reason it is useful to be able to assess the individual's level of readiness and specify related and relevant treatment objectives at each session. One way of assessing the individual's readiness at each session is in terms of treatment or intervention targets. This scheme is more sensitive than the stages of readiness for change described in Chapter 1 and is considerably modified from the hierarchy of treatment targets described by Linehan (1993). She described five sets of progressive treatment targets: parasuicidal; behaviors interfering with the conduct of treatment, such as missing sessions or medication noncompliance; escape behaviors that interfere with making or maintaining changes outside of treatment, such as substance abuse or illegal actions; skills acquisition that are necessary to function more effectively in and outside of treatment; and achievement of the individual's personal goals.

Clearly, individuals who are parasuicidal or continually acting out in treatment are not as ready for work on schema change as individuals who are sufficiently engaged in treatment and have the requisite skills to collaborate in processing regressive issues like emotional and sexual abuse. The suggested treatment strategy for using these treatment targets is to assess the individual's current level of treatment readiness and then focus on that level as long as necessary before preceding to the next level. Thus, if the individual reports or admits to any suicidal ideation, no other "higher" level issues, such as the individual's social security disability application or lost welfare check, can be discussed until the "lower" or more basic treatment issue is reasonably resolved.

Medication Strategies

Medication is commonly used in the treatment of this disorder. Usually the treatment targets are affective instability, interpersonal sensitivity, impulsivity, aggressivity, transient psychotic episodes, and self-harming behavior.

Lithium and carbamazepine have targeted affective instability, while sero-tonergic agents have been effective with impulsivity and aggressivity. Sero-tonergic agents, like fluoxetine and sertraline, are effective for reducing the interpersonal sensitivity and reactivity (Reich, 2002). For those with rejection sensitivity, and a history of good treatment compliance, a trial of an MAOI can be considered if all other approaches have failed. Serotonergic agents have some efficacy in lower functioning histrionic individuals who exhibit impulsivity and affective instability (Reich, 2002). Transient psychotic epi-sodes, including mild thought disorders and dissociation, are best addressed with atypical antipsychotics instead of traditional neuroleptics which have the risk of tardive dyskinesia. Finally, for self-harming behavior, trials of SSRIs have been helpful. If not, an adjunctive trial of naltrexone can be considered, if necessary (Reich, 2005).

In recent years, quetiapine (Seroquel) has become the most commonly prescribed medication for borderline personality disorder probably because it reduces various symptoms such as anxiety, presumably because it has a sedating effect. It is an antipsychotic medication that is generally well toler-ated. That means it has few adverse effects and specifically has low potential for extrapyramidal (tremor and stiffness) symptoms. However, it can cause weight gain (Diamond, 2009). Very well-designed research has been reported that confirms what clinicians have known for some time. In a randomized controlled trial it was found that low dose quetiapine (150 mg/day) was effec-tive in reducing the overall severity of symptoms in those with borderline personality disorder. Most improvement was noted in verbal and physical aggression but less on impulsivity and depression (Black, Zanarini, Romine, Shaw, Allen & Schulz, 2014).

There are some potential complications or disadvantages with pharma-cotherapy in the treatment of borderline individuals. First is the matter of noncompliance either related to side effects or to secondary gain. Medica-tions can serve as leverage to control the prescribing clinician or other caregivers. Demands for frequent changes in dosage or type of medication, overdosing, and failure to take the medication prescribed are all means of transference acting out. Second, borderline individuals may appear to oth-ers to have improved from medication but report they feel worse, or vice versa. Gunderson (1989) suggested that this apparent paradox may ensue to the extent the individual believes that symptomatic improvement will result in undesirable consequences, such as loss or abandonment of depen-dent gratifications.

Schema Change Strategies

Once the borderline individual has achieved a sufficient measure of stability, it is then possible to address more traditional therapeutic issues. As noted earlier, schemas of abandonment/loss, unlovability/defectiveness, and depen-dence/incompetence are often seen in borderline individuals. There are two general approaches to modifying such schemas. The more traditional is the psychodynamic approach in which the strategy is clarification, confrontation, interpretation, and working through. According to Klein (1989), therapeutic confrontation is the most effective psychodynamic tactic for working with borderline individuals.

The other basic approach to modifying schemas is the cognitive therapy strategy. Layden et al. (1993) described the use of memory reconstruction, schema identification, imagery exercises, and the use of physical cues for modifying borderline schemas. Five extended case examples illustrate the cognitive therapy strategy of schema modification. Turner (1992) described an interesting integrative approach which he called dynamic–cognitive behavior therapy of the borderline personality disorder. In this approach, schemas are modified with both dynamic and cognitive therapy methods.

Group Treatment Strategies

The general consensus is that group therapy can be extremely effective with borderline-disordered individuals. Group therapy has a number of advantages over individual therapy. Particularly noteworthy is that group tends to "dilute" intense transferences that otherwise would be directed to the individual clinician. Instead, affects like rage are diluted and directed toward other group members. Borderline individuals also find it easier to accept feedback and confrontation from group peers than from an individual clinician. Groups also provide opportunities to understand and master such borderline defenses as splitting and projective identification.

There are some disadvantages and difficulties in treating borderline individuals in groups. First, because of their propensity for acting out, these individuals can be quite disruptive in traditional therapy groups consisting of high-functioning individuals. Second, they may feel deprived amidst the competition of other group members for the group leader's nurturance. Third, these individuals may be easily scapegoated because of their primitive manner of expression. And they may maintain a certain distance in the group because of their privacy attachment to their individual psychotherapist. For that reason, borderline individuals seem to fare better in homogeneous groups consisting; of all or mostly borderline individuals.

Behaviorally oriented groups for borderline individuals focus less on intrapsychic and interpersonal dynamics and more on disordered patterns and symptomatic behavior. Accordingly, they are particularly suited for helping these individuals acquire the specific skills necessary to control their affects, reduce their cognitive distortions and projective identifications, and find alternatives to self-destructive behaviors. Linehan (1993, 2015) provided a manual-guided strategy for the treatment of self-destructive behavior and impulsivity. Group sessions use didactic instruction, skill training, and behavioral rehearsal techniques. Some of these social skills training interventions, such as distress tolerance training and interpersonal skills training, are described in Chapter 4 of this book. These twice-weekly sessions for 1 year are complemented with weekly individual counseling.

Research supports the clinical observation that these intervention strategies are remarkably effective (Linehan et al., 1991, 1993). Parasuicidal female borderline individuals were randomly assigned to Dialectical Behavior therapy groups or to traditional community treatment. Those in the behavioral therapy groups had fewer incidents of parasuicide, and had significantly fewer inpatient psychiatric days compared with those in traditional treatment. They were also more likely to remain in individual therapy (Linehan et al., 1991, 1993).

Marital and Family Therapy Strategies

Parents and siblings of borderline individuals have high incidence of affective disorders, alcoholism, antisocial personality disorder, and borderline personality disorder or traits. Usually, the parent–child relationship in borderline families is characterized by both neglect and overprotectiveness. Borderline families are also noted to display increased impulsivity, affective instability as well as significant problems with individuation, boundary violations, and enmeshment. Thus, involving the borderline individual's family or partner can be useful in decreasing enmeshment, respecting boundaries, and facilitating individuation. Family therapy can also increase overall family functioning and communication, and provide education about the nature of the disorder, while supporting compliance with medication or other treatment modalities. Family therapy can also be useful, and in some instances necessary, in maintaining borderline individuals in outpatient psychotherapy. This is particularly the case when borderline individuals remain financially and/or emotional dependent on their parents. To the extent that the family is motivated and has some capability of modulating affects and controlling projections, they may be a helpful adjunct to the overall treatment plan. Glick, Clarkin, and Goldsmith (1993) suggested that a mixture of systems, psychodynamic, behavioral, and psychoeducational family therapy intervention is preferable to a single approach to family therapy. Following are three different approaches for working with borderline individuals in the context of their families.

Everett, Halperin, Volgy, and Wissler (1989) described a psychodynamically oriented approach with five specific treatment goals: increasing the family's ability to reduce the systemic splitting process; increasing family members' capacities for owning split-off objects and moving toward interacting with others as a "whole person"; reducing oppositional and stereotypic behavior of all family members; "resetting" external boundaries for both unclear and intergenerational systems and internal boundary for spousal, parent-child, and sibling subtypes; and permitting a clearer alliance between the parents and limiting reciprocal intrusiveness of children and parents. Five treatment strategies for accomplishing these goals in an outpatient family treatment setting are developing and maintaining a therapeutic structure; reality testing in the family; interactional disengagement; intervening in the intergenerational system; and solidification of the marital alliance and sibling subsystem.

Solomon (1998) and Lachkar (1998) also described psychodynamically based treatments for troubled relations when one of the partners meets criteria for borderline personality disorder while the other meets criteria for narcissistic personality disorder. Both of these approaches emphasize the self-psychology perspective but recognize that systemic dynamics need to be considered.

A structural family approach is particularly useful for couples where the partner with borderline pathology is overly involved in the relationship while the other is distant and disengaged. Issues such as inclusion and rejection, nurturance and neglect, and symbiosis and abandonment become the basis for structurally rebalancing the couple subsystem within the larger family system (Sperry, 1995).

Relationship enhancement therapy is a potent psychoeducational intervention that has also been shown to be particularly useful in couple's relationships when one partner has borderline pathology. Because borderline individuals have major deficits in self-differentiation and communication, relationship enhancement's focused on skill building seems promising, particularly for mildly to moderately dysfunctional borderline individuals. The clinician functions largely as a coach to develop the necessary relational skills in the course of 2-hour conjoint sessions (Waldo & Harman, 1993, 1998).

A history of childhood abuse can complicate efforts to use family modalities, especially if family members were party to the trauma. When the abuse has been particularly malevolent, family involvement probably should not be encouraged. However, if the trauma has been less malevolent family sessions may eventually be possible (Perry et al., 1990).

Combined and Integrative Treatment Strategy

There is growing consensus that combined treatment is essential for effective outcomes with the borderline personality disordered individual (Koenigsberg, 1993). This consensus reflects the severity of this condition and its apparent treatment resistance. Clinical experience suggests that there are clear differences between the prognosis and treatability of the high-functioning borderline individuals (i.e., GAF over 65) and the low-functioning borderline individuals (i.e., GAF below 45). Use of long-term psychoanalytically oriented psychotherapy may be possible with the highest-functioning borderline individuals, but it is likely to be too regressive for lower functioning borderline individuals. In line with the basic premise of this book, the lower the individual's functioning and motivation and readiness for treatment, the greater the likelihood that treatment must be integrated and combined for it to be effective.

Combined treatment for borderline individuals is indicated for those with severe symptoms for which symptom relief has been slow with psychosocial treatment, for those with overmodulated affects, for those with impulsive aggressivity, and for those with transient psychotic regression. These individuals should have combined medication and individual therapy. Similarly, borderline individuals with significant interpersonal disturbance and identity issues should be considered for combined medication, individual, and group treatment modalities. Furthermore, to increase medication compliance and to more accurately assess the effects of medication, conjoint treatment in which family sessions or sessions with a significant other, roommate, or job supervisor should also be considered.

Contraindications to combined treatment include a variety of clinical presentations. Individuals with high overdose potential who cannot be controlled with limit setting are probably not candidates for combined individual and medication treatment. Group treatment, including partial hospitalization, may be an alternative. Individuals who may be responsive to medication but have a history of negative therapeutic reactions probably should not be offered individual psychotherapy. Similarly, individuals who use medication to precipitate crises in therapy or where medication becomes the central focus of therapy probably should not be offered combined treatment (Koenigsberg, 1993).

Combining medication with individual therapy is the most common integrative modality. Klein (1989) skillfully described the integration of pharmacotherapy within an individual psychotherapy context. He provided three guidelines for the effective use of medication: careful attention to diagnostic precision, evaluation of objective signs rather than subjective symptoms when determining when and which medication to use, and controlled awareness of the risks to therapeutic medication. Several case examples are provided that illustrate these guidelines.

A variety of transference phenomena can complicate combined treatment efforts with borderline individuals. Individuals with a history of transference enactments should probably be offered a trial of medication prior to the introduction of intensive individual psychotherapy to avoid or reduce such enactments. Otherwise, the clinician should consider using a structured medication management protocol in an individual format. Furthermore, issues of splitting are particularly common with borderline individuals when medication is monitored by one clinician and psychotherapy is provided by another. However, splitting can also become manifest when the prescribing clinician also provides formal psychotherapy. In the case of two clinicians, when both clinicians are able to integrate psychological and biological perspectives and regularly collaborate with one another to present a "united front," splitting can be reduced or eliminated (Woodward, Duckworth, & Guthiel, 1993). When there is a single clinician, splitting is only possible when the clinician has a split view (i.e., biological vs. psychological) of treatment.

Further complicating matters is the task differential between medication prescribing and practicing psychotherapy. Whereas psychotherapy favors spontaneous discourse and activity on the part of the individual, medication monitoring is much more directive and requires considerable clinician activity. Because borderline individuals may find it disruptive and difficult to move between these two tasks, it can be useful to set aside a few minutes at the beginning of a session to review medication effects and arrange for prescription, and then shift to the more obvious psychotherapeutic mode of discourse (Koenigsberg, 1993).

Medication compliance is often a problem in combined treatment with borderline individuals, especially when medication is perceived by the individual as a chemical means by which the clinician can exert control over the individual's mind and will. Thus, medication compliance can be viewed as acquiescing to the control of the clinician, whereas noncompliance is viewed as taking back that control. For this reason, it is important for the clinician to elicit specific fantasies the individual has about medication and its effects, as well as the meaning of medicating the individual for the clinician in the countertransference (Koenigsberg, 1991). The interested reader is referred to Koenigsberg (1991, 1993) for a more detailed discussion of combined treatment issues with borderline individuals.

Finally, combined treatment for lower functioning borderlines can be accomplished in a community-based setting. Usually, several treatment modalities will need to be combined. These often include individual therapy, group therapy, medication, drug and alcohol services, psychosocial rehabilitation, crisis intervention, and crisis housing. These modalities are often provided concurrently and usually are coordinated by a case manager (cf. Nehls & Diamond, 1993, for a detailed description of this strategy).

Pattern Maintenance and Termination Strategies

Termination Issues

Termination can be extremely difficult and distressing for borderline individuals. Because abandonment is an essential dynamic in borderline pathology, modifying the abandonment schema has to be the central focus of treatment. For this reason, it is essential that the treatment plan include provision for dealing with past interpersonal losses. Saying good-bye and grieving are skills most borderlines have never developed, and so therapy becomes the place where these skills and this corrective emotional experience usually begins. It must also deal with the anticipated loss of the current clinician(s) in the final phase of treatment. Losses need to be reframed as "necessary losses" and abandonment as "memories" that are treasured and not forgotten. Necessary losses are viewed as developmental opportunities to trade a secure, predictable experience and set of feelings for newer, growth opportunities that can only occur when an earlier experience is relinquished, but never really forgotten. In short, necessary losses and past memories are a prerequisite for personal growth and development.

Even in treating lower functioning and more severely disordered borderline individuals who will require continued medication long after formal psychotherapy is completed, the matter of loss is still germane. Even though the individual may have quarterly medication monitoring sessions, the intensity of daily or weekly meetings with one or more clinicians no longer exists, and so it is perceived as a loss. Usually, the hypersensitivity that many borderline individuals experience with the anticipation of loss can be, in part, desensitized by weaning sessions. In longer term therapies, this may mean reducing the frequency of sessions from daily to weekly to biweekly to monthly and then even quarterly over the last year of a 2- to 3-year course of treatment, or for the last half or third of therapy for 1- to 2-year treatment courses. When only 12 to 20 sessions per year are possible, it may be possible to meet weekly for 5 to 10 sessions and then spread the remaining sessions out on a biweekly and then monthly basis for the remainder. Spacing out sessions allows individuals to "contain" their abandonment fears. It also allows them the opportunity to use transitional objects and develop a sense of self-constancy between sessions, something they never would have believed was possible.

Finally, it is helpful for clinicians and borderline individuals to collaboratively develop a plan of self-therapy and self-management following termination. It is recommended that these individuals set aside an hour a week to engage in activities that continue the progress made in formal treatment. They might keep a diary or work on selected exercises. They could observe, monitor, and analyze obstacles and thoughts that interfered. Or, they might look ahead at the coming week and predict which situations could be troublesome, and plan ways to cope with feelings of loss or impulses to act out. The goal of such effort is, of course, to maintain treatment gains and maintain the newly acquired pattern.

Relapse Prevention Strategies

Another essential aspect of the treatment plan and process is relapse prevention. Because borderline individuals can easily revert to their maladaptive pattern, it is necessary to predict and plan for relapse. The final phase of treatment should largely focus on relapse prevention. An important goal of relapse prevention is predicting likely difficulties in the time period immediately following termination. Borderline individuals need to be able to analyze specific external situations such as new individuals, unfamiliar places, as well as internal states such as specific avoidant beliefs and fears and other vulnerabilities that increase the likelihood of them responding with avoidant behavior in the face of predictable triggers. Once predicted, individuals can develop a contingency plan to deal with these stressors. Clinicians may find it useful to have individuals think and talk through the following questions: What can I do if I find myself resorting to my previous pattern? What should I do if I start believing my old beliefs more than my new beliefs? What should I do if I relapse?

A belief that is particularly troubling for borderline individuals is, "I'll be alone forever. Everyone that I really need abandons me." This belief is easily activated and borderline individuals need to dispute it whenever it comes to mind. Furthermore, they need to anticipate the situations and circumstances when this belief is likely to arise and plan for it.

Good News About Treatment Outcomes

There has been more research published on this disorder than any other personality disorder. A recent study of the outcomes of treatment of this disorders has considerable clinical value for practicing clinicians. Zanarini and colleagues (Zanarini, Frankenburg, Reich, & Fitzmaurice, 2010) followed nearly 300 individuals prospectively over a 10-year period, interviewing them at 2-year intervals. They looked at both symptom remission and attainment of an adequate level of social and vocational functioning for at least two years. Both of these are indicative of a cure, not simply improvement. For symptom remission they found that nearly seven of eight borderline individuals achieved symptom remission that lasted at least four years. Half the patients achieved total recovery. That meant that they no longer met diagnostic criteria for this disorder and also attained reasonable social and occupational functioning. They found that symptom recovery occurred sooner than resolution of style-temperament features like self-mutilation, suicide gestures and attempts, impulsive actions like shoplifting and careless sexual encounters were resolved within 1–2 years with medication and/or psychotherapy. In contrast, modulating style features like emotional dysregulation, mood lability, demandingness, intense anger, and abandonment concerns took considerably longer. They also found that substance abuse issues were slow to resolve and lead to a more ominous prognosis, with more relapse and suicidality (Zanarini et al., 2010).

The good news of this important prospective study is that for individuals with this disorder, treatment can often be successful. In fact, there is a good chance that those with this disorder can be cured, i.e., they no longer meet diagnostic criteria and can function effectively in daily life! It also validates a basic premise of this book: that successful treatment must address both character and temperament features of the disorder.

Case of Tammy

Tammy R. is a 25-year-old, single Caucasian female with a 6-year history of inpatient and outpatient psychiatric treatment. Soon after she was married she experienced abandonment feelings and suicidal ideation and that led to the first of six hospitalizations. It appears to have been precipitated by her husband leaving her for an out-of-town business meeting. Since then she has been in continuous treatment of one sort or another with four different therapists and three different psychiatrists. Her most recent therapist of 2 years has focused on a number of regressive issues, including early childhood emotional abuse, which probably accounts for the four hospitalizations during that time.

At the time of the current evaluation she complained of vague, occasional suicidal ideation, dysphoria, initial insomnia, and confusion about life and career goals. She was notably deficient in the skills of symptom management, interpersonal effectiveness, and self-management of affect regulation and impulse control. Skill deficits in affect regulation and impulse control were noted as were in her mood lability with chronic dysphoria and suicidal behaviors which included impulsive wrist-cutting, binge drinking, and overdosing with prescribed medications. She regularly engages in projective identification and splitting. Records suggest she had been functioning at the Moderate Impairment Level prior to her first admission but over the past 2½ years has fluctuated between that and the Severe Impairment Level. Currently, she is receiving Social Security Disability and is living alone in an apartment. She reports receiving regular morning phone calls from her mother asking "if I made it through the night without hurting myself."

Developmentally, she is an only child from a chaotic family environment.

She reports that her alcoholic father abandoned her when she was 5 years old. Her mother appears to have an inconsistent and overly enmeshed relationship with Tammy. Although she reports being an honor student in high school, she had considerable difficulty maintaining friendships with female peers. She also described a series of ill-fated relationships with boyfriends. She married right after graduation from high school. The relationship lasted 18 months before her husband left her "because of my crazy, clinging behavior." After that, she worked at various part-time jobs while attending college. During the past 6 years, she has accumulated over 90 semester hours but had changed majors enough that it might require as many as 15 more courses to complete degree requirements.

Her medical history was noncontributory. She binges on wine and beer usually on weekend evenings when she is "lonely and mad that everyone else is going out and having fun." She had smoked marijuana in high school for a while but denies any current use of it or other substances, including various over-the-counter medications. She denied the use of nicotine and admitted that she consumes no more than the equivalent of two cups of coffee/caffeine a day. She has had trials of several antidepressants, neuroleptics, and mood stabilizers all with limited or no symptom relief. At the time of the evaluation, she was being prescribed Lyrica, a mood stabilizer. Medication compliance appears to have been inconsistent, although compliance with therapy sessions—individual twice weekly—was relatively consistent. She indicated that she had been compliant with medication prior to her first overdose on it, and thereafter was ambivalent about filling prescriptions believing that if she had medications around her apartment she might be tempted to overdose again. At one point, family therapy had been suggested but her mother refused it and the matter was never broached again.

Comprehensive Assessment and Diagnosis. A comprehensive diagnostic and functional assessment was completed. Her DSM-5 diagnoses were Borderline Personality Disorder with histrionic and dependent traits, and Other Specified Depressive Disorder: Depressive episodes with insufficient symptoms. Figure 6.1 portrays her profile.

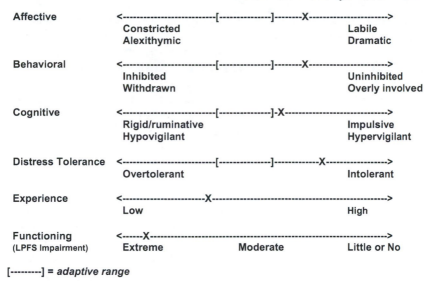

Figure 6.1 ABCDEF Profile of Borderline Personality Disorder: Case of Tammy

Engagement Process

Like many borderline-disordered individuals, Tammy believed the purpose of therapy was for the therapist to take responsibility for making her feel better. However, because of her dependency needs, Tammy also needed to please her therapist. Thus, she had good attendance for partial hospital programs and appeared to collaborate with treatment. But she did not really collaborate. For example, she would "forget" to fill prescriptions and "misunderstand" how she was to keep a diary of her feelings, thoughts, and behaviors, and otherwise had difficulty taking responsibility for herself.

Turning to the matter of her expectations for treatment: When queried about her expectations, she indicated that even though she had tried individual therapy in the past, it did not seem to have worked for her. That somehow the treatment "just got stuck" and she was not sure that it really would be any different this time. Still, she recognized that she needed help and that she didn't believe she could make it without some kind of treatment.

Pattern Analysis

Her pattern was characterized by abandonment and dependency schemas and a dysregulated temperament. Her developmental history suggested that she wanted to be loved, taken care of, and directed. And, although she had attempted to individuate from her family, she was doubtful of her ability to function independently. An underlying belief—a core schema—was that if she functioned autonomously her mother, husband, or significant other would rebuke and abandon her. She learned that to obtain love she had to be compliant and emotionally needy, whereas being self-reliant led to being reproached and abandoned. Although she wanted to be independent and make her own decisions, taking control of her life frightened her because she was unsure of what she would do with her life. Her struggle to establish a college major reflected this conflict. Consequently, she vacillated between submission and depression. Unfortunately, neither her early environment nor later life fostered the development of necessary self-regulation and relational skills. This, along with her maladaptive schemas of abandonment and dependency, led to her vulnerability toward acting out and self-harm as well as submissiveness and depression. Finally, it appears that actual or perceived rejection involving close relationships triggers this maladaptive pattern and her impulsive acting out.

Concise Case Conceptualization. Tammy's long history of suicidal gestures, dysphoria, and social and occupational impairment about life (*presentation*) appears to be her response to being lonely and not getting the caring and support she expects from others (*precipitant*). When under increased stress she experiences intense feelings of abandonment and rage and acts out demanding that others—including therapists—take care of her and "fix" her (*pattern*). This is a strong externalizing pattern assessed as between "severe impairment" and "extreme impairment" on the Level of Personality Functioning Scale. Her suicidal behavior and dysphoria is understandable when viewed in light of her beliefs and biological vulnerability. She views herself as defective, needy, and neglected. She views others as dangerous, unpredictable, unhelpful, and rejecting. She is biologically vulnerable to impulsivity, emotional dysregulation, acting out behaviors, and distress intolerance. She has consistently experienced invalidating and inconsistent parenting. While she has the intellectually capacity to succeed in college and the workplace, she is hampered by her inability to control her emotional outburst, impulsiveness, and distress about negative emotional states (*predisposition*). Given her low level functioning, long history of psychiatric treatment, and six prior suicide attempts, referral was made for intensive outpatient treatment with the goal of decreasing her undercontrol style and increasing her self-control and resilience (*treatment goal*). She has never been offered Dialectical Behavior Therapy before, and it is more likely to empower and increase her self-control than her previous treatments. CBASP will also focus on increasing her capacity to learn from experience, and replacing her self-defeating thoughts and behaviors regarding relationships with more adaptive ones (*treatment interventions*).

Pattern Change

Because Tammy had essentially failed in weekly outpatient individual therapy sessions in the past, it was unlikely that she would have a positive outcome now, even if therapy was specifically directed toward modifying her maladaptive schemas. Her impulsive acting out suggested an unmodulated style or temperament, which needed to be addressed prior to schema issues. Regarding treatment modalities, her negative beliefs about past treatment outcomes and her low expectations for the efficacy of current psychopharmacotherapy and psychotherapy in an individual format were sufficient to warrant a change in modality. Clearly, tailored, combined treatment was indicated.

Accordingly, she was referred to an intensive outpatient program with a focused treatment program for severe personality-disordered individuals. It was a modified DBT program which emphasized focus on group skill training in emotion regulation, mindfulness, distress tolerance, and interpersonal effectiveness. In addition, there was a weekly medication group and individual therapy sessions that focused only on her progress in the program and on issues and concerns that Tammy was unable to discuss in group sessions. Twice-weekly occupational therapy and pre-employment training was also part of the programming. Tammy quickly responded to the consistency and stability of the program structure. Her binge drinking and fear of overdosing on prescribed medication subsided in the first 2 weeks. Thus, plans for substance abuse counseling were shelved. After 6 months in the program, Tammy's Level of Personality Functioning Scale was assessed at just above the Some Impairment level. She then moved to the partial hospital's aftercare program for approximately 12 months. It consisted of twice-weekly programming involving occupational training, a relapse-prevention group, as well as individual and group therapy sessions that focused on her abandonment and dependency schemas. During this time, three family evaluation sessions were held with Tammy and her mother to foster more functional boundaries between mother and daughter. Even though she was somewhat reluctant, Tammy's mother agreed that it would be more helpful for Tammy the adult to make phone contact with her at least once a week instead of mother's usual daily wake-up call. These, efforts appear to have been successful.

Tammy's maladaptive pattern—driving others away with unrealistic demands for caring and closeness for fear of being abandoned—was interpreted as a learned response, rather than an immutable trait, which could be changed through self-observation, cognitive replacement and restructuring, and skills training. Medication was considered to be an essential component of treatment because of her dysphoria and insomnia. It was felt that combined medication and group treatment could probably replace the negative beliefs she had toward medication. Therefore, she was begun in a medication group in the partial hospital program that emphasized symptom management training for persistent symptoms. For Tammy, these included chronic dysphoria and suicidality. Because of its recently reported success with borderline symptoms, a trial of Seroquel was begun (Black et al., 2014). However, the mainstay of treatment was group skill training and individual sessions with CBASP.

Pattern Maintenance and Termination

Not surprisingly, termination issues for Tammy will inevitably involve abandonment fears. After completing 18 months in the intensive outpatient and aftercare program, she continued with monthly individual sessions that included medication monitoring. It is anticipated that after 1 year, these monthly sessions will be decreased to quarterly sessions. Because much of her individual and group therapy was directed toward the abandonment schema and because the intensity of treatment has been weaned from daily to monthly, Tammy will be reasonably desensitized to rejection/abandonment.

In establishing a plan for preventing relapse, it is necessary to target the situations and circumstances in the individual's pattern that triggered relapse. Tammy was most vulnerable to relapse on weekend nights when she was lonely and angry and felt abandoned by others and had access to alcohol. The plan Tammy developed in her relapse prevention group included arranging to have a planned activity scheduled for weekends, even if it was just going out to a movie by herself, and not keeping alcohol in her apartment.

After 12 months, she was able to return to college full time, work part time at a low-stress retail sales job, and continue in a twice-weekly relationship skills group and a monthly medication group. Seven months later, Tammy's Level of Personality Functioning Scale was assessed at the Little or No Impairment level when she was "graduated" to monthly individual therapy sessions including medication monitoring. She graduated from college a year later and began working full-time as an elementary school teacher. Although she dates occasionally, she has no plans for remarrying. She has established gratifying friendships with two other teachers at her school, and has been able to set and maintain limits on phone calls from her mother. As noted above, she will probably continue on medication indefinitely with quarterly follow up. Finally, no hospitalizations nor suicide gestures were reported.

Case of Jesse

The following case and session transcription demonstrates how a modified form of CBASP can be used as the mainstay of outpatient treatment for a higher functioning individual with Borderline Personality Disorder.

Jesse is a 23-year-old, never married Caucasian female. She graduated from high school and has been consistently employed for 5 years as a bookkeeper in a small factory. She was referred for therapy to the county mental health clinic by a physician at her primary care clinic. At intake, Jesse complained of low self-esteem, insomnia, and difficulties with intimate relationships. She also reported suicidal ideation dating back to age 15, with two suicide gestures including cutting her wrists "to make a statement to my parents." While she had been evaluated in the emergency room after these attempts, no referral for any psychiatric treatment was made presumably because of the "minor nature of the cutting behavior" as the ER report for the first episode noted. Her DSM-5 diagnosis was Borderline Personality Disorder. Her ABCDEF Profile showed affective and cognitive styles in the low "optimal self-control" but that that dimension of behavioral/interpersonal style and distress tolerance was at the low end of the "undercontrol" range. Her functioning on the Experience dimension was midway between low and high. Her Level of Personality Functioning Scale was assessed at between the Some Impairment and the Moderate Impairment levels.

Because she did not want to jeopardize her job by taking off to be involved in the day-long, intensive outpatient program, her therapist agreed to a plan of treatment that involved individual sessions—twice a week—that would also include skills training in distress tolerance and interpersonal skills. Her therapist had considerable experience with incorporating DBT group skill training in individual therapy (Marra, 2005). It was mutually agreed that if this form of individual skills training was insufficient, Jesse to would attend the 2-hour group skill training 3 days per week. She understood and agreed that participation in treatment required that she would not engage in any self-injurious behavior. The following transcript is from the sixth therapy session. Prior to this session, no suicidal gestures had been made.

Therapist: Okay, Jesse. Why don't you go ahead and tell me about the situation that just happened that was so upsetting to you.

Jesse: My boyfriend and I had an argument about him going back again to Puerto Rico for a job he has down there. When we were done arguing, I tried to hug and kiss him, but he said wouldn't let me because he said it's against his religion.

Therapist: Okay, let me make sure I have this right . . . First, you and Jose had an argument. Following the argument, you tried to hug and kiss him, but he would not allow you to do that based on his religious beliefs. Do I have that right?

Jesse: Yes, that's basically what happened.

Therapist: Okay, now tell me your thoughts and interpretations of that situation.

Jesse: Well, I thought to myself, "why can't I show affection?"

Therapist: So, your thought was "I should be able to show affection."

Jesse: Yeah.

Therapist: Okay, good, that's a good one. Did you have any other interpretations?

Jesse: Yeah. I know he's kissing women in Puerto Rico.

Therapist: Okay, you thought to yourself, "I know he's kissing other women in Puerto Rico." What is your interpretation of that thought? What does that mean to you?

Jesse: He's cheating on me.

Therapist: Okay, so when you were in the situation and Jose refused to return your affection, you thought to yourself "I know he's cheating on me in Puerto Rico and kissing other women." Did you have any other thoughts or interpretations?

Jesse: We've kissed in the past, but everything has changed since he returned from Puerto Rico the first time.

Therapist: Okay, so that's good. Now we have three interpretations to work with. Let's look at your behaviors? When you tried to hold Jose's

	hand and he would not let you, what did you say and do in the situation?
Jesse:	I told him to go and kiss his Puerto Rican friends!
Therapist:	And how did you say that? What was your tone?
Jesse:	I don't know. I just said it.
Therapist:	If I was there, what would I have seen and heard?
Jesse:	I guess! Sounded sort of sarcastic or cocky, like, fine . . . whatever . . . go kiss whomever you want. I don't care!
Therapist:	Okay. What else did you say and do?
Jesse:	I turned away from him.
Therapist:	Did you say anything else?
Jesse:	Well, when he got up to leave I said, "If you leave now, then it's over for good!" I also told him that if he left, I would kill myself.
Therapist:	And what was your tone when you said that?
Jesse:	The same as before, I wasn't really yelling, but I was letting him know that I was angry.
Therapist:	Okay, so your tone was angry and forceful.
Jesse:	Yeah, I wanted him to know that I was serious.
Therapist:	So, let me make sure I have all of this down. After you and Jose had an argument, you reached out to him and tried to hug him, but he wouldn't show affection saying it was against his religious beliefs. You responded by turning away from him and telling him to kiss his female friends in Puerto Rico. When he got up to leave, you told him that if he left it would be over between you for good, and that you would kill yourself.
Jesse:	Well, when you say it like that it sounds pretty bad.
Therapist:	I'm not trying to make it sound bad or good. I just want to make sure that I have an accurate account of the facts.
Jesse:	Yeah, I guess that's what happened . . . but it wasn't my fault.
Therapist:	No one is assigning blame here, Jesse. Let's go on and see how this situation ended up. What was the actual outcome in this situation?
Jesse:	He left and I got drunk and went to the store and bought a bottle of sleeping pills.
Therapist:	Did you take the pills?
Jesse:	No.
Therapist:	What kept you from taking the pills?
Jesse:	I passed out before I had a chance to take them.
Therapist:	So, it sounds like there were some other thoughts that we may have missed the first time through.
Jesse:	What do you mean?
Therapist:	How did you get from telling him you were going to kill yourself? What else were you thinking?
Jesse:	That I'll tell him I'm going to kill myself, unless he stays.

Therapist:	Okay, I hear that, and we'll come back to that in a couple of minutes. Before we do that, what did you want to happen? What was your desired outcome?
Jesse:	That he would have stayed to discuss it.
Therapist:	So what you wanted was for Jose to stay and discuss what had just happened, and what actually happened was that he left without discussing it. Is that accurate?
Jesse:	Yes.
Therapist:	So, the question is: did you get what you wanted in this situation?
Jesse:	No!
Therapist:	Okay, are you willing to look at your thoughts to see whether they helped you or hurt you in getting your desired outcome of Jose staying to discuss the situation with you? (Yeah). The first thing you told me was that you thought. "Why can't I show affection?" Did that thought help you or hurt you in achieving your desired outcome of Jose staying to discuss the situation?
Jesse:	I don't know. I don't really think it hurt.
Therapist:	I'm not sure either, let's put it this way . . . do you think it helped you to get Jose to stay?
Jesse:	I guess not.
Therapist:	It doesn't sound like it did. What do you think you could have thought instead?
Jesse:	I don't know . . . maybe, "I really want to show him how much I care about him".
Therapist:	Good! I think that's a great thought! Can you think of anymore?
Jesse:	Hugging is a sign of affection . . . I just still don't understand why unmarried people are not allowed to touch each other!
Therapist:	What could you have thought that could have helped you understand his beliefs?
Jesse:	Maybe . . . I should ask him to explain his religion to me.
Therapist:	Great! Thinking, "I really want to show him how much I care about him" and "I should ask him to explain his religion to me" would have helped you to get your desired outcome of Jose staying to discuss things with you.
Jesse:	Yeah. I agree.
Therapist:	Now, let's look at your thoughts. "I know he's cheating on me and kissing other women in Puerto Rico" and "we've kissed in the past, but everything has changed since he returned from Puerto Rico." Do you think those thoughts helped you or hurt you in getting your desired outcome of Jose staying to discuss the situation with you?
Jesse:	They hurt me. (pause). They really pissed me off.
Therapist:	I agree with that. What would have been a more helpful interpretation?
Jesse:	(pause) Maybe that's the way people greet each other in Puerto Rico.

Therapist:	Okay, that's great! What are some other helpful thoughts?
Jesse:	I trust Jose. He loves me.
Therapist:	Great! It sounds to me that if you were thinking those thoughts, it definitely would have helped you to achieve your desired outcome. Now, let's look at the thought "If I tell him I'm going to kill myself, he'll stay." Do you think that one helped you or hurt you?
Jesse:	I suppose it hurt.
Therapist:	You don't sound convinced.
Jesse:	It's just hard to give that one up.
Therapist:	I know, Jesse, (pause). That strategy of hurting yourself has seemed to work for you in the past. But I agree with you. It didn't help you to achieve your desired outcome in this situation. What do you think you could have thought instead?
Jesse:	I don't know . . . I don't think there was anything I could have thought that would really have made him stay.
Therapist:	I know this is hard. Just try to think about some helpful thoughts that may have helped you to regulate your emotions and the way you were interacting with him.
Jesse:	Maybe just thinking, "I really want him to stay and talk to me."
Therapist:	That sounds good. Is there anything else?
Jesse:	How about, "I want us to work this out."
Therapist:	I think that's a great one! You are really getting better at this! I know it is hard to come up with these alternative thoughts, especially in the heat of the moment, but you are doing a great job so far. It's only going to get easier the more we practice. Let's move on to your behaviors. You said that you told him "Why don't you go kiss your Mexican friends!" Was that helpful or hurtful in getting your desired outcome?
Jesse:	Hurtful.
Therapist:	What could you have said to help you get your desired outcome of Jose staying to talk with you?
Jesse:	Maybe I could have asked him to explain why he didn't want to show affection. To explain the rules of his religion to me.
Therapist:	Sounds like that would have been a helpful thing to say. (Pause). Let's move on to the last thing you said. "If you leave now, then it's over for good and I'm going to kill myself!" Do you think that one was helpful or hurtful?
Jesse:	We both know it was hurtful.
Therapist:	What could you have said instead?
Jesse:	Jose, I just really want you to stay and talk to me!
Therapist:	Good. Is there anything else?
Jesse:	I could have told him that I love him.
Therapist:	I agree, Jesse, I think that would have helped you get your desired outcome. Now, let's wrap things up . . . What have you learned from this situation?

Jesse: I guess that, if I want to work things out with Jose, I need to be honest about how I feel and to be respectful to him. Threatening to kill myself is not fair to him and, it didn't get me what I wanted.

Therapist: Good work today. I know this isn't easy for you, but you are making a lot of progress. If you keep working on these homework assignments here and in your group, things will get easier!

Table 6.1 Treatment Interventions for Borderline Personality Disorder

ENGAGEMENT	Typically engage in treatment to feel better but not to get better. Demonstrate treatment-interfering behaviors. Shift from idealization to devaluation and with over-dependence on therapist. **Tx:** Confrontation and limit-setting; Treatment contract and holding environment
Transference	Overt efforts to derive nurturing and caring from therapist. Dependency and merger fantasy with therapist. Resistance to getting better leading to abandonment feelings so they demand more from therapist. **Tx:** Process: confront and interpret; Set limits
Countertransference	Tendency to feel overwhelmed by clients' strong emotions and intense needs. May feel angry or high levels of anxiety, tension, and personal and professional violations. May feel incompetent or inadequate and often experience a sense of confusion, frustration, or guilt. May have rescue fantasies or go the extra mile and do things not done for other individuals. **Tx:** Self-monitor; therapist support group
PATTERN ANALYSIS	*Triggers:* personal goals, close relations
PATTERN CHANGE	*Treatment Goals:* increase stability & cohesiveness
Schema/Character	Abandonment/loss schema, Unlovability/defective schema, Dependency/Incompetence schema **Tx:** Schema change and/or Interpretation strategy
Styles/Skills	
a. *Affective Style*	Overmodulated affects; Impulse dyscontrol **Tx:** DBT—emotion regulation training; Impulse control training
b. *Behavioral/ Interpersonal Style*	Self-mutilation and parasuicidality; Interpersonal deficits; vulnerability **Tx:** DBT—Interpersonal skill training
c. *Cognitive Style*	Overmodulated thinking and projective identification **Tx:** DBT—Mindfulness training
d. *Distress Tolerance*	Overly sensitive or intolerant of distress **Tx:** DBT—Distress tolerance training
MAINTENANCE/ TERMINATION	Abandonment fears about termination; relapse proneness **Tx:** Interpret; Support relapse prevention plan; Wean and space out sessions

Summary

Effective treatment of the Borderline Personality Disordered individual requires the establishment of a collaborative therapeutic relationship fostered by focal treatment interventions to modify the maladaptive pattern and then to maintain the more adaptive pattern. Borderline-disordered individuals have considerable difficulty focusing on the individual-clinician relationship to the extent necessary to work within a traditional individual psychotherapeutic mode. Usually, it is not until they experience some degree of modulation of their affective, behavioral, and cognitive styles that they are amenable to modifying or changing their character structure. Thus, an integrative and combined approach, usually including medication, can be effective in treating even symptomatic, lower functioning borderline individuals. Table 6.1 summarizes the treatment intervention strategies most likely to be effective with this disorder.

7   Dependent Personality Disorder

Basically, individuals with dependent personality disorder are passive, self-sacrificing, and non-assertive. While treatment of such individuals involves a number of unique therapeutic challenges, it can be highly effective and successful. This chapter describes a framework for effective treatment of this disorder from a cognitive behavioral perspective. It includes sections on assessment, case conceptualization, and treatment interventions. The section on assessment includes behavioral and cognitive factors, as well as a DSM-5 description and a prototypic description of this disorder. A prototype is a brief description that captures the essence of how a particular disorder commonly presents. Prototypic descriptions are useful and convenient and clinicians commonly rely on them rather than lists of behavioral criteria and core beliefs (Westen, 2012). The section on case conceptualization provides both cognitive and behavioral formulations of this disorder. The longest section is on treatment. It emphasizes engagement, pattern analysis, pattern change, and pattern maintenance and termination strategies for effectively managing and treating this disorder. In addition to individual psychotherapeutic strategies and tactics, group, marital and family, medication, and integrative and combined treatment strategies are included. An extensive case example illustrates the treatment process.

Assessment

Behavioral

A behavioral assessment of this disorder emphasizes individual and interpersonal behaviors. Individuals with this disorder are characterized by submissiveness, passivity, and non-assertiveness. They tend to be excessively docile, insecure, and isolated individuals who become overly dependent on others. Interpersonally, they tend to be pleasing, self-sacrificing, clinging and constantly requiring the assurance of others. Their compliance and reliance on others lead to a subtle demand that others assume responsibility for major areas of their lives. While initially acceptable, their behavior can become controlling, appear hostile, and even blend into a passive-aggressive pattern. In females the dependent style often takes the form of submissiveness, while in males the dependent style is more likely to be autocratic, such as when the husband and boss depends on his wife and secretary to perform essential tasks that he himself cannot accomplish. In either case, this disorder is likely to lead to anxiety and depression when the dependent relationship is threatened (Sperry, 2003).

Cognitive

A cognitive assessment of this disorder emphasizes core beliefs, particularly those about their views of self and of others. Typically, they view themselves as inadequate, weak, helpless, incompetent, and needy. They view others as strong, nurturing, supportive, and able to care for them. Related beliefs include needing the assistance of strong and caring individuals in order to survive and to make decisions for them. They also are convinced that one must remain close to and not displease such individuals. Not surprisingly, such beliefs are reflected in their main strategy or pattern of subordinating themselves and pleasing others (Beck, 2015; Brauer & Reinecke, 2015).

DSM-5 Description

Individuals with this personality disorder are characterized by an excessive and unremitting need to be cared for and cling to others because of their fear of separation. They constantly seek the advice and reassurance of others when making decisions. More than anything, they want others to take responsibility for most major areas of their lives. Not surprisingly, they seldom express disagreement with others for fear they will lose their support and approval. Because they lack confidence in their own judgment and ability, they have difficulty starting projects and doing things on their own. These individuals will even engage in actions that are difficult and unpleasant in order to receive support and caring from others. Because of unrealistic fears of being unable to take care of themselves, they feel helpless or uncomfortable when faced with being alone. When a close relationship is about to end, they immediately seek out another caring and supportive relationship. Finally, they become preoccupied with fears of being left to take care of themselves (American Psychiatric Association, 2013).

Prototypic Description

These individuals feel inadequate, weak, and needy. They don't take very good care for themselves. They find it nearly impossible to make their own decisions, and they don't feel good about being alone. Their neediness makes them submissive and subservient. So they are more than willing to put others' needs and views above their own. Basically, they will do whatever it takes to get others to care for them, to give them affection, and give direction to their lives (Frances, 2013).

Case Conceptualization

According to Beck (2015), the dependent personality is rooted in basic assumptions about the self and the world. These individuals typically view themselves as helpless and inadequate, and the world as too dangerous for them to cope with alone. Accordingly, they conclude that they must rely on someone else who is stronger and more adequate to take care of and protect them. They must pay a considerable price for this security: First, they must relinquish responsibility and subordinate their own needs. Second, they must relinquish opportunities to learn such skills as assertiveness, decision making, and problem solving. Finally, they must contend with fears of rejection and abandonment if their clinging relationship ends. The main cognitive distortion of such dependent individuals is dichotomous thinking with respect to independence (Brauer & Reinecke, 2015). For example, they believe that they are both totally connected to another and dependent or totally alone and independent, with no gradation between. Also, they believe that things are either "right" or "wrong," and that there is either "absolute success" or "absolute failure." Another cognitive distortion observed among dependent personalities is "catastrophizing," particularly regarding relationships. Common cognitive distortions are: "I never would be able to do that," "I can't," and "I'm too dumb to do that."

Turkat (1990) suggests a behavioral formulation for this disorder that centers on a pervasive fear of decision making and an inability to act assertively. Because these individuals have not previously learned either of these skills, these become basic therapeutic tasks, after their overwhelming anxiety is effectively managed.

Treatment

Engagement Strategies

Early Session Behavior

In early sessions, especially the first, dependent personality disordered individuals typically wait for the clinician to begin the conversation. After the clinician inquires about the reason for coming to the sessions, these individuals can present an adequate description of their current situation. But, then are likely to become silent. Predictable comments include, "I'm not sure what to say. I've never been in therapy before," or "Ask me something, then I'll know how to answer your question." When the clinician asks other questions, the cycle tends to be repeated.

Nevertheless, interviewing these individuals and establishing rapport can be relatively easy and enjoyable. After experiencing some initial anxiety, these individuals can quickly establish a bond of trust with the clinician. For this reason, individuals with dependent personalities are among the easiest of the personality disorders to engage in the therapeutic process. Presuming the clinician provides pleasant advice and support, as well as being empathic in the face of their indecisiveness and failures, the interview will flow smoothly. Yet, as the clinician moves to explore the detriments of their submissiveness, these individuals predictably become noticeably uncomfortable—particularly in the early phase of treatment. If the dependency isn't pursued with an empathic ear, these individuals may change to another clinician. But if pursued empathically, these individuals are likely to cooperate and meet their clinician's expectations. They can be expected to respond to questions and to clarify and elaborate. They can also tolerate abrupt transitions and will allow deep feelings to be probed. However, they do not easily tolerate confrontation and interpretation of their dependency needs and behaviors (Othmer & Othmer, 2002).

Facilitating Collaboration

Unlike treatment with most other personality disorders, collaboration can be achieved or at least approximated rather early in the course of treatment of the dependent personality disorder. Largely because of their strong needs to please and be accepted by others (particularly authority figures), dependent personality disordered individuals are likely to be quite willing to respond favorably with the expectations and demands of clinicians. Thus, they will, more likely than not, collaborate with psychotherapeutic and medication regimens if the clinician requests and expects collaboration. However, because they have an equally strong propensity to enlist others in taking care of and making decisions for them, dependent individuals may not really want to assume the degree of responsibility that real therapeutic collaboration requires. So they may be passively compliant and take prescribed medications as directed, but not actively follow through on other treatment matters that were "mutually agreed" on, nor initiate self-responsible behaviors unless reminded by the clinician. In other words, compliance is much easier than collaboration for dependent individuals, and both individuals and clinicians may mistake compliance for collaboration. Clearly, the distinction between the two must be pointed out, and the transference issue underlying it must be dealt with (Sperry, 2003).

Transference and Countertransference

Predictable transference and countertransference problems are noted to arise in treating dependent personality disordered individuals. Perhaps the most common transference involves individuals' efforts to engage clinicians in assuming responsibility for all their personal decisions. Unfortunately, this transference can provoke a countertransference in which clinicians succumb to these efforts either because they feel exasperated by individuals' protestation of their inadequacy or because of their wish to be idealized. These responses not only reinforce overreliance on clinicians but also their belief that they really don't have to become independent nor self-sufficient. Another transference involves individuals' failure to make progress in treatment, while maintaining their attachment to clinicians. So, as noted above, they may passively respond to the clinical directive but not take initiative or become truly active in the treatment process (Gabbard, 2005). Unfortunately, as noted earlier, this compliant attitude may be mistaken for collaboration with treatment goals.

The countertransference involved here is the clinician's failure to confront the lack of actual change and unwitting reinforcement of the individual's refusal to be responsible and become more self-reliant. A final transference involves the sheer number of requests for advice, nurturance, and guidance that these individuals make early in the course of treatment. Bornstein (2012) identified that dependent personality disordered individuals are much more likely to request between-session contact with their therapist than compared with other clients. The clinician must modulate these requests—which are essentially demands—early in treatment in order to prevent the individual from becoming overly disappointed, which could result in the client's premature termination. This transference invites the clinician's countertransference response of emotional withdrawal, which subsequently reinforces the individual's neurotic guilt about their neediness (Perry, 1995). Generally speaking, it is useful for the clinician to make aspects of the individual's dependent transference explicit. Although an open discussion of the individual's dependency needs may not always be appropriate very early in treatment, this discussion is both useful and necessary after a working relationship has been established. Timing of the feedback is important. Typically, such feedback is best communicated in the context of the situation that has arisen wherein the individual's dependent behaviors have been problematic.

Pattern Analysis Strategies

Pattern analysis with dependent personality disordered individuals involves an accurate diagnostic and clinical evaluation of schemas, styles, and triggering stressors as well as their level of functioning and readiness for therapeutic change. Knowledge of the optimal DSM-5 diagnostic criterion along with the maladaptive pattern of the dependent personality disordered individual is not only useful in specifying diagnosis but also in planning treatment that is tailored to the individual's unique style, needs, and circumstances. The optimal criterion specified for the dependent personality disorder is that the individual needs others to assume responsibility for most major areas of his or her life (Allnutt & Links, 1996). This reliance on others serves to alleviate anxiety around making decisions while maintaining a subservient posture in the relationship. With this criterion in mind, the clinician can plan and direct treatment to focus on these deficits in self-confidence and overreliance on others.

Pattern refers to the predictable and consistent style and manner in which an individual thinks, feels, acts, copes, and defends the self. Pattern analysis involves both the triggers and response—the "what"—as well as a clinical formulation or explanatory statement—the "why"—about the pattern of a given dependent individual. Obviously, such a clinical formulation specifies the particular schemas and temperamental styles unique to a given individual rather than the more general clinical formulation that will be noted here (Sperry, 2006).

Triggers

Generally speaking, the "triggers" or "triggering" situations for dependent individuals are stressors related to self-reliance and being alone. This means that when dependent-disordered individuals are engaging in behaviors, discussing, or even thinking about being alone or relying on their own resources, and they become distressed; their disordered or maladaptive pattern is likely to be triggered and their characteristic symptomatic affects, behaviors, and cognitions are likely to be experienced or exhibited. For instance, the thought "I hate to be alone" triggers anxious, panicky feelings and the likelihood of giving up their own aspirations and goals to cling to another for guidance (Othmer & Othmer, 2002).

Schemas

Generally speaking, the underlying schemas of dependent disordered individuals involve a self-view of weakness, defectiveness, and inadequacy. Their worldview is that others will protect and care for them (Sperry, 2015). Among the most frequently encountered schemas in dependent individuals are functional dependency/incompetence and failure to achieve. The *dependency/incompetence schema* refers to the core set of beliefs that one is incapable of handling daily responsibilities competently and independently, and so must rely on us to make decisions and initiate new tasks. *Failure to achieve* refers to the core set of beliefs that one cannot perform as well as others so no attempt is made out of fear of failure (Bricker, Young, & Flanagan, 1993; Young, Klosko, & Weishaar, 2003). Hundreds of published studies on Dependent Personality Disorder have identified some of the common traits associated with this disorder: insecurity, fear of abandonment, trait anxiety, insecurity, fear of negative evaluation, high levels of agreeableness, and loneliness (Bornstein, 2011).

Style/Temperament

There are four unique style dimensions in the ABCDEF Profile that characterize individuals with this personality disorder: Affective, Behavioral-interpersonal, Cognitive, and Distress tolerance. Dependent personality disordered individuals are prone to overmodulated anxiety. Regarding the biological aspect of temperament, no studies have yet examined biological markers among the Dependent Personality Disordered population (Bornstein,

2011). Their cognitive style is one of uncritical cognitive appraisal and the naive perception of others' capacity and desire to care for them. Cloninger (2004) noted that their behavioral response style is characterized by harm avoidance. As such, they are considerably inhibited and are unlikely to show initiative or to function independently. Accordingly, they tend to be limited in assertiveness and deficient in the problem-solving skills like planning, decision-making, and implementing decisions, and other self-management skills related to independent functioning. Relationally, they have been so consistently overreliant on others and thus need to please others that they have not developed adequate skills in assertive communication nor in negotiation nor conflict resolution (Sperry, 2003). They also tend to be distress overtolerant meaning they can tolerate high distress that results in adverse long-term consequences (Lynch & Mizon, 2011). Overall, their pattern reflects an internalizing disorder.

Pattern Change Strategies

In general, the long-range goal of psychotherapy with a dependent personality is to increase the individual's sense of independence and ability to function interdependently. At other times, the clinician may need to settle for a more modest goal. That is, helping the individual become a "healthier" dependent personality. Treatment strategies typically include challenging the individual's convictions or dysfunctional beliefs about personal inadequacy, and learning ways in which to increase assertiveness. A variety of intervention strategies are useful in achieving these goals.

After the maladaptive pattern has been identified and analyzed in terms of schemas and style and skill deficits, the therapeutic process involves relinquishing that pattern and replacing it with a more adaptive pattern. Thus, the pattern change process involves modifying schemas, modulating style dysregulations, and reversing skill deficits. The process of modifying the maladaptive schemas of dependent personality disordered individuals usually follows efforts to modify style and skill-deficit dimensions because schema change early in the course of treatment is often resisted by the client (Sperry, 2006).

Schema Change

The functional dependency/incompetence and failure to achieve schemas are supported by such injunctive beliefs as "I'm helpless when I'm left alone," "Somebody must be around at all times to help me do what I need to do or in case something goes wrong," "I must not do anything that offends my supporters and helpers," and, particularly, "I can't make decisions on my own" (Beck, 2015). In the schema change process, the clinician and individual work collaboratively to understand the developmental roots of the maladaptive schemas. Then these schemas are tested through predictive experiments, guided observation, and reenactment of early schema-related incidents. Finally, dependent individuals are directed to begin to notice and remember counter-schema data about themselves and their social experiences.

CBASP Strategies

Cognitive Behavioral Analysis System of Psychotherapy (CBASP) utilizes cognitive and behavioral replacement strategies to effect change among dependent personality disordered individuals' maladaptive patterns (Driscoll, Cukrowicz, Reardon, & Joiner, 2004). This approach examines the individual's dependent schema dynamics and pattern by focusing on situations in which their pattern caused harm in their daily functioning or led to an undesirable outcome. The process is started through use of a situation analysis, in which thoughts, behaviors, their desired outcome, and the actual outcome information is gathered. Secondly, the remediation phase elicits the client to create more useful and adaptive thoughts and behaviors that support the desired outcome. CBASP can ultimately assist individuals with Dependent Personality Disorder to better meet their own needs through realistic thinking and behaviors that are in accordance with their goals. This approach is a brief model of therapy that can effect change among extremely challenging clients.

Style-Skill Change

Unlike borderline personality disorder and narcissistic personality disorder in which temperaments are markedly overmodulated in all four style dimensions of affective, behavioral/relational, and cognitive, the dependent personality disorder does not display as much dysregulation (Sperry, 2003). Nevertheless, skill-training interventions are quite effective in modulating styles and reversing skill deficits.

Anxiety dysregulation can be modulated with the graded exposure strategy that is a core feature of anxiety management training. Assertive communication training and problem-solving training are useful in reducing dependent individuals' harm avoidance and inhibition and thereby increase their capacity to function more energetically and independently. This training also reduces their skill deficits in problem solving, particularly decision-making. Cognitive awareness training and pinpointing and challenging automatic beliefs can be helpful in redirecting their cognitive style marked by naive, uncritical appraisal.

Medication Strategies

Currently, there are no psychotropic medications specifically indicated for treating individuals with dependent personality disorder (Silk & Feurino, 2013). Nevertheless, medications are used that target specific troubling symptoms associated with the disorder, such as depression, anxiety, or sleep problems. Generally, these medications are used as an adjunct to psychotherapy and skills training. Because troubling symptoms often respond to medications sooner than most psychological interventions, medications are usually prescribed at the onset of treatment (Sperry, 1995b). Unfortunately, there is little research evidence to provide guidelines for the use of such medications (Silk & Feurino, 2012).

Group Treatment Strategies

Group treatment can be particularly effective with dependent personality disordered individuals. In deciding if group treatment should be extended, and if it is, two factors need to be considered. The first involves the individual's motivation and potential for growth. If it is reasonably high, a more interactional psychotherapy group may be indicated. This type of group provides a therapeutic milieu for exploring the inappropriateness of passive-dependent behavior and for experimenting with greater assertiveness (Yalom, 1985). On the other hand, if dependent traits reflect severe personality impairment and/or the absence of prosocial behavior (such as assertive communication, decision making, and negotiation) an ongoing supportive problem-solving group) or a social skills training group might be indicated. The second involves whether the group should be homogeneous—treatment targeted at dependency issues shared by all group members—or heterogeneous wherein group members have different personality styles or disorders. Clinical lore suggests that dependent individuals tend to get "lost" in heterogeneous groups, whereas time-limited assertiveness training groups that are homogenous and have clearly defined goals have been shown to be very effective (Lazarus, 1981).

Marital and Family Therapy Strategies

There is a very limited literature on family therapy interventions involving individuals with the dependent personality. Clinical experience suggests that dependent personality disordered individuals are brought to family therapy by their parents. These individuals are frequently older adolescents or young adults between the ages of 20 and 35 who present with a neurotic or psychotic symptom. Changing the enmeshed family relationship tends to be anxiety provoking for all parties, and thus, there is considerable resistance from other family members when only one member of the family is in therapy (Harbir, 1981).

Similarly, there is relatively little literature on marital therapy with dependent personality disordered individuals. Clinical experience suggests that a dependent partner can function adequately if their marital partner consistently meets their needs, but he or she often becomes symptomatic and impaired when the marital partner's support is withdrawn or withheld. Accordingly, it is useful to engage the cooperation of the marital partner in treatment because of the negative impact on the relationship as the dependent partner becomes less anxious and more independent, and because treatment progress results when the marital partner is also committed to the treatment goals (Sperry, 2006).

Nurse (1998) described the marital dynamics between a partner who meets criteria for dependent personality disorder and a partner who meets criteria for narcissistic personality disorder. He also offered an interesting approach to planning treatment based on the Millon Multiaxial Clinical Inventory (MMCI-III). This approach to treatment emphasizes the use of feeding back MMCI-III data to the couple, communication training, and homework assignments.

Barlow and Waddell (1985) described a 10-session couples group intervention for the treatment of agoraphobia where the symptomatic partner exhibits dependent personality features. This intervention encourages the nonsymptomatic partners to function in a coaching role collaborating on treatment goals, which effectively discourages the role of reinforcing their partner's agoraphobia and dependency. Over the course of this group treatment, panic and agoraphobia symptoms remit while the marital relationship shifts from dependency to interdependency.

Combined and Integrative Treatment Strategies

Barlow and Waddell's (1985) effort to combine Behavior Therapy in a group setting with dependent couples is one of many examples combining modalities with dependent personality disordered individuals. However, there is relatively little research published on integrative treatment strategies with dependent individuals. Nevertheless, there have been some case reports of efforts to use anxiety reducing strategies in both dynamic and cognitive therapies (Sperry, 2006).

One such example was reported by Glantz and Goisman (1990). They described their effort to integrate relaxation techniques within psychodynamic psychotherapy with dependent individuals. A controlled breathing and progressive muscle relaxation strategy was used to merge split self-representations in the course of exploration psychotherapy. The strategy was introduced after signs of split self-representation had been identified. Individuals practiced the strategy and were prescribed it as homework. When they achieved an adequate level of relaxation in the session they were asked for visual images of both conflicting self-representations. After clear images were elicited and discussed, they were instructed to merge the images. The results of this strategy were noteworthy in that most dependent individuals responded with improved interpersonal relationships.

Pattern Maintenance and Termination Strategies

Termination Issues

Termination can be very difficult for dependent individuals, because termination represents relinquishing an important, necessary relationship with a nurturing, caretaking figure. Recall that dependent individuals erroneously view independence as being totally alone and without the support of anyone, while dependence means being totally cared for and supported. Not surprisingly, termination can be particularly anxiety producing for dependent individuals. Consequently, the clinician must endeavor to minimize the negative effects of termination, and frame termination as a therapeutic intervention in and of itself. Three therapeutic strategies can facilitate treatment termination with the dependent individual. First, termination will be made easier if the clinician makes it clear that termination does not require a permanent break in the therapeutic relationship. However, the clinician does not want to send a mixed message, indicating that the individual is ready to terminate but is not "really" terminating. Rather, the clinician must frame the termination in a manner that emphasizes the individual's successful work during treatment (Bornstein, 1993, 1994).

Second, the clinician should offer the predictive interpretation that dependency needs may complicate the termination process. Conveying this prediction to the individual in a matter-of-fact, nonjudgmental fashion can simultaneously preempt the individual's conscious or unconscious wish to subvert termination and continue therapy indefinitely, and provide the individual with useful feedback regarding the ways in which dependency strivings can adversely affect other important interpersonal relationships.

Third, spacing out sessions allows individuals to become more independent of the clinician and the treatment process. In this process of becoming less reliant on the clinician's direct support during weekly sessions, they learn to rely more on their own resources as well as develop or maintain other support systems. As they become increasingly able to tolerate this separation, their maladaptive dependency pattern shifts to a more adaptive and healthier pattern of interdependence. A variant of spacing sessions is to set a specific termination date at the very outset of treatment. Mann (1973) described this option for higher functioning individuals with relatively focal issues, including dependency, for the 12-session dynamically oriented treatment he called "time-limited psychotherapy." With higher functioning dependent personality disordered individuals, it is possible to set a specific termination date and then focus treatment on increasing self-reliance; however, clinical experience indicates that considerably more than 12 sessions are needed.

If they would continue to be prescribed medication, they might slowly shift to scheduled medication monitoring appointments at 3- to 6-month intervals. If they were not receiving, or have already been weaned from, medication they might have booster sessions scheduled at 3-, 6-, or 12-month intervals.

Finally, it is helpful for clinicians and dependent individuals to collaboratively develop a plan of self-therapy and self-management following termination. It is recommended that these individuals set aside an hour a week to engage in activities that continue the progress made in formal treatment. They might work on selected exercises. They might look ahead at the coming week and predict which situations could be troublesome and plan ways to cope with dependent behaviors. The goal of such effort is, of course, to maintain treatment gains and maintain the newly acquired pattern.

Relapse Prevention Strategies

Another essential aspect of the treatment plan and process is relapse prevention. Because dependent individuals can easily revert to their previous avoidant pattern, it is necessary to predict and plan for relapse. The final phase of treatment should largely focus on relapse prevention. An important goal of relapse prevention is predicting likely difficulties in the time period immediately following termination. The individual needs to be able to analyze specific external situations such as new individuals, unfamiliar places, as well as internal states, such as specific avoidant beliefs and fears and other vulnerabilities that increase the likelihood of responding with dependent behavior in the face of predictable triggers. Once predicted, individuals can develop a contingency plan to deal with these stressors. Clinicians may find it useful to have individuals think and talk through the following questions: What can I do if I find myself resorting to dependent patterns? What should I do if I start believing my old dependency beliefs more than my new beliefs? What should I do if I relapse?

A belief that is particularly troubling for dependent individuals is, "I can't stand being alone." This belief is typically activated when dependent individuals face situations that require self-reliance or being alone. In such instances, it can be helpful for individuals to imagine what their clinician might have them think and do in such a circumstance. With this imaginal strategy, the individual will no longer feel totally alone nor feel that they must be totally self-reliant.

Case of Janet

Janet R., the 29-year-old mother of a 4-year-old daughter, experienced her first panic attack while on a business trip with her husband. Sweating, difficulty breathing, numbness and tingling of the extremities, and chest pain convinced her that she was having a heart attack. She was quickly transported to a local emergency room, where physical examination ruled out a myocardial infarction. After intramuscular Valium partially relieved her symptoms, the trip was aborted and she returned home. In the subsequent week, her sleep and anxiety improved to some extent. But because she had experienced anxiety episodes of increasing severity and had begun to avoid crowded places and shopping malls over the previous 2 years, she readily accepted her family physician's referral for a psychiatric evaluation.

Comprehensive Assessment and Diagnosis. A comprehensive diagnostic and functional assessment was completed. Janet met DSM-5 criteria for Other Specified Anxiety Disorder as well as Dependent Personality Disorder. Figure 7.1 portrays Janet's ABCDEF Profile.

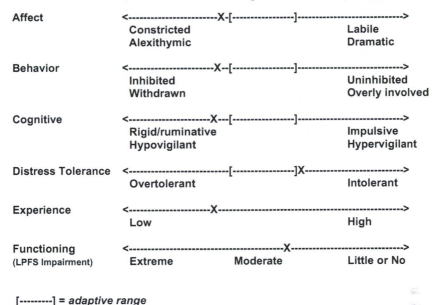

Affect	<------------------------X-[----------------]---------------------------->		
	Constricted		Labile
	Alexithymic		Dramatic
Behavior	<-----------------------X--[---------------]---------------------------->		
	Inhibited		Uninhibited
	Withdrawn		Overly involved
Cognitive	<--------------------X---[---------------]---------------------------->		
	Rigid/ruminative		Impulsive
	Hypovigilant		Hypervigilant
Distress Tolerance	<---------------------------[----------------]X----------------------->		
	Overtolerant		Intolerant
Experience	<---------------------X-->		
	Low		High
Functioning	<---------------------------------------X---------------------------->		
(LPFS Impairment)	Extreme	Moderate	Little or No

[---------] = *adaptive range*

Figure 7.1 ABCDEF Profile for Dependent Personality Disorder: Case of Janet

Engagement Process

Before ending their initial session, the psychiatrist asked her to keep a daily log of the sensations, events, thoughts, and feelings associated with each episode of anxiety and what she did about it. The expectation was that accomplishing this task would not only provide Janet a sense of control, but also assess her readiness and capacity for treatment. One week later, she reported moderate improvement in symptoms: no panic attacks, decreased anticipatory anxiety, less fitful sleep, and better concentration.

Pattern Analysis

The psychiatric evaluation elicited a family history of treatment for anxiety, and depression in her mother. Recent stressors included having few friends because they had just moved from another city, her daughter's starting kindergarten, and anticipatory anxiety about the recent business trip. She was unable to tell her husband she was frightened of accompanying him, and felt guilty when the trip had to be rescheduled because of her panic attack. Needless to say, she had considerable difficulty expressing negative feelings, particularly toward authority figures, including her husband. She met DSM-5 criteria for panic disorder with agoraphobia and dependent personality disorder.

Janet recalled being reprimanded as a child whenever she directly expressed her feelings: From an early age, as the oldest child, she assumed many parental duties because of her mother's long-term psychiatric hospitalizations. As a result, she had little opportunity to develop an identity distinct from that of looking after others. She believes she is inadequate as a parent, wife, and person. Similarly, she believes that she needs others not only to survive but to be happy. In addition to the core schema of dependency/incompetence that is typical of the dependent personality disorder, Janet also internalized the self-sacrifice schema. Furthermore, she uses the defenses of denial and suppression to cope with anger. These defenses underlie her maladaptive pattern, which was to refrain from expressing her needs, avoid confronting others to garner their support and avoid their rejection, as well as to enlist others in making decisions for her. She has noticeable skill deficits in assertiveness and anxiety modulation. Figure 7.1 summarizes these style features.

Concise Case Conceptualization. Janet's panic attack symptoms (***presentation***) while on a business trip with her husband seem to be her reaction to struggling to communicate her anxiousness and concerns about going on the trip (***precipitant***). Her reaction is understandable given her history of being the primary caretaker for her siblings while concurrently struggling with expressing her own needs and feelings. She places a high demand on pleasing others, while disregarding her own needs (***pattern***). This is an internalizing pattern assessed as "moderate impairment" on the *Level of Personality Functioning Scale*. Her pattern can be understood in light of emotionally unavailable parents, strong parental injunctions against disclosing emotions and communicating needs to others, caretaking for her siblings and friends, and schemas of self-sacrifice and incompetence. Her family history of anxiety and depression may biologically predispose her to panic attacks, as did the underdevelopment of assertiveness skills and conflict resolution skills (***predisposition***). This pattern is maintained by her dependence on relationships, her limited assertiveness skills, and her chronic disregard of her own needs to assume a caretaking role in her close relationships. A referral was made for intensive outpatient treatment with the goal of decreasing her overcontrolled style and also to increase her ability to communicate her own needs and feelings (***treatment goals***). Cognitive Behavior Therapy with an emphasis on assertive communication skills, anxiety management, conflict resolution skills, self-soothing skills, and interpersonal effectiveness are interventions aimed at modifying her pattern to express her needs while also coping with stress. Individual therapy (CBASP) would focus on increasing her capacity to learn from experience, and replacing her self-defeating thoughts and behaviors regarding relationships with more adaptive ones (***treatment interventions***).

Pattern Change

In the second session the psychiatrist then prescribed relaxation training to help Janet regulate her psychological and physiologic arousal and an antidepressant to block panic attacks and her anticipatory anxiety. Between sessions she had considerable difficulty with the controlled breathing exercises; and rather than deep breathing, she hyperventilated. Fearful she will have another panic attack, she abandons the exercise. Subsequently, adjunctive group treatment is discussed in the third session. With some hesitation, Janet agrees to participate in an 8-session anxiety modification group in addition to biweekly individual sessions with the psychiatrist. The group sessions emphasized relaxation and assertive communication. By the fourth session, she had few symptoms but was still fearful of a panic attack. Needless to say, she continued to depend on the antidepressant to "keep me safe and secure." Her response to the assertiveness training was equivocal. For example, she had been able to refuse a request to coordinate a school event, yet she still could not stand up to her husband and felt guilty when she contemplated confronting him about his burdensome demands. Janet and her group therapist collaboratively developed a desensitization program for her phobic avoidance. She developed a hierarchy of fear-provoking activities and situations, and then used her new relaxation skills to avert anxiety in each activity and situation. She was able to begin shopping in relatively uncrowded stores and dining out during off-peak hours. During the last group session, Janet developed a relapse prevention plan.

Meanwhile, in individual sessions, the psychiatrist helped Janet explore her dependency/self-sacrificing schema. During the 6th session, Janet recognized the intensity of her anger and became more anxious for several weeks. But in the 11th session, she reported a new confidence having been able to cope principally by relying on her ability to control symptoms with relaxation rather than on medication alone. By now the antidepressant was changed from daily dose to an as-needed or prn dose. In the 13th session she indicated that she thought she needed to stop treatment, citing expense and her new-found confidence. The psychiatrist hypothesized that she had been frightened by a glimpse of her anger at her parents and her husband, but she rejected this interpretation. She said that despite her husband's appreciation of her symptomatic improvement, he seemed annoyed by what he perceives as her growing reliance on treatment, but he refused a conjoint session to discuss the matter. The clinician acceded to her request to stop treatment but emphasized his availability should she wish to explore further the psychological predisposition of her illness.

Two months later, Janet returned to treatment in dismay. Her anxiety had recurred following news of her sister's impending divorce. There had been continuous phone calls at all hours of the day and night. Janet had to frequently interrupt her daily responsibilities "to be available to my sister in her time of need." Janet's husband, who up to this point had been supportive, was becoming exasperated. In 12 further individual sessions spread out over 5 months, Janet explored these conflicts and the underlying schemas of dependence/incompetence and self-sacrifice in a focal dynamic psychotherapy mode. Her objective was to understand that she was identifying with the psychiatrist's caretaking role to the detriment of both her sister's needs and her own. Was this not a familiar pattern? And was this behavior not alienating her husband, the one person who was receptive to her needs? The transference interpretation struck home. She advised her sister to seek psychiatric treatment. With her husband's help, she set limits on her sister's intrusion. Janet identified how her compliance with the clinician's statements was, in fact, a defense against her rage when he did not gratify her dependency needs.

Pattern Maintenance and Termination

By the 25th individual session, she was relatively symptom-free. More important, she understood how to manage her emotions and personal relationships. The earlier conceived relapse plan was reviewed and revised. Fully active again, Janet terminated treatment. Follow-up consisted of participation in an assertiveness-training group in which she functioned as the group facilitator. In the ensuing months, she rarely used the antidepressants she had been given. One year later, she reported an increased capacity to deal with anxiety and her concerns about self-sufficiency. She continued to practice assertive communication and relaxation. To her surprise, she noted the beneficial effect of her new insight and competence with her husband and family members.

Summary

Effective treatment of dependent personality disordered individuals requires the establishment of a trusting client-clinician relationship fostered by focal treatment interventions to modify the maladaptive pattern and then maintain the new pattern. Higher functioning dependent individuals may be reasonably adaptive and functional at work and socially, and thus may be able to profit from single modality treatment. However, many dependent individuals have concurrent symptom disorders in addition to their personality disorder and are much less adaptive and functional. These individuals have considerable difficulty making progress in traditional individual psychotherapy. Thus, an integrative and combined approach, which may include medication, can be effective in treating the majority of dependent personality disordered individuals. Table 7.1 summarizes the treatment intervention strategies most likely to be effective with this disorder.

Table 7.1 Treatment Strategies for Dependent Personality Disorder

ENGAGEMENT	Silent demand for therapist to make decisions and solve their problems. Will comply rather than collaborate. They demonstrate a strong need to please and be accepted. **Tx:** Allow measured amount of dependence at first and gradually introduce collaboration theme. Empathically explore dependency style. Distinguish collaboration from compliance.
Transference	Clients' efforts to engage therapist in assuming responsibility for all their personal decisions while little therapeutic improvement may be present. Will often develop a co-dependent relationship with the therapist, make multiple requests, and idealize them. **Tx:** Set clear limits on therapist–client relationship by refusing to collude.
Countertransference	Therapists may have rescue fantasies or will take on a more directive role in sessions. They may fail to confront individual's limited progress outcomes. Therapist may disclose their feelings or self-disclose more about their personal life than with their other individuals. They may feel nurturant towards the client and even take on a parental role with them. They may experience a sense of incompetence and inadequacy and feel anxious or frustrated. **Tx:** Monitor own thoughts/feelings regarding rescue/directive role and confront client's limited progress.
PATTERN ANALYSIS	***Triggers:*** Expectations of self-reliance and/or being alone
PATTERN CHANGE	***Treatment Goals:*** Autonomy with interdependency/healthier dependence
Schemas	Dependency/incompetence schema; Failure to achieve schema **Tx.:** Schema change strategy and/or Interpretation strategy
Styles/Skills	
a. *Affective Style*	Anxiety dysregulation **Tx:** Anxiety management training; Graded exposure
b. *Behavioral/ Interpersonal Style*	Docile, passive, nonassertive, lack of self-confidence **Tx:** Assertiveness training; Problem-solving training; Involve significant others in treatment process
c. *Cognitive Style*	Naive, uncritical cognitive appraisal **Tx:** Pinpoint/challenge automatic thoughts
d. *Distress Tolerance*	Distress overtolerant **Tx:** RO-DBT-Distress Tolerance training
MAINTENANCE/ TERMINATION	Fear of termination/abandonment with paradoxical worsening of progress **Tx:** Predictive interpretation; Weaning/spacing out sessions; Time-limited format with target termination date; Scheduled booster session

8 Histrionic Personality Disorder

Basically, individuals with histrionic personality disorder are exhibitionistic, superficial, and attention-seeking. While treatment of such individuals involves a number of unique therapeutic challenges, it can be highly effective and successful. This chapter describes a framework for effective treatment of this disorder from a cognitive behavioral perspective. It includes sections on assessment, case conceptualization, and treatment interventions. The section on assessment includes behavioral and cognitive factors, as well as a DSM-5 description and a prototypic description of this disorder. A prototype is a brief description that captures the essence of how a particular disorder commonly presents. Prototypic descriptions are useful and convenient and clinicians commonly rely on them rather than lists of behavioral criteria and core and instrumental beliefs (Westen, 2012). The section on case conceptualization provides both cognitive and behavioral formulations of this disorder. The longest section is on treatment. It emphasizes engagement, pattern analysis, pattern change, and pattern maintenance and termination strategies for effectively managing and treating this disorder. In addition to individual psychotherapeutic strategies and tactics, group, marital and family, medication, and integrative and combined treatment strategies are included. An extensive case example illustrates the treatment process.

Assessment

Behavioral

A behavioral assessment of this disorder emphasizes individual and interpersonal behaviors. Individuals with this disorder are characterized as dramatic, expressive, attention-seeking, while also being demanding, self-indulgent, and inconsiderate. Mood lability, capriciousness, and superficiality further characterize their behavior. While they may initially seem likeable, charming, energetic, and seductive, as time passes they are likely to be seen as emotionally unstable, immature, and egocentric. This disorder is more common in females, and presents with a caricature of femininity in dress and manner. They are easily suggestible and rely heavily on hunches and intuition. They avoid awareness of their own hidden dependency and tend to be "other-directed" with respect to the need for approval from others. Therefore, they can easily dissociate their "real" or inner self from their "public" or outer self. Interpersonally, these individuals tend to be exhibitionistic and flirtatious in their manner, with attention-seeking and manipulativeness being most prominent. Although they are constantly seeking reassurance that they are loved, they typically respond with only superficial warmth and charm and are generally emotionally shallow. Finally, they are exceedingly rejection-sensitive (Sperry, 2003).

Cognitive

A cognitive assessment of this disorder emphasizes core beliefs, particularly those about their views of self and of others. Typically, they view themselves as inadequate and vulnerable to others' neglect. To compensate, they project an image of being glamorous or impressive. They view others as useful to them as long as others are attentive, affectionate, and positively responsive. Related beliefs include needing others to admire them so they can be happy, and believing that their worth depends on others responding positively to them. Not surprisingly, such beliefs are reflected in their main strategy or pattern of being dramatic and demonstrative to bind others to them. If that does not work they may resort to tears, assaultive behavior, or impulsive suicide gestures to command attention (Beck, 2015; Sungar & Gunduz, 2015).

DSM-5 Description

Individuals with this personality disorder are characterized by an unremitting pattern of attention-seeking and emotionality. They tend to be uncomfortable in situations where they cannot be the center of attention. Their emotional reactions tend to be shallow and rapidly shifting. Typically, they draw attention to themselves with the way they dress. Their manner of speech tends to be impressionistic with few details. These individuals are easily influenced by others or circumstances. They are likely to perceive relationships as more intimate than they really are. They often engage in provocative and inappropriate seductive sexual behavior. Furthermore, they are dramatic and overly exaggerate their emotional expressions (American Psychiatric Association, 2013).

Prototypic Description

These individuals are the exhibitionists in life. If they are female they use charm, physical appeal, and seductiveness to command attention. There is an intensity to their relationships and emotions, but a shallowness at the same time. If they are male, they are more likely to command attention by bragging about a business deal or investment, or their prowess in sports or sex. Their interests and attitudes are easily influenced by what others think and value.

They come on strong and seek intimacy quickly, but such intimacy wears thin quickly, which leaves them feeling unappreciated (Frances, 2013).

Case Conceptualization

Beck (2015) describes a cognitive therapy view of the Histrionic Personality Disorder based on specific underlying assumptions and cognitive distortions. Two underlying assumptions are posited: "I am inadequate and unable to handle life by myself" and "I must be loved by everyone to be worthwhile." Believing they are incapable of caring for themselves, histrionic individuals actively seek the attention and approval of others and expect others to take care of them and their needs. Believing they must be loved and approved by others promotes rejection sensitivity. Finally, feeling inadequate and desperate for approval, they are under considerable pressure to seek attention by "performing" for others. These beliefs also give rise to a thinking style characterized as impressionistic, global, and unfocused, which is not conducive to a differentiated sense of self. Not surprisingly, this global, exaggerated thinking style engenders common cognitive distortions (Beck, 1976) such as dichotomous thinking, overgeneralization, and emotional reasoning.

Taking a more behavioral tack, Turkat (1990), differentiates this disorder in two types: the controlling type in which the basic motivation is achieving total control through the use of manipulative and dramatic ploys; and the reactive type in which the basic motivation is seeking reassurance and approval. Turkat does not believe the controlling type is amenable to behavior treatment. Unable to read other's emotions and interventions accurately, these individuals remain shallow, self-centered, and uncomfortable when reinforcement is not immediately forthcoming from others. In short, they suffer from a primary deficit in empathy.

Treatment

Engagement Strategies

Early Session Behavior

Interviewing histrionic individuals can be enjoyable, but it is always quite challenging. The challenge is that these individuals are more interested in admiration and approval than in establishing a therapeutic relationship. The clinician can expect exaggerated emotionality, vagueness, and superficiality in the first session. Histrionic females are likely to be flirtatious, obsequious, or playful with a male clinician, whereas they are more likely to engage in a power struggle with a female clinician (Sperry, 2006). Eliciting sufficient history and information to complete the diagnostic evaluation usually requires the clinician to neutralize the histrionic individual's vagueness, dramatics, or control. The clinician's use of open-ended and unstructured questions should be limited or avoided because these individuals easily become sidetracked. Rather, it is more productive to pursue a basic theme, such as interpersonal conflict or a work issue, and then elicit specific examples while curbing their ramblings and contradictions. Confronting their contradictions may result in hostility and even loss of rapport, and thus it is preferable to express empathy and understanding. It should be anticipated that when they experience that empathy and understanding diminishing, they will return to vagueness or dramatization (Othmer & Othmer, 2002). Several strategies to reduce counter-therapeutic behaviors include discussing problem behavior in-session, shortening sessions into shorter periods, completing homework tasks in session, and using non-verbals to redirect the clients monologue discussion or other problematic behavior (Bilsen & Thomson, 2011).

Because histrionic individuals tend to regard the self as a recipient of the actions of others rather than as an agent of action, they report symptoms as caused or represented outside of the self. Accordingly, by repetitions and structured questioning the clinician can begin assisting these individuals to clarify their experience, to provide everyday labels for them, and to recognize that thoughts and feelings come from within the self (Horowitz, 1995).

Facilitating Collaboration

Establishing a collaborative relationship with histrionic individuals is somewhat similar to establishing such a relationship with dependent personality disordered individuals. At the outset of treatment, both types of individuals are likely to view clinicians as all-powerful rescuers who will make everything better for them. And, because of their global, impressionistic cognitive style and sense of specialness, histrionic individuals tend to believe and expect that clinicians will somehow intuitively be able to appreciate and understand their needs and concerns without any or much intrapsychic exploration of these needs and concerns. For this reason it is essential that the clinician assume an active role at the outset of treatment (Othmer & Othmer, 2002). The more this active role is evidenced, the quicker the fantasy of the all-powerful rescuer will fade.

Histrionic individuals must undergo a socialization process in which they experience the phenomenon of collaboration, which is quite foreign to them. Whenever histrionic individuals beg and demand that they be helped or rescued, clinicians use questioning to assist them in arriving at their own solutions. Furthermore, clinicians would be well to reinforce every instance of assertive and competence behaviors manifest in the early phase of treatment, but not reinforce any helping–demanding behaviors. The cognitive therapy strategy of guided discovery in which clinicians work with individuals to understand the connection between individuals' thoughts, images, feelings, and behaviors is particularly effective in facilitating collaboration with these individuals (Davis & Beck, 2015).

Transference and Countertransference

Two common transferences noted with histrionic individuals are rescue fantasy and the erotic or eroticized transferences. When histrionic individuals bring a series of problems to clinicians expecting quick solutions, or otherwise feign helplessness, it is easy for clinicians to respond to their rescue fantasy by assuming an all-powerful/messianic or rescuer role. In the role of rescuer, clinicians may provide advice, give in to specific demands, make decisions, and even assume blame for their individuals' failure to work toward change. As a result, clinicians may feel angry, manipulated, and deceived. Not surprisingly, by assuming the rescuer role, clinicians not only inadvertently reinforce feelings of helplessness among these individuals, but also become embroiled in a reenactment of their earliest relationship pattern (Davis & Beck, 2015). Redirecting and refocusing the individual toward finding their own solutions is recommended.

In hysterical individuals, the erotic transference—or transference love, which is a mixture of tender, erotic, and sexual feelings toward the clinician—tends to develop over a gradual period of time along with feelings of shame and embarrassment. On the other hand, histrionic personality disordered individuals can develop an erotized transference, which, unlike transference love, is characterized by the expectation of sexual gratification with the clinician. Typical countertransferences with erotic and eroticized transferences are aloofness, anxiety, and exploitation. Essentially, these transferences need to be analyzed and understood, and the countertransferences monitored rather than acted out. A detailed discussion of the resolution of these erotic/erotized transference–countertransferences can be found in Gabbard (2005).

Pattern Analysis Strategies

Pattern analysis with histrionic personality disordered individuals involves an accurate diagnostic and clinical evaluation of schemas, styles, and triggering stressors, as well as level of functioning and readiness for therapeutic change. Knowledge of the optimal DSM-5 criterion along with the maladaptive pattern of the histrionic personality disordered individual is not only useful in specifying diagnosis but also in planning treatment that is tailored to the histrionic individual's unique style, needs, and circumstances. The optimal criterion specified for the histrionic personality disorder is discomfort in situations in which he or she is not the center of attention (Allnutt & Links, 1996). Both planned treatment goals and interventions should reflect this theme of attention-getting and specialness.

Pattern refers to the predictable and consistent style and manner in which an individual thinks, feels, acts, copes, and defends the self. Pattern analysis involves both the triggers and response—the "what"—as well as an explanatory statement—the "why"—about the pattern of a given histrionic individual. Obviously, such a clinical formulation specifies the *particular* schemas and temperamental styles unique to a given individual rather than the more *general* clinical formulation that will be noted here (Sperry, 2006).

Triggers

Generally speaking, the "triggers" or "triggering" situations for straight histrionic individuals are stressors related to heterosexual relationships (Othmer & Othmer, 2002). This means that when histrionic-disordered individuals are engaging in behaviors, discussing, or even thinking about certain opposite sex relationships and they become distressed, their disordered or maladaptive pattern is likely to be triggered, and their characteristic symptomatic affects, behaviors, and cognitions will be experienced or exhibited. Generally speaking, while histrionic individuals tend to engage in help-seeking, seductive, or attention-getting behavior with opposite sex individuals, they are more likely to engage in power struggles with same sex individuals.

Schemas

Generally speaking, the underlying schemas involve a self-view of needing to be noticed by others, and a view of the world as the provider of special care and consideration because life makes them nervous (Sperry, 2015). Among the most frequently encountered schema in histrionic individuals is the entitlement/self-centeredness schema. Often, features of the emotional deprivation schema are also noted. The *entitlement/self-centeredness schema* refers to the core set of beliefs that one is entitled to take or receive whatever is wanted irrespective of the cost to others or society. The *emotional deprivation schema* refers to the core set of beliefs that one's need for nurturance and emotional support will never be met by others (Bricker, Young, & Flanagan, 1993; Young, Klosko, & Weishaar, 2003).

Style/Temperament

There are four unique style dimensions in the ABCDEF profile that characterize individuals with this personality disorder: Affective, Behavioral-interpersonal, Cognitive, and Distress tolerance. Histrionic personality disordered individuals have affective styles characterized with superficial, overmodulated affects. Behaviorally, they tend to be unfocused and inconsistent, whereas relationally they are likely to have difficulty relating to others except in a superficial, manipulative manner. In addition, they tend to have empathic deficits. Finally, their cognitive style is marked by the capacity for global, impressionistic thinking, and vividness of imagination (Sperry, 2003). They also experience considerable difficulty focusing on specifics and details. When impulsivity is also present, it further exacerbates the other style dysregulations. The most notable skill deficits in this disorder are problem-solving skills and self-management skills. Other skill deficits that may be present include empathy and time and money management. They also tend to be distress intolerant meaning they have difficulty tolerating high levels of distress (Lynch & Mizon, 2011). Overall, their pattern reflects an externalizing disorder.

Pattern Change Strategies

In general, the overall goal of treatment with histrionic personality disordered individuals is to increase their capacity for reflection, interdependence, and self-management. In other words, the first goal is to "feel less and think more," which is the converse of the goal for the obsessive-compulsive personality disorder. The goal of interdependence is met when the histrionic individual is able to establish and maintain more functional intimate relationships. That means that instead of relating to others in the demanding but distancing role of princess or sex object, the female histrionic can relate more as an intimate, equal partner taking the risks that mutually giving relationships require. Accomplishing these goals involves modifying maladaptive beliefs about specialness and attention-getting, and learning ways in which to increase self-management.

After the maladaptive pattern has been identified and analyzed in terms of schemas, style, and skill deficits, the therapeutic process involves relinquishing that pattern and replacing it with a more adaptive one. Thus, the pattern change process involves modifying schemas, modulating style dysregulations, and reversing skill deficits. The process of modifying the maladaptive schemas of histrionic personality disordered individuals usually follows efforts to modify style and skill-deficit dimensions because schema change early in the course of treatment is often resisted by the client.

Schema Change

The entitlement/self-centered schema is supported by such injunctive beliefs as "I'm interesting and exciting," "Intuition and feeling are more important than rational planning," "If I'm entertaining others won't notice my weaknesses," and, particularly, "To be happy I need other people to pay attention to me" (Beck, Freeman, Davis, & Associates, 2004). The emotional deprivation schema fosters such histrionic beliefs as "I'll never get enough love and attention" and "I'm only capable of having superficial relationships" (Young et al., 2003). In the schema change process, the clinician and individual work collaboratively to understand the developmental roots of the maladaptive schemas. Then these schemas are tested through predictive experiments, guided observation, and reenactment of early schema-related incidents. Finally, histrionic individuals are directed to begin to notice and remember counter-schema data about themselves and their social experiences.

CBASP Strategies

Cognitive Behavioral Analysis System of Psychotherapy (CBASP) utilizes cognitive and behavioral replacement strategies to effect change among histrionic personality disordered individuals' maladaptive patterns (McCullough, 2000; McCullough, Schramm, & Penberthy, 2015). This approach examines the individual's histrionic schema dynamics and pattern by focusing on situations in which their pattern caused harm in their daily functioning or led to an undesirable outcome. The process is started through use of a situation analysis, in which thoughts, behaviors, their desired outcome, and the actual outcome information is gathered. Secondly, the remediation phase elicits the client to create more useful and adaptive thoughts and behaviors that support the desired outcome (Driscoll, Cukrowicz, Reardon, & Joiner, 2004). This approach is a brief model of therapy that can effect change among histrionic individuals.

Style-Skill Change

Because histrionic individuals tend to exhibit superficial but intense and overly modulated affects, emotional awareness training along with "dramatic behavioral experiments" can be effective interventions. Because of their flair for the dramatic and dread of protocol and detail, histrionic individuals will likely respond to homework assignments if they are given permission to use their vivid imagination particularly with behavioral experiments and behavioral rehearsal. Sungar and Gunduz (2015) illustrated the use of dramatic behavioral experiments with histrionic individuals.

Problem-solving training can be effective in assisting histrionic individuals to become more organized and exert more consistent effort in daily life. Adding a measure of structure in their lives can reasonably modulate their free-spirited, inconsistent, and manipulative style (Marra, 2005). Because impulsivity is usually part of this style and can also exacerbate other style dysregulation, impulse control training may be necessary. Furthermore, because they tend to have some deficits in assertiveness, empathy, and intimacy; assertive communication training, empathy training, and intimacy promoting activities may be indicated.

Setting specific treatment goals and learning the skill of listing advantages and disadvantages or pros and cons are common cognitive therapy interventions for modifying the personality's cognitive style (Beck et al., 2004). As noted below, medication may also be a useful adjunct in modulating these style dimensions.

Medication Strategies

Currently, there are no psychotropic medications specifically indicated for treating individuals with histrionic personality disorder (Silk & Feurino, 2012).

Histrionic personality disordered individuals may exhibit anxiety disorders, depressive disorders, or somatoform symptoms. Nevertheless, medications are used that target specific troubling symptoms associated with the disorder, such as depression, anxiety, or sleep problems. Generally, these medications are used as an adjunct to psychotherapy and skills training. Because troubling symptoms often respond to medications sooner than most psychological interventions, medications are usually prescribed at the onset of treatment (Sperry, 1995b). Unfortunately, there is little research evidence to provide guidelines for the use of such medications (Silk & Feurino, 2012).

Group Treatment Strategies

Group treatments have a number of advantages over individual treatment. First, group treatment frustrates the histrionic's wish and demand for the exclusive attention of the therapist. Group dynamics inevitably challenge the approval-seeking posture of these individuals. Accordingly, the likelihood that an eroticized transference will develop is relatively small in contrast with individual therapy. Second, the histrionic individual's global cognitive style and related defenses of denial and repression can be more effectively modified in a group rather than an individual treatment context. These features are frustrating for group members who will subsequently confront the histrionic individual's distorted self-perceptions, omission of details, and thematic thinking. Third, because histrionic individuals crave positive maternal transference, they expect, and even demand, that the group provide them with the maternal nurturance they missed as children. While the nurturing maternal transference can be particularly challenging in individual therapy, the group treatment context effectively diminishes this transference (Gabbard, 2005). These advantages are particularly relevant with lower to moderate functioning histrionic individuals.

The following are some indications and contraindications for group treatment of the histrionic personality. Indications for group treatment include higher functioning histrionic individuals who can express affects directly and spontaneously, and those who can draw others out and manifest concern for other group members. Such individuals tend to be highly valued by other group members. Contraindications include histrionic individuals who cannot participate in a group process without monopolizing or disrupting it. Nevertheless, clinical experience suggests that concurrent individual psychotherapy with group therapy can be useful for histrionic individuals who are likely to monopolize or be disruptive in group settings. It should also be noted that skill-oriented groups are well-suited for lower functioning histrionic individuals, particularly in partial hospitalization and day-treatment programs.

Marital and Family Therapy Strategies

Little has been written about family therapy, per se, with histrionic individuals. However, there is considerable literature on couples therapy with histrionic individuals. Typically, the marriage consists of a histrionic wife and an obsessive-compulsive husband, wherein the obsessive-compulsive partner has assumed increasing responsibility for the relationship while the histrionic partner has assumed an increasingly helpless or irresponsible role (Sperry & Maniacci, 1998). Treatment is often sought after a primitive outburst, which usually involves some actual or threatened self-destructive behavior, often in the context of a separation or divorce. The perceived or actual loss of a stable dependent person in their lives is a major stressor for histrionic individuals. Thus, they will engage in various forms of attention-seeking behavior—including suicide gestures and promiscuity—in an effort to get the other partner's attention (Harbir, 1981). Generally, the goal of treatment is to change this pattern and redirect the energies of both partners. Usually, this goal can better be accomplished in conjoint rather than individual treatment. Sperry and Maniacci (1998) described an integrative dynamic, cognitive–behavioral and systems treatment approach for this type of couple.

Combined and Integrated Treatment Strategies

Integrated and combined treatment strategies are not only useful for higher functioning histrionic individuals, they can considerably shorten the course of treatment. However, with lower to moderate functioning histrionic individuals, integrated and combined treatment strategies are necessary for effective treatment outcomes. The most common combination of treatment modalities for moderate to higher functioning histrionic individuals are individual therapy and couples or marital therapy, and heterogeneous group therapy. For lower functioning histrionic individuals, skill-focused group treatment is particularly useful. Typically, this modality is combined with individual treatment. Previously, it was mentioned that concurrent individual psychotherapy is a necessary adjunct to group therapy for histrionic individuals who monopolized the group process or were otherwise disruptive in group settings. Finally, medications may be a useful adjunct to psychotherapy, either concurrent or in tandem, if specific symptoms are prominent.

Pattern Maintenance and Termination Strategies

Termination Issues

Treatment termination can be difficult and challenging for clinicians and histrionic individuals, largely because the therapeutic relationship provided individuals with undivided attention and concern. As the termination phase begins, a repetition of the maladaptive histrionic pattern is inevitable as they begin to realize that they must soon relinquish the attention and nurturance that treatment has come to represent. Fantasies of rescue and nurture that previously had remained veiled will now be disclosed (Sperry, 2006).

Particularly prominent are fantasies of a continued relationship with the clinician following termination. But since they have already relinquished much of their maladaptive pattern, these fantasies and yearnings are no longer as compelling as before. Presumably, they have also developed more adaptive relationships with significant others since treatment began. Accordingly, they can better tolerate the perceived loss of the therapeutic relationship. Subsequently, residual symptoms will finally be relinquished during this last phase of treatment, particularly those symptoms that were maintained because of secondary gain.

Allen (1977) noted that "the patient may have a covert wish for indefinite continuation of treatment, and only in the termination phase is it possible to examine and resolve the desperate need for an enduring, sustaining relationship" (p. 320). Furthermore, all the individual's dilemmas about relating to others, getting attention, and authentic sexuality can now be reviewed in the context of terminating the therapeutic relationship. Not surprisingly, as termination nears and their anxiety mounts, some individuals attempt to continue a transference as a defense against the risk of establishing and maintaining real relationships outside the treatment context.

Two therapeutic strategies can facilitate the termination process. First, the clinician can offer the predictive interpretation that attention-getting and dependency needs may complicate the termination process. Conveying this prediction to the individual in a matter-of-fact, nonjudgmental fashion can simultaneously preempt the individual's conscious or unconscious wish to subvert termination and continue therapy indefinitely, and provide the individual with useful feedback regarding the ways in which their strivings can adversely affect other important interpersonal relationships. Second, spacing out sessions allows individuals to become less reliant on their relationship with the clinician and more on relationships outside the treatment context. As they become increasingly able to tolerate this separation, their maladaptive pattern shifts to a more adaptive and healthier pattern of interdependence (Sperry, 2006).

Relapse Prevention Strategies

Another essential aspect of the treatment plan and process is relapse prevention. Because histrionic individuals can easily revert to their maladaptive pattern, it is necessary to predict and plan for relapse. The final phase of treatment should largely focus on relapse prevention. An important goal of relapse prevention is predicting likely difficulties in the time period immediately following termination. Histrionic individuals need to be able to analyze specific external situations such as persons, times, places, and internal states such as specific histrionic beliefs and fears, and other vulnerabilities that increase the likelihood of them responding with histrionic behavior in the face of predictable triggers. Once predicted, a contingency plan to deal with these stressors can be developed. Clinicians may find it useful to have individuals think and talk through the following questions: What can I do if I find myself wanting to impress others or show off? What should I do if I start placing unreasonable demands on important relationships? What should I do if I start believing my old histrionic beliefs more than my new beliefs? What should I do if I relapse? Finally, because interpersonal relationships are triggers for the histrionic pattern, the relapse plan should also include provisions for increasing and maintaining intimacy and commitment (Sperry, 2006).

Case of Kristy

Kristy G. is a 44-year-old, married female who worked as a beauty consultant for a major cosmetics distributor. She had been married to Warren G. for 19 years and had an 18-year-old son. For the past 5 years she had been in psychiatric treatment for chronic, recurrent depression. Irrespective of the medications used, she experienced only partial remission of her symptoms and reported episodic periods of dysphoria, vague suicidal ideation, and chronic dissatisfaction with her life. She had also received adjunctive supportive psychotherapy from a social worker who claimed that "adjustment to her condition" was all she could expect from treatment. During her third year of treatment, Kristy realized that while she was not improving, her marriage was deteriorating. Her husband, who has been always been a pillar of strength for her, was becoming quite symptomatic himself and their relationship had become even more distant. Accordingly, she decided to stop her current treatment and try couples therapy. Subsequently, she and her husband met with a couples therapist who, after evaluating them as a couple in a conjoint session and then also individually, recommended a course of conjoint couples and also dynamically oriented individual psychotherapy for both spouses. The course of couples therapy is described in some detail in conjunction with the case of Warren G. in Chapter 10 of this book, while the course of individual treatment with Kristy is described here.

Comprehensive Assessment and Diagnosis. A comprehensive diagnostic and functional assessment was completed. Kristy met DSM-5 criteria for Persistent Depressive Disorder as well as Histrionic Personality Disorder. Figure 8.1 portrays Kristy's ABCDEF Profile.

Engagement Process

Kristy was an attractive woman who was quite fashionably dressed yet appeared somewhat older than her stated age. She appeared to be considerably pleased with the prospect of working with a male clinician. Despite her somewhat depressed mood, she forced smiles, gesticulated with her hands, made facial expressions that seemed exaggerated, and gave the impression she was performing for an admiring but unseen audience. Initially skeptical of combining dynamically oriented individual therapy with couples sessions, Kristy agreed to the treatment plan.

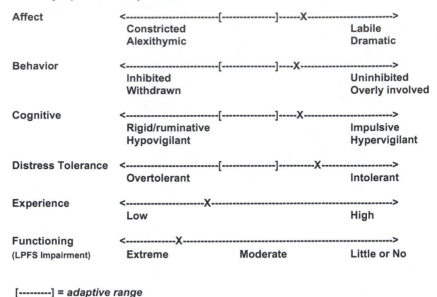

[---------] = *adaptive range*

Figure 8.1 ABCDEF Profile for Avoidant Personality Disorder: Case of Kristy

Pattern Analysis

Kristy was the youngest of four siblings and a prized daughter, particularly of her father. She was especially cute and received considerable attention for her brightness and vivaciousness. Shortly after her third birthday, her mother was admitted for the first of several hospitalizations for depression. This illness took its toll on the rest of the family. The father was forced to take on an additional job and withdrew much of his attention from Kristy. While she was still the favorite grandchild of her grandparents, she secretly envied her mother's new, privileged position. Her mother gained considerable sympathy and seemed to be excused from much of the burden of being a housewife and mother. Her needs always seemed to prevail, and, not surprisingly, the family byword was "Don't upset your mother!" Kristy's first episode of depression occurred when she 15 years old following the breakup of an intense relationship with her 18-year-old boyfriend who had left to attend a distant university. She felt devastated and claimed to have never fully gotten over this loss. She eventually completed training as a cosmetologist and after which she has been successfully employed as a beauty consultant.

Her earliest memory involved her fourth birthday party. She was wearing a party dress and everyone was looking admiringly at her. She felt special, loved, and amazed by all the gifts and the cake that were placed before her. Her next memory involved her first day of school. She recalls walking into class, feeling pretty in a new dress. The female teacher told her she needed to take a seat near the back of the room since her name was near the end of the alphabet.

Her first reaction was to look at the teacher, but then at herself, thinking she wasn't dressed "nice enough" to be up front. She felt angry and sad. These early recollections, along with other developmental history data, suggested that Kristy had internalized the schemas of entitlement/self-centeredness and emotional deprivation indicative of the histrionic personality. Her overmodulated affects, impressionistic thinking, and deficits in intimacy, empathy, and other interpersonal skills were also indicative of the histrionic personality. She met criteria for dysthymic disorder as well as histrionic personality disorder with narcissistic features. Her current level of functioning was fair although she had functioned better earlier in the year. Her current level of distress she was experiencing in herself and in her family, along with her husband's willingness to seek couples therapy with her, suggested that her motivation and readiness was reasonably high and predictive of a positive treatment outcome.

The following pattern formulation served as basis for planning individual treatment. Kristy grew up feeling special but cheated. Although she was aware that she could get attention for her specialness, she was also aware of how fleeting it could be. Getting attention was wonderful, but being able to hold on to it was another matter. She measured life and others by how they could care for her and notice her. Not surprisingly, she mastered the art of attracting others' attention. As she grew older, she thought her specialness, particularly her beauty, youth, and energy were beginning to fade. She felt abandoned by her husband who worked long hours, and anticipated she would also be abandoned by her son who would soon be leaving for college, as her first love had. She was using depression as a coping device to deal with life, to draw others to her as she had seen modeled by her mother. She was probably genetically loaded for depression and had become skilled, like her mother, in using it to rally support for herself. Figure 8.1 summarizes these style features.

Concise Case Conceptualization. Kristy's increased depressive symptoms (*presentation*) seem to be her reaction to the news that her son would be moving away to college, and that her marriage was increasingly deteriorating (*precipitant*). Throughout her life, she received attention for her specialness, she experienced a sense of belonging and validation through attracting men and getting them to be of service to her (*pattern*); as result she presented with deficits in intimacy, empathy skills, and other interpersonal skills. This is an externalizing pattern assessed as falling between the "moderate impairment" and "severe impairment" on the Level of Personality Functioning Scale. Her pattern can be understood in light of receiving considerable attention from her father and grandparents as a child. At the age of three, she lost her "center of attention" position due to her mother's psychiatric condition, as a result she learned that attention and feeling special can be fleeting and temporary. Her family history of depression may biologically predispose her to sadness and her mother also modeled the secondary gain benefits of receiving attention and care by being in the patient position (*predisposition*). This pattern is maintained by her small support system, her limited empathy and interpersonal skills, and her perception that her beauty is deteriorating (*perpetuants*). A referral was made for intensive outpatient treatment with the goal of decreasing her undercontrolled style and increasing her ability to experience authentic intimacy in relationships (*treatment goals*). Cognitive Behavior Therapy will emphasize skills training in intimacy, empathy, interpersonal skills, self-management, and interventions aimed at increasing her sense of interdependence and relational intimacy. Individual therapy (CBASP) would focus on increasing her capacity to learn from experience, and replacing her self-defeating thoughts and behaviors regarding relationships with more adaptive ones (*treatment interventions*).

Pattern Change

Because she had experienced only partial symptomatic relief from several antidepressant trials over the previous 5 years, Kristy's depressive symptoms were framed as persistent symptoms that were more likely to respond to psychosocial interventions like symptom management training and cognitive therapy. Accordingly, individual treatment sessions initially focused on learning the symptom management skill of distraction, which she agreed to practice between sessions. Concurrently, treatment also focused on her dysthymic features using the short-term cognitive therapy treatment protocol for dysthymia described by Freeman (1992b). Kristy was helped to identify her negative thoughts and cognitive distortions and challenge them. The 26 individual sessions, supported by her couples therapy, allowed Kristy to gain considerable control over her chronic depression and dissatisfaction. Her scattered, inconsistent behavior style, which was reinforced by her impressionistic cognitive style, was modulated to some degree with problem-solving training and assertive communication training. In the course of these in-session and between-session activities, she learned to take more control of her life by being better organized and more decisive. Empathy training and work on intimacy skills was accomplished in conjoint sessions with her husband (cf. the case example in Chapter 10). Finally, schema change strategies were used to modify her entitlement/self-centeredness and emotional deprivation schemas.

Pattern Maintenance and Termination

During the termination phase, Kristy's dysthymia became more under her control and she experienced more satisfaction in life and with her marriage. Her relationship with her husband was greatly improved, in part because of the couples therapy, and part because he was now working out of a home office which meant he and Kristy were able to spend more time together. She also reported less fear about her future, her marriage, and her son. She began to feel more consistency and balance in her life. While she still enjoyed dressing fashionably and remained free-spirited, she experienced herself as more connected and valued as a person. A planned termination from individual treatment occurred after 26 sessions. These sessions had been spaced over a period of 18 months. Four months prior to termination, couples therapy had been terminated. It was mutually agreed that quarterly follow-up sessions would be scheduled over the next year.

Table 8.1 Treatment Strategies for Histrionic Personality Disorder

ENGAGEMENT	Expect exaggerated emotionality, vagueness, and superficiality in the first session. Quickly develops therapeutic alliance and often believe therapist should be able to understand them intuitively, nonverbally, without intrapsychic exploration. **Tx:** Role induction and socialization; Reflection vs. impressionistic reporting
Transference	Bring a series of problems to therapist expecting quick solutions, or otherwise feign helplessness (rescue fantasy). Challenge and belittlement are likely in same-sex therapeutic relationships, while erotic or eroticized transference are likely with opposite sex relationships. **Tx:** Redirect and refocus; Analyze and explain
Countertransference	Erotic and erotized transferences are common while rarely feeling bored or distracted. Therapists tend to be overinvolved and have difficulty setting boundaries because the clients require so much attention. **Tx:** Essentially, these transferences need to be analyzed and understood, and the countertransference monitored rather than acted out.
PATTERN ANALYSIS PATTERN CHANGE	**Triggers:** Intimate relationships *Treatment Goals:* Feel less, think more; Increased interdependence and self-management
Schemas	Entitlement/self-centeredness schema; Emotional deprivation schema **Tx:** Interpretation or schema change strategy
Styles/Skills a. *Affective Style*	Superficial, overmodulated affects **Tx:** Emotional awareness training; Dramatic behavioral experiments; Externalization of voices
b. *Behavioral/ Interpersonal Style*	Inconsistency; Over-/underassertive; Empathy and intimacy deficits **Tx:** Problem-solving training; Intimacy skills; Empathy training
c. *Cognitive Style*	Global/impressionistic Impulsivity **Tx:** Set specific treatment goals; Pros and cons analysis; Impulse control training
d. *Distress Tolerance*	Distress overtolerant **Tx:** RO-DBT-Distress Tolerance training
MAINTENANCE/ TERMINATION	Fantasies of a continuing relationship; Fear of termination **Tx:** Predictive interpretation; Weaning, spaced sessions; Encourage other healthy relationships

Summary

Effective treatment of histrionic personality disorder requires that these individuals become sufficiently committed to a treatment process that is tailored and focused on modifying their maladaptive histrionic pattern. Because these individuals tend to have considerable difficulty engaging in and profiting from traditional psychotherapy, an integrative-combined approach that focuses on characterological, temperament, and skill dimensions is usually essential for effective treatment outcomes. The case example illustrates the common challenges that these individuals present, and the kind of clinician flexibility and competence as well as treatment resources required. Table 8.1 summarizes the treatment intervention strategies most likely to be effective with this disorder.

9 Narcissistic Personality Disorder

Basically, individuals with narcissistic personality disorder are typically grandiose, entitled, and self-centered. While treatment of such individuals involves a number of unique therapeutic challenges, it can be highly effective and successful. This chapter describes a framework for effective treatment of this disorder from a cognitive behavioral perspective. It includes sections on assessment, case conceptualization, and treatment interventions. The section on assessment includes behavioral and cognitive factors, as well as a DSM-5 description and a prototypic description of this disorder. A prototype is a brief description that captures the essence of how a particular disorder commonly presents. Prototypic descriptions are useful and convenient and clinicians commonly rely on them rather than lists of behavioral criteria and core and instrumental beliefs (Westen, 2012). The section on case conceptualization provides both cognitive and behavioral formulations of this disorder. The longest section is on treatment. It emphasizes engagement, pattern analysis, pattern change, and pattern maintenance and termination strategies for effectively managing and treating this disorder. In addition to individual psychotherapeutic strategies and tactics, group, marital and family, medication, and integrative and combined treatment strategies are included. An extensive case example illustrates the treatment process.

Assessment

Behavioral

A behavioral assessment of this disorder emphasizes individual and interpersonal behaviors and it recognizes two variants or types: the overt and covert types (Levy, 2012). While the DSM-5 describes the overt or classic type, the covert type is not uncommon in clinical practice. The behavior of individuals with the overt type is characterized by grandiosity, attention-seeking, entitlement, arrogance, conceit, boastfulness, and snobbishness. This type comes across as self-assured and self-centered, and will dominate conversation, seek admiration, and act in a pompous and exhibitionistic fashion. They are also impatient, arrogant, and thin-skinned or hypersensitive. Interpersonally, they tend to be socially facile, pleasant, and endearing. They quickly establish relationships that tend to be superficial and exploitative. This means they use others to indulge themselves and their desires. They can quickly become dissatisfied with others, especially when others are not responsive to their demands. Typically, they are unable to respond with true empathy to others. When stressed, they can be disdainful, exploitive, and generally irresponsible in their behavior. When their needs are not met, they become depressed, develop somatic symptoms, have brief psychotic episodes, or display extreme rage. While often symptom-free and well-functioning, they tend to be chronically unsatisfied due to a constant need for admiration and unrealistic expectations (Sperry, 2003).

In contrast, the covert or closet type tends to be hypersensitive to others' evaluations, inhibited, and outwardly modest. These individuals tend to be shy but quietly grandiose, yet are highly sensitive to criticism and slights. Unlike the overt type, they avoid the limelight and drawing attention to themselves. They may express their grandiosity through an overidentification with suffering and distress. Accordingly, they insist that they suffer more than everyone else. While different in some respects, both overt and covert types are overly self-absorbed and harbor unrealistic, grandiose expectations of themselves (Levy, 2012).

Cognitive

A cognitive assessment of this disorder emphasizes core beliefs, particularly those about their views of self and of others. Typically, they view themselves as special, superior, and entitled to special favors and treatment. They view others as potential admirers who recognize their superiority and grandiosity. Related beliefs include deserving special treatment and dispensations because of their specialness. It also includes believing that they are not bound by the rules and social conventions that govern others. Not surprisingly, such beliefs as are reflected in their main strategy or pattern of seeking prestige, power, position, and wealth. If necessary, they will use manipulation and guile to achieve these goals (Beck, 2015; Behary & Davis, 2015).

DSM-5 Description

Individuals with this personality disorder are characterized by an unremitting pattern of self-centeredness and grandiosity. More specifically, they have an exaggerated sense of their own abilities and achievements. They may have a constant need for attention, affirmation, and praise. Typically, they believe they are unique or special and should only associate with others of the same status. They are likely to have persistent fantasies about attaining success and power. These individuals can exploit others for personal gain. A sense of entitlement and the expectation of special treatment is common. They may come across as snobbish or arrogant. They appear to be incapable of showing empathy for others. In addition, they can be envious or think that others are envious of them (American Psychiatric Association, 2013).

The Alternate DSM-5 Model for Personality Disorders—in Section III— better reflects the emerging research on Narcissistic Personality Disorder (Ronningstam, 2011). The updated definition of narcissistic personality disorder includes "variable and vulnerable self-esteem, with attempts at regulation through attention and approval seeking, and either overt or covert grandiosity" (American Psychiatric Association, 2013, p. 767). This definition includes additional styles of narcissism that were not in DSM-IV-TR. In Section III of the DSM-5, vulnerability of self-esteem is now emphasized as a core feature of narcissistic personality disorder and recognizes the covert type. In contrast, Section II of the DSM-5 emphasizes the dimension of grandiosity and only includes the overt type.

Prototypic Description

These individuals are the center of their worlds. They believe and act as if they are special in every way. They can be showoffs and name droppers. Without a doubt, they are legends in their own minds. There is no limit to their sense of self-importance and entitlement. They are haughty, high-handed, and superior, and expect others to show deference and admiration. They seldom recognize the needs, concerns, or feelings of others. Not surprisingly, they experience disappointments and anger when others fail to live up to their highly unrealistic expectations (Frances, 2013).

Case Conceptualization

According to Young, Klosko, and Weishaar (2003), the Narcissistic Personality Disorder stems from a combination of schemas about the self, world, and future. The central schema is the superior/special schema that develops from direct and indirect messages from parents, siblings, and significant others as well as by experiences that mold beliefs about personal uniqueness and self-importance. The schema of being superior can be shaped by flattery, indulgence, and favoritism. Similarly, the schema of being special can be shaped by experiences of rejection, limitations, exclusion, or deficits. The common denominator for such beliefs about self is that the individual perceives himself or herself as different from others in significant ways. The actual presence of some culturally valued—or devalued—talent or attribute tends to elicit social responses that reinforce the superior/special schema. Feedback that could modify this schema may be lacking or distorted. Being insulted from negative feedback may contribute to the narcissistic vulnerability to criticism and evaluation. Behavior is affected by difficulty in cooperation and reciprocal social intervention and by excesses in self-indulgent, demanding, and aggressive behavior. Problems emerge when this self-schema is overactive and not balanced by more integrative judgments.

Taking a more behavioral tack, Turkat (1990), differentiates this disorder into three types: the self-centered impulsive type, the ruthless impression management type, and the acceptance-oriented impression-management type. Of these, he considers the last type to have the best therapeutic prognosis. Nevertheless, he formulates each type as behavioral manifestations of an impulse control deficit that is learned in early childhood. Specifically, these individuals learned to seek reinforcers without having to work for them. This resulted in their development as self-indulgent, egocentric, and impulsive individuals (Turkat & Maisto, 1985). Turkat notes that individuals with the second and third types focus on creating a favorable impression on others. However, they are unable to maintain close relationships because while they have excellent skills at reading superficial cues, they have empathic deficits (Turkat, 1990).

Treatment

Engagement Strategies

Early Session Behavior

Effectively interviewing narcissistic individuals requires considerable ability to recognize, understand, and respond to their unique dynamics. Throughout the interview, they give the distinct impression that the interview has only one purpose: to underscore their self-promoted importance (Othmer & Othmer, 2002). These individuals often present themselves as self-assured, pretentious, and entitled to having their needs met, and they appear indifferent to the clinician's perspective. Typically, they are unwilling to conform to expectations associated with the "patient" role but have well-defined expectations for the clinician's role. They expect clinicians to mirror or reflect their specialness, and will respond by idealizing them—at least temporarily—as wonderful clinicians and human beings. However, should a clinician confront their grandiosity early in the treatment process, they will inevitably respond with rage and possibly terminate treatment prematurely. Not surprisingly, narcissistic individuals prefer open-ended questions that permit them extended descriptions of their many talents, accomplishments, and future plans.

Narcissistic individuals may present for treatment in pain following a narcissistic injury. They want and expect that the clinician will soothe this wrenching pain. When the clinician fails to recognize the need for or fails to provide sufficient soothing, the individual is likely to react angrily or leave treatment. Not surprisingly, rapport and engagement into the treatment process occurs only after a considerable period of mirroring and soothing. One of the reasons the establishment of rapport and engagement is so difficult is because of clinician countertransference. Clinicians can easily become bored, exasperated, and even angry in the initial interviews as they try to listen attentively to the individual's monologue of self-promotion. If the clinician can remain patient through this period and sufficiently mirror the individual, engagement can be achieved and the formal work of confronting and interpreting their grandiosity can begin (Sperry, 2006).

Facilitating Collaboration

Developing a collaborative relationship with narcissistic individuals can be extraordinarily challenging. The notion of collaboration is distasteful to them because collaboration implies some measure of equality, and they have a vested interest in maintaining their sense of superiority over everyone, including clinicians. Rather than view treatment as a collaborative endeavor, narcissistic individuals are more likely to perceive it as a competitive endeavor in which they fight to establish and maintain their position of superiority. Not surprisingly, they will avoid, derail, or deride the clinician's efforts to directly influence them to collaborate. Furthermore, these individuals have usually had limited experience in cooperative interactions and very likely have skill deficits in this cooperation and collaboration. Accordingly, the clinician does well to mirror these individuals, "join" with their grandiosity, and not act out on their countertransference during the early period of treatment. Once the clinician passes this therapeutic test, the individual is less likely to view the clinician as a competitor (Sperry, 2003). Then, the clinician will be more likely to convey to the individual that both might be able to work together in the best interest of the individual.

Transference and Countertransference

Common transferences involve idealization, devaluation, and projective identification. Narcissistic individuals typically idealize clinicians when they provide them with mirroring and other emotional supplies, but they can quickly shift to devaluing clinicians when they are confronted or emotional supplies are withheld. Similarly, in projective identification the individual excludes the clinician just as she was once excluded by her own parents. An aspect of the individual is projected onto the clinician who identifies with that self before helping the individual to re-introject it (Gabbard, 2005).

Four countertransferences that can be activated in working with narcissistic individuals are described by Gabbard (2005). The first, failure of clinicians to recognize their own narcissistic needs, may be operative as early as the initial session. The narcissistic individual may idealize his current clinician while devaluing previous clinicians. Rather than viewing this as a defensive maneuver, the clinician who longs for idealization may uncritically believe that she has unique talents that were lacking in the individual's previous providers. Another countertransference is boredom that can arise when the individual appears to be oblivious to the clinician's presence. When clinicians must endure serving as a sound board function for narcissistic individuals for long periods of a session, they may easily experience boredom and subsequently respond critically or by not mirroring. In addition, clinicians may also struggle with feelings of being controlled by narcissistic individuals. This occurs when individuals interpret the clinician's body language and paralanguage as indicators of the clinician's rejection or boredom, resulting in the clinician feeling coerced into focusing entirely on their every movement. Gabbard (1994) suggested saying something like: "It seems to hurt your feelings when I clear my throat or fidget in my seat because you feel I am not giving you my full attention" (p. 520). Finally, clinicians may have to contend with countertransference feelings, such as anger, hurt, or feeling impotent, in response to a client's devaluing comments of them.

Pattern Analysis Strategies

Pattern analysis with narcissistic-disordered individuals involves an accurate diagnostic and clinical evaluation of schemas, styles, and triggering stressors as well as level of functioning and readiness for therapeutic change. Knowledge of the optimal DSM-5 criterion along with the maladaptive pattern of the narcissistic-disordered individual is not only useful in specifying diagnosis but also in planning treatment that is tailored to the narcissistic individual's unique style, needs, and circumstances. The optimal criterion specified for the narcissistic personality disorder is that the individual has a grandiose sense of self-importance (Allnutt & Links, 1996). Both planned treatment goals and interventions should reflect this theme of grandiosity and specialness.

Pattern refers to the predictable and consistent style and manner in which an individual thinks, feels, acts, copes, and defends the self. Pattern analysis involves both the triggers and response—the "what"—as well as an explanatory statement—the "why"—about the pattern of a given narcissistic individual. A full-scale case conceptualization that articulates the client's narcissistic/maladaptive pattern will guide treatment strategies and interventions to ultimately foster a more adaptive pattern in the client's interpersonal and intrapersonal style (Sperry & Sperry, 2012). Obviously, such a clinical formulation specifies the *particular* schemas and temperamental styles unique to a given individual rather than the more *general* clinical formulation that will be noted here. Cognitive behavior therapy can assist a narcissistic client to modify their pattern to increase psychological flexibility, decrease compulsivity, and ultimately modulate their behavior to get more of what they want in life (Freeman & Fox, 2013).

Triggers

Generally speaking, the "triggers" or "triggering" situations for narcissistic individuals involve evaluations of self. This means that when narcissistic-disordered individuals are engaging in behaviors, discussing, or even thinking about being alone or relying on their own resources and become distressed, their disordered pattern is likely to be triggered and their characteristic symptomatic affects, behaviors, and cognitions are likely to be experienced or exhibited

(Sperry, 2003). For instance, an actual or perceived threat to the "I'm the only one that counts" can trigger rageful thoughts and affects, along with lowered self-esteem, and compensatory self-centered and even retaliatory behavior.

Schemas

Generally speaking, the underlying schemas involve a self-view of grandiosity, specialness, and entitlement, and a worldview in which the individual expects special treatment and dispensation from the rules and regulations that govern others (Sperry, 2015). Among the most frequently encountered schema in narcissistic individuals is the entitlement/self-centeredness schema. Occasionally, the insufficient self-control/self-discipline schema or abuse/mistrust also is observed. The entitlement/self-centeredness schema refers to the core set of beliefs that one is entitled to take or receive whatever is wanted irrespective of the cost to others or society. The insufficient self-control/self-discipline schema refers to the core set of beliefs that one has such limited control and ability to tolerate frustration that achieving goals or controlling impulses and emotional outbursts is unlikely. The abuse/mistrust schema is noted in the hypervigilant and suspicious narcissist. This schema refers to the core set of beliefs that others will hurt, humiliate, or take advantage of one (Bricker, Young, & Flanagan, 1993; Young et al., 2003).

Style/Temperament

There are four unique style dimensions in the ABCDEF Profile that characterize individuals with this personality disorder: Affective, Behavioral-interpersonal, Cognitive, and Distress tolerance. Narcissistic personality disordered individuals tend to be prone to overmodulated anger to the point of ragefulness. Behaviorally, they tend to be manipulative, whereas relationally they are likely to have difficulty relating to others except in a superficial manner. In addition, they tend to have significant empathic deficits. Finally, their cognitive style is marked by the capacity for cognitive distortion and projective identification. When impulsivity is also present, it further exacerbates the other style dysregulations. The most notable skill deficit in this disorder is the skill of empathic responding. Other skill deficits that may be present include negotiation and conflict resolution (Sperry, 2003). They also tend to be distress intolerant meaning they have difficulty tolerating high levels of negative emotion (Lynch & Mizon, 2011). Overall, their pattern reflects an externalizing disorder.

Pattern Change Strategies

In general, the long-range goal of treatment with narcissistic personality disordered individuals is to increase their capacity and willingness to share and identify with others. Treatment strategies typically include challenging the individual's dysfunctional beliefs about specialness and grandiosity and learning to become more empathic (Sperry, 2006).

After the maladaptive pattern has been identified and analyzed in terms of schemas, style, and skill deficits, the therapeutic process involves relinquishing that pattern and replacing it with a more adaptive pattern. Thus, the pattern change process involves modifying schemas and style-skill dimensions. The process of modifying the maladaptive schemas of narcissistic personality disordered individuals usually follows efforts to modify style and skill-deficit dimensions because schema change efforts early in the course of treatment are usually resisted by the individual (Sperry, 2006).

Schema Change

The entitlement/self-centeredness schema is supported by such injunctive beliefs as "It's essential that I get others' admiration, praise, and recognition," "I'm above the rules," "Others have no right to criticize me," and, particularly, "Since I am special, I deserve special dispensations, privileges and perogatives" (Beck, 2015). In the schema change process, the clinician and individual work collaboratively to understand the developmental roots of the maladaptive schemas. Then these schemas are tested through predictive experiments, guided observation, and reenactment of early schema-related incidents. Finally, narcissistic individuals are directed to begin to notice and remember counter-schema data about themselves and their social experiences.

Modification of the entitlement schema does not mean these individuals become selfless and no longer believe themselves to have special talents or capacity to influence and control others. It means that while they continue to view themselves with some degree of specialness, they are able to use their talents and capacities to influence others more for the common good rather than their own personal gratification (Behary & Davis, 2015; Sperry, 2006).

CBASP Strategies

Cognitive Behavioral Analysis System of Psychotherapy (CBASP) utilizes cognitive and behavioral replacement strategies to effect change among narcissistic individuals (McCullough, 2000; McCullough, Schramm, & Penberthy, 2015).This approach examines the individual's narcissistic schema dynamics and pattern by focusing on situations in which their pattern caused harm in their daily functioning or led to an undesirable outcome. The process is started through use of a situation analysis, in which thoughts, behaviors, their desired outcome, and the actual outcome information is gathered. Secondly, the remediation phase elicits the client to create more useful and adaptive thoughts and behaviors that support the desired outcome. CBASP provides a feedback loop regarding an individual's narcissistic style and how it negatively impacts different social situations and corresponding outcomes. By examining various social situations, individuals can actually modify their ego-syntonic and narcissistic pattern by choosing new behavioral responses and more helpful and realistic cognitions to achieve desired outcomes. This process includes learning from previous experiences and also places the locus of control in the individual's hands. This approach is a brief model of therapy that can effect change among extremely challenging clients (Driscoll, Cukrowicz, Reardon, & Joiner, 2004).

Style-Skill Change

Because narcissistic individuals tend to cognitively distort and overuse the defenses of splitting and projective identification, cognitive awareness training can be quite useful. With regard to emotional style wherein narcissistic rage is prominent, anger management training can be an effective intervention strategy. Because empathic deficits greatly affect relational style, empathy training and increasing intimacy-promoting behavior is indicated. And, because impatience and impulsivity often exacerbate other style dysregulation, impulse control training may be necessary. As noted below, medication may also be a useful adjunct in modulating these style dimensions.

Medication Strategies

Stylistic or temperament treatment targets for this disorder tend to be affective instability, interpersonal sensitivity, impulsivity, and aggression. The less their impulsivity, the more likely they will be able to control their ragefulness and resulting projective identifications. Currently, there are no psychotropic medications specifically indicated for treating individuals with narcissistic personality disorder (Silk & Feurino, 2012).

Nevertheless, medications are used that target specific troubling symptoms associated with the disorder, such as depression, anxiety, or sleep problems. Generally, these medications are used as an adjunct to psychotherapy and skills training. Because troubling symptoms often respond to medications sooner than most psychological interventions, medications are usually prescribed at the onset of treatment (Sperry, 1995b). Unfortunately, there is little research evidence to provide guidelines for the use of such medications (Silk & Feurino, 2012).

Group Treatment Strategies

Group treatment has a role in the treatment of narcissistically disordered individuals. Alonso (1997) contended that group therapy is as effective as individual modes in treatment of narcissistic personality. Nevertheless, recent developments in conjoint marital therapy suggest that group treatment may have fewer indications than individual and couples therapy (Sperry, 2003).

Nevertheless, several factors contribute to the effectiveness of group treatment with these individuals. First of all, peer rather than clinician feedback tends to be more acceptable to the individual. Second, transferences—particularly negative transferences—tend to be less intense in group compared with individual therapy. Working through intense affects is facilitated in groups because of the increased potential for positive attachments within the group and because of peer-group scrutiny of the individual's disavowed affects. Third, a group provides narcissistic individuals with sources of mirroring, objects for idealization, and opportunities for peer relationships. Finally, the group provides ready-made opportunities for narcissistic individuals to increase their ability to empathize with others, and to enhance both self-esteem and self-cohesion.

Not surprisingly, narcissistic individuals can make unreasonable demands for attention in group treatment. These demands can be very taxing for other group members, particularly in heterogeneous groups. Accordingly, it is advisable to begin narcissistic individuals in individual therapy as preparation for entrance into group treatment. Even though narcissistic pathology can strain efforts to achieve group cohesion, a properly run group can function as a container for splitting and projective processes. Nevertheless, the dropout rate for narcissistic personality disordered individuals is higher in long-term ongoing groups than in time-limited groups. Accordingly, concurrent individual psychotherapy that focuses on helping individuals to remain in group therapy is often useful.

Horowitz (1987) outlined the following four indications and contraindications for group treatment of narcissistic individuals: the presence of demandingness, egocentrism, social isolation and withdrawal, and socially deviant behavior. While these traits may be taxing to both clinician and group members, Horowitz contended that individuals with such traits tend to be quite responsive to group treatment. Finally, attending to the unique needs of the narcissistic individual usually means that the clinician will place less emphasis on interpreting overall group dynamics and more on individual dynamics as they affect the group process (Sperry, 2003).

Marital and Family Therapy Strategies

Reports on the use of family therapy with narcissistic personality disorder individuals emphasized the treatment of adolescents in families with severe narcissistic pathology, wherein the adolescent was the identified patient on whom family members projected their own devalued view of themselves. More recent applications of family therapy to narcissistic personality disorder emphasize treatment of the entire family system from a systemic perspective (Jones, 1987).

Much has been published about marital therapy with the narcissistic spouse or couple. Solomon (1989, 1998) described a conjoint treatment strategy for narcissistic partners from a self-psychology perspective. Conjoint sessions are structured to function as a "holding environment" for the distorted projections and other conflictual manifestations in the relationship.

The therapist's empathic self is the basic tool of this kind of psychodynamic treatment.

Kalojera and his colleagues (Kalojera et al., 1998) described an integrative blending of self-psychology and the systemic approach to the narcissistic couple that is noteworthy. Lachkar (1998) offered a number of clinically useful considerations for the treatment of couples where one partner meets criteria for narcissistic personality disorder while the other meets criteria for borderline personality disorder. This type of couple is increasingly common today. Nurse (1998) described the dynamics and treatment strategies for another common variant of the narcissistic couple: One partner meets criteria for narcissistic personality disorder while the other meets criteria for dependent personality disorder.

Relationship enhancement therapy has also been adapted to couples therapy with narcissistic spouses (Snyder, 1994). This approach emphasizes the learning and application of four basic interpersonal skills: (a) effective expression, (b) empathy, (c) discussion—mode switching between empathic and expresser roles, and (d) problem solving/conflict resolution. The clinician's role is to explain, demonstrate, and coach each skill in the conjoint session, whereas the partner's role is to practice these skills during and between sessions with progressively difficult issues. It should not be surprising that empathic skills and the subjective aspect of the expresser skill are notably deficient in narcissistically vulnerable couples. The clinician provides a "holding environment" in which narcissistic vulnerability is experienced and addressed productively rather than acted out. This results in both partners learning to express feelings with less risk of shame, while increasing their capacity to empathize with their partner (Snyder, 1994).

Combined and Integrative Treatment Strategies

There is seldom a single treatment strategy, such as mirroring or empathy training, that can ensure positive treatment outcomes with narcissistically disordered individuals. Rather, depending on the individual's overall level of functioning, temperamental patterns, defensive style, and skill deficits, a focused, specific, and sequentially coordinated tailored treatment protocol is usually necessary to accomplish treatment goals and objectives in a timely manner and fashion (Sperry, 2006). As noted earlier, higher functioning individuals who meet either DSM-5 or dynamic criteria for a personality disorder have fewer troubling temperamental patterns, skill deficits, and defensive styles than the lower functioning individual. Consequently, the higher the functioning and the fewer skill deficits, the less likely a combined approach is necessary; whereas the lower the functioning and the more skill deficits/temperament dysregulation, the more an integrative, tailored, and combined approach is necessary. This section describes such integrative and combined strategies.

Generally speaking, the psychodynamic approaches have largely emphasized the interpretation of narcissistic vulnerability regarding grandiosity, entitlement, and soothing and mirroring frustrations to reduce narcissistic rage. The cognitive approaches have focused on modifying narcissistic vulnerability, emphasizing modification of schemas, moderating narcissistic expectations, and reducing cognitive distortions, particularly projective identification. The behavioral and psychoeducational approaches have emphasized skill training, particularly empathy training. Combining all three of these modalities is relatively easy to implement and quite acceptable to individuals (Sperry, 2006). The usual time sequence for using these modalities is as follows: Begin with mirroring and mirroring interpretations to engage the individual in treatment. Next, focus on reducing skill deficits and temperament dysregulation that would otherwise hinder the treatment process. This may include medication but almost always involves skill training, particularly empathy training (Snyder, 1994). This training can be accomplished in individual, group, or couples sessions. Then continue with the schema change strategy and other interpretation strategies. The case example that follows illustrates this sequencing of modalities.

Pattern Maintenance and Termination Strategies

Termination Issues

Planned termination is usually not particularly difficult for narcissistic individuals. Rather, for the reasons described in the *engagement* section, narcissistic individuals tend to be premature terminators. There are some who, because of the clinician's early confrontative stance or failure to mirror sufficiently, experience treatment as another narcissistic injury and leave at the outset. But for all narcissistic individuals, the therapeutic challenge is to engage these individuals in the treatment process long enough to achieve basic treatment objectives. To that end, it may be necessary to conceptualize the treatment process as a series of discrete phases and establish treatment contracts for these phases. The initial phase usually involves resolution of distress. Many narcissistic individuals present for treatment with such sufficient distress that they will remain until it has lessened. For instance, they come for treatment because of depression, a serious narcissistic injury, or because of the distress they have created in the lives of others, such as a spouse who threatens divorce if treatment is not sought. These individuals will likely remain in treatment until they have achieved sufficient soothing or amelioration of their anxiety or depressive symptoms. Many of them terminate after experiencing relief of their distress. Accordingly, it is advisable to establish a treatment agreement for a given number of sessions focused on distress resolution and then re-evaluate and re-negotiate another series of sessions to focus on more general concerns. Needless to say, the clinician's challenge is to sufficiently "join" with the individual's entitlement so that the individual comes to believe that therapeutic change is in his or her best interest (Sperry, 2006).

Relapse Prevention Strategies

Relapse prevention is essential in the effective treatment of narcissistic individuals. Even though effective treatment greatly reduces their interpersonal sensitivity and narcissistic vulnerability, these individuals are still prone to narcissistic injury. The final phase of treatment should therefore emphasize relapse prevention. An important goal of relapse prevention is predicting likely difficulties in the time period immediately following termination. The individual needs to be able to analyze specific factors such as persons, places, circumstances, as well as specific narcissistic beliefs that can trigger their maladaptive pattern. Once predicted, individuals can develop a contingency plan to deal with these stressors.

Case of James

James K. is a 49-year-old, married chairman of the department of plastic and reconstructive surgery at a university school of medicine. He grudgingly came for psychotherapy because of depressive symptoms and because of ultimatums from his wife and boss. His wife demanded that he get help or she would divorce him. He had been married for 7 years to his current wife, and prior to that was married for approximately 5 years during the last 2 years of medical school and the first 3 years of his surgical residency. Recently his wife complained that she would no longer tolerate his constant need for attention nor his increasing rage and verbal abuse, which consisted of blaming, insults, and name-calling. Lately, their time together was marked by either destructive conflict or cold distancing for days to weeks. In addition, the dean of the medical school had also warned him if he didn't adopt a "more consultative management style" he would be removed as chair of his department. Apparently, Dr. K. had increasingly alienated a number of his faculty over the past few years by his arrogant, demanding style and because he had recently fired two junior faculty for insubordination. The university grievance committee that reviewed the firings found that due process was not followed and recommended that the two faculty be reinstated. Dr. K. was furious with the committee's recommendation and demanded that the dean ignore it. It was then that the dean gave him the ultimatum. Dr. K.'s rage turned to depression manifested by dysphoria, insomnia, some anhedonia, and loss of energy. Although he had refused his wife's demand for couples therapy, he reluctantly agreed to individual psychotherapy.

Comprehensive Assessment and Diagnosis. A comprehensive diagnostic and functional assessment was completed. James met DSM-5 criteria for Other Specified Depressive Disorder as well as Narcissistic Personality Disorder. Figure 9.1 portrays James' ABCDEF Profile.

Engagement Process

Like many narcissistic personality disordered individuals who enter treatment, Dr. K. was deeply narcissistically wounded and mildly to moderately depressed.

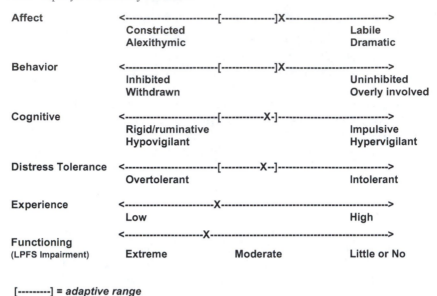

Figure 9.1 ABCDEF Profile for Narcissistic Personality Disorder: Case of James K.

Nevertheless, they usually seek treatment with great reluctance and demand that it be on their terms. Dr. K. announced during the first session that he was there against his better judgment and that he had no problems except for a wife who was a "bedeviling shrew" and a boss who was a "wimpish idiot." Reluctantly, he admitted that he was embarrassed and hurt by recent events particularly at the medical school but said these would pass. Mainly, he was concerned about his depressive symptoms, which were worsening over the past 3 weeks. He wanted an antidepressant. By the second session, his sleep was normalizing and he was more energetic but still was quite wounded. He responded to the clinician's mirroring and attentiveness and agreed to return for a third session. The clinician was a member of the school's psychiatry faculty and had responded to an emergency that resulted in being about six minutes late for Dr. K.'s third appointment. Dr. K. immediately launched into an attack on the clinician's character and competence, and stated he should never have trusted himself to the care of a junior faculty member, when he should have been seen by the chair of the department or at least a faculty psychiatrist who was listed in *Best Doctors in America*. The clinician successfully soothed Dr. K. and apologized for the delay. Later that session, Dr. K. announced his depression had lifted and he would no longer need treatment. The clinician offered a mirroring interpretation and suggested it might still be in Dr. K.'s best interest to consider some alternative ways of dealing with his wife, colleagues, and dean that would ease the current situation and prevent their recurrence. Dr. K. agreed it was in his best interest to "do some damage control" and committed to eight additional sessions after which the treatment contract would be reviewed.

Pattern Analysis

Although he did not meet criteria for major depressive disorder, he did meet criteria for minor depressive disorder as well as narcissistic personality disorder. A review of his early childhood and later developmental history as well as his early recollections indicated a self-view of specialness and a worldview in which others were to cater to his needs. His maladaptive pattern involved increasing self-aggrandizement, manipulation, and demands of others whenever he felt the slightest discomfort or lack of others' recognition. When criticized or otherwise narcissistically wounded he would engage in projective identification and ragefulness. This pattern reflects the maladaptive schema of entitlement/self-centeredness and, to some extent, the schema of insufficient self-control/self-discipline. This pattern also reflects style/skill deficits in accurate attributions, impulse control, and empathic communication. Figure 9.1 summarizes these style features.

Concise Case Conceptualization. James' depressive symptoms (*presentation*) seem to be his reaction to ultimatums given to him by his wife and boss (*precipitant*). In particular, James was narcissistically injured after the dean of his department and corresponding committee declined his recommendation to fire two junior faculty members. His initial response was rage and verbal abuse towards his wife, which was shortly followed by depressive symptoms. Throughout his life, he placed high demands on others, while frequently manipulating them to meet his needs (*pattern*); as a result he presents with skill deficits in self-soothing, impulse control, and empathic communication. This is an externalizing pattern assessed as between "moderate impairment" and "severe impairment" on the *Level of Personality Functioning Scale*. His pattern can be understood in light of his self-view of specialness and worldview in which others cater to his needs, maladaptive schema of entitlement/self-centeredness and, to some extent, the schema of insufficient self-control/self-discipline (*predisposition*). This pattern is maintained by his sense of entitlement, the fact that his wife is chronically unhappy in their marriage, his limited self-soothing skills, and his poor empathic communication skills. Given his severe presentation, his lack of insight into his narcissistic pattern, and major vulnerability to slights from others, a referral was made for intensive outpatient treatment with the goal of decreasing his undercontrolled style and increasing his empathy and relational skills (*treatment goals*). Cognitive Behavior Therapy will emphasize skills training in empathic responding, impulse control, assertiveness, and conflict resolution. Distress tolerance interventions are aimed at increasing his impulse-control and relational skills. Group therapy will be used to help increase his awareness and responsiveness to others' needs. Individual therapy (CBASP) would focus on increasing his capacity to learn from experience, and replacing his self-defeating thoughts and behaviors regarding relationships with more adaptive ones (**treatment interventions**).

Pattern Change

The eight sessions were arranged to include four individual weekly sessions and four weekly conjoint sessions. The individual sessions focused on cognitive awareness training and impulse control training skills. Even though he had previously refused couples therapy, Dr. K. was receptive to the conjoint sessions because the focus would be limited to interpersonal skills. Dr. K. agreed that the purpose of these sessions was to give him "another set of people skills" that he could "use when it was expedient." After all, he was proud of his persona of toughness and arrogance and didn't want to give it up. Empathy training exercises were the focus of four such conjoint sessions. In these sessions, both spouses were helped to understand their narcissistic vulnerability, expectations, and needs underlying their narcissistic defense. The clinician modeled empathic listening as well as empathic responding for them, and coached them in both listening and responding from the others' frame of reference. In part, this was accomplished by role playing and role reversal in which Dr. and Mrs. K. played themselves expressing their feelings and concerns and then reversed roles. They agreed to practice these skills at least 30 minutes per day.

During the last of the four individual sessions, the eight-session treatment agreement was reviewed. The focal intensity of the individual and conjoint sessions, as well as their daily skill practice, resulted in a significant shift in the relationship between Dr. K. and his wife. It had become much more respecting and caring, and they had been able to handle the few conflicts that had arisen in a more adaptive fashion. Dr. K. was also pleased that his work relationships were also less charged, and he congratulated himself for "reinventing myself," by which he meant he now had a "good guy persona" too. Through mirroring interpretations, the clinician set the stage for discussing a continuation of the treatment contract. The modality would be individual psychotherapy, with a focus on further enhancement of the skills and understanding of self that had already been started. Not surprisingly, Dr. K. declined the invitation saying he had gotten what he had come for and was fine. The clinician offered to resume treatment if and when Dr. K. might find it beneficial.

Approximately 5 months later, Dr. K. was back in treatment. Two weeks earlier, following a stormy confrontation with him, Mrs. K. had filed for divorce. Dr. K. was crushed. He was dysphoric and panicky at the prospect of losing "the jewel of my life." Furthermore, he had begun experiencing palpitations that diagnosed as a cardiac arrhythmia for which medication was prescribed. He was agreeable to anything now, even couples therapy. Individual psychotherapy was begun with a focus on maladaptive schemas. The antidepressant was reintroduced for a short time until depressive and anxiety symptoms were ameliorated and then weaned. Twice weekly sessions were scheduled. These sessions continued for the next 11 months, after which they were reduced to weekly sessions for an additional 3 months.

Pattern Maintenance and Termination

During the course of this treatment period, Mrs. K. dropped the divorce action. A planned termination ensued. He had developed considerable insight into his need for specialness and control along with concomitant changes in his behavior. Dr. K. did not believe a scheduled follow-up appointment was necessary but agreed to call the clinician in 6 months. At that time, he reported that things were going reasonably well at work and even better at home. His son and daughter-in-law who had gotten married just after he started the long-term therapy had just visited and had brought their infant daughter. He and Mrs. K. were quite excited by the prospect of being grandparents.

Summary

Effective treatment of narcissistic personality disordered individuals requires the establishment of a trusting client–clinician relationship fostered by focal treatment interventions to modify the maladaptive pattern and then maintain the new more adaptive pattern. Because these individuals may have considerable difficulty engaging in and profiting from traditional psychotherapy, an integrative-combined approach that focuses on characterological, temperament, and skill dimensions may be essential for effective treatment outcomes. The case example illustrates the common challenges that these individuals present, and the kind of clinician flexibility, resourcefulness, and level of competence required. Table 9.1 summarizes the treatment intervention strategies most likely to be effective with this disorder.

Recent research indicates that that CBT leads to symptom reduction among narcissistic personality disordered individuals with a dual diagnosis (Cukrowicz, Poindexter, & Joiner, 2011). Besides symptom improvement, additional improvements include enhanced impulse control, improved interpersonal relationships, and increased treatment compliance. Unfortunately, barriers to improved treatments with this population are due to the lack of randomized control trials that compare the efficacy of CBT versus other therapeutic modalities (Cukrowicz et al., 2011). Hopefully future research and subsequent publication will fill the gaps among the efficacy of CBT and other treatments for narcissistic personality disorder.

Table 9.1 Treatment Strategies for Narcissistic Personality Disorder

ENGAGEMENT	Present as self-assured, pretentious, and entitled to having their needs met. Appear indifferent to the clinician's perspective. Often demand mirroring and are easily narcissistically wounded.
	Tx: Mirroring and soothing
Transference	Demand support and admiration, wish to control treatment, and show intense anger at therapist's failure to meet their needs. Also, a high likelihood of withdrawing from treatment when it becomes difficult.
	Tx: Self-monitor and interpret
Countertransference	Tendency to experience boredom, distraction, and annoyance with these clients. May not be sufficiently engaged when working with them adding to the frustration. May also experience feeling ineffectual, deskilled, or invisible.
	Tx: Monitor countertransference
PATTERN ANALYSIS	*Triggers:* Evaluation of self
PATTERN CHANGE	*Treatment Goals:* increased awareness and responsiveness to others' needs
Schemas	Entitlement/self-centeredness; insufficient self-control/self-discipline; Abuse/mistrust
	Tx: Interpretation or schema change strategy
Styles/Skills	
a. *Affective Style*	Narcissistic rage
	Tx: Anger management
b. *Behavioral/ Interpersonal Style*	Empathic deficits
	Tx: Empathy training
c. *Cognitive Style*	Cognitive distortion; Projective identification; Hypervigilance
	Tx: Cognitive awareness training; Sensitivity reduction training
d. *Distress Tolerance*	Overly sensitive or intolerant of distress
	Tx: DBT—Distress tolerance training
MAINTENANCE/ TERMINATION	Premature termination
	Tx: "Join" client's entitlement

10 Obsessive-Compulsive Personality Disorder

Basically, individuals with Obsessive-Compulsive Personality Disorder are rigid, stubborn, perfectionistic, and judgmental—all factors that can impede personal change. While treatment of such individuals involves a number of unique therapeutic challenges, it can be highly effective and successful. This chapter describes a framework for effective treatment of this disorder from a cognitive behavioral perspective. It includes sections on assessment, case conceptualization, and treatment interventions. The section on assessment includes behavioral and cognitive factors, as well as a DSM-5 description and a prototypic description of this disorder. A prototype is a brief description that captures the essence of how a particular disorder commonly presents. Prototypic descriptions are useful and convenient and clinicians commonly rely on them rather than lists of behavioral criteria and core and instrumental beliefs (Westen, 2012). The section on case conceptualization provides both cognitive and behavioral formulations of this disorder. The longest section is on treatment. It emphasizes engagement, pattern analysis, pattern change, and pattern maintenance and termination strategies for effectively managing and treating this disorder. In addition to individual psychotherapeutic strategies and tactics, group, marital and family, medication, and integrative and combined treatment strategies are included. An extensive case example illustrates the treatment process.

Assessment

Behavioral

A behavioral assessment of this disorder emphasizes individual and interpersonal behaviors. Individuals with this disorder are characterized as inhibited, stubborn, perfectionistic, judgmental, overconscientious, rigid, and chronically anxious. They are likely to be workaholics. In addition to dependability, they tend to be stubborn and possessive. They can be indecisive and procrastinating. Interpersonally, these individuals are exquisitely conscious of social rank and status and modify their behavior accordingly. That is, they tend to be deferential and obsequious to superiors, and haughty and autocratic to subordinates and peers. They may insist that others do things their way, without an appreciation or awareness of how others react to their insistence. They tend to avoid intimacy and the expression of feelings. Not surprisingly, they experience little pleasure from life. While they may be successful in their work, success in relationships is seldom achieved or even possible given their perfectionism and demands on others. Often they are perceived as cold and reserved. At best, they are polite and loyal to the organizations and the ideals they espouse (Sperry, 2003).

Cognitive

This perspective emphasizes core beliefs, particularly those about their views of self and of others. Typically, they view themselves as responsible and account-able for most everything in their lives. At the same time they believe they are inadequate, helpless, or defective. They view others as incompetent, care-less, and less concerned about matters than they are. Related beliefs include needing rules and regulations in order to survive. They also believe that they must be in control and perfect, and if they fail at a task, they are a failure and worthless. Not surprisingly, such beliefs are reflected in their main strategy or pattern of exercising maximum control over themselves and others through the use of directiveness, coercion, and disapproval (Beck, 2015; Simon, 2015).

DSM-5 Description

Individuals with this personality disorder are characterized by an unremit-ting pattern of perfectionism, orderliness, and control instead of flexibility, openness, and efficiency. They are overly preoccupied with details, rules, and schedules. Their perfectionism interferes with completing tasks due to their overly strict standards. They are overly devoted to work and productivity to the exclusion of leisure activities and friendships. When it comes to matters of values, morality, or ethics, these individuals are inflexible, scrupulous, and overconscientious. Often, they are unable to discard worn-out or worthless objects that have no sentimental value. They will not delegate tasks or work with others unless it can be on their terms. Not surprisingly, these individu-als are also rigid and stubborn. Finally, they are misers with money, and it is hoarded in the event of future catastrophes (American Psychiatric Associa-tion, 2013).

Prototypic Description

These individuals are perfectionists and unyielding control freaks. They can-not rest until they get every detail exactly right. Because they insist that others can never be careful or competent enough, they never delegate or trust impor-tant matters to others. Their lives are controlled by schedules, rules, and rigid routines. Because of their scrupulous attention to details and their projects, they cannot relax, be spontaneous, or enjoy close and intimate relationships. They are unusually tight with money, feelings, and affection. They make it clear they must always have their way or else (Frances, 2013).

Case Conceptualization

Beck (2015) identified some schemas held by obsessive-compulsive individuals: perfectionism and control. The perfectionism scheme involves beliefs such as: "To be worthwhile I must avoid making mistakes because to make a mistake is to fail which would be intolerable," and "If the perfect course of action is unclear, it is better to do nothing." The control scheme involves beliefs such as: "I must be perfectly in control of myself and my environment, because loss of control is intolerable and dangerous." "Without my rules and rituals, I'll collapse into an inert pile." "Magical rituals or obsessive ruminations prevent the occurrence of catastrophes."

Guidano and Liotti (1983) provide a similar but different cognitive formulation which involves three maladaptive schemas. They are: perfectionism, the need for certainty, and the belief that there is an absolute correct solution for human problems. Guidano and Liotti note that these individuals received mixed, contradictory messages from at least one parent. They also describe typical automatic thoughts of obsessive-compulsive individuals. "I need to get this assignment done perfectly"; "I have to do this project myself or it won't be done right"; "That person misbehaved and should be punished"; and "I should keep these old reports because I might need them some day." In addition to these schemas and automatic thoughts, individuals with this personality pattern often utilize the cognitive distortions of dichotomous thinking and magnification or catastrophizing.

Turkat (1990) and Turkat and Maisto (1985) suggest a behavioral formulation of this pattern. These individuals are noted to have been reared in families that emphasized productivity and rule-following at the expense of emotional expressivity and interpersonal relationships. Accordingly, these individuals did not acquire adequate levels of empathy skills or skills in interacting with others on an emotional basis.

Treatment

Engagement Strategies

Early Session Behavior

The characteristic features of circumstantiality, perfectionism, and ambivalence make interviewing obsessive-compulsive individuals difficult and challenging. Their preoccupation with details and their need for control often results in a seemingly endless struggle about facts, issues, and power struggles. Clinicians who persist in asking open-ended questions will note that while they become frustrated, obsessive-compulsive individuals become confused. These patients are better able to handle more focused questions, although they have a tendency to interpret them too narrowly. They may bring copies of past treatment records or a notebook that details their medical history, diet, and exercise pattern, and possibly their dreams. Usually, they expect the clinician to review these documents or topics in detail. Because these details are important to the obsessive-compulsive's self-definition, it is important that the clinician acknowledges this offer rather than dismissing it. Expressing affects are difficult because these individuals believe emotional expression is dangerous or at least suspect. Although they may admit that affects are associated with details, they will discount the value of expressing those affects, much less talking about them. Furthermore, it is difficult for them to overcome their ambivalence because they will not easily accept the clinician's assurance that their problems are solvable or that relinquishing control of their life is tolerable (Sperry, 2006).

Because they insist they are objective and have no feelings, they are perturbed at the clinician's expression of empathy and reject it as irrelevant. The clinician's only effective therapeutic leverage with these patients is to get and keep them in touch with their anger and other affects. Initially, they will defend against or deny these affects, and use additional obsessionality to neutralize such therapeutic leverage. In sum, forming a therapeutic alliance is difficult and early sessions may consist of aborted attempts, frustrations and struggles (Othmer & Othmer, 2002).

Facilitating Collaboration

True collaboration is extremely difficult to achieve early in the course of treatment of the obsessive-compulsive personality disorder. Rather, pseudo-collaboration tends to occur quickly. *Pseudo-collaboration* refers to behaviors that, at first, may appear to be collaborative and cooperative behaviors but are not. These patients may appear to be eager to be "model" patients and attempt to please the clinician by being "prepared" for sessions. For example, they may come to sessions with lists of items that they are prepared to discuss, diaries that detail dreams, and the like, or they may have overachieved on a between-session or homework assignment. However, the veneer of their "collaboration" is quickly revealed when the clinician endeavors to ask about their feelings and fears, or attempts to focus on the present rather than the past. Typically, they will resist requests to share affects and are uncomfortable commenting on the "here and now" of the clinician–patient relationship. Such responses are reflective of their ambivalence, the need to please vs. the need to control, as well as their belief that life is unpredictable and so they must take control or, at least, resist efforts to be controlled. For the obsessive-compulsive individual, rational expression is much more predictable and comfortable than expression of affects, which are much less predictable and comfortable. Whereas facts can bolster their perceived sense of self-worth, feelings threaten to embarrass or even injure them. Similarly, the individual will "structure" sessions with their planned agenda to reduce the unpredictable.

True collaboration will occur only when the obsessive-compulsive individual experiences minimal threat in treatment. Accordingly, the clinician is advised to establish a "collaborative contract," which is based on the patient's goal for treatment. The goal, a method for achieving the goal, and specific role expectations for both clinician and individual are stated (Sperry, 2003). For example, the patient's goal might be "to increase my efficiency," while problem solving is indicated as the primary treatment strategy or method to achieve the goal. A problem-solving treatment strategy is an excellent way of operationalizing the collaborative contract. It consists of stating a goal or analyzing a problem, identifying options, weighing the options, deciding on a course of action, and then implementing it. Besides being effective, this treatment strategy is usually quite acceptable to the obsessive individual since it is rational and is relatively nonthreatening. In addition, the clinician needs to structure sessions in such a way that threat is minimized and treatment goals can be achieved. This means focusing on one topic at a time and confronting resistances as they arise. Not surprisingly, the cognitive-behavioral approach is well suited for working with obsessive-compulsive patients.

Transference and Countertransference

Predictable transference and countertransference problems are noted in treating obsessive-compulsive personality disordered individuals. Perhaps the most common transference involve their tendency to engage in rambling speech, often in a monotone. The defenses of intellectualization and isolation of affect are commonly noted. In the process, they wander from their original point and create an "anesthetizing cloud," which serves both as a smoke screen to mask their feelings and to sidetrack the clinician's attention (Gabbard, 2005). Not surprisingly, the related countertransference to this rambling is boredom, daydreaming, and disengagement. Sometimes, these monologues may have high interest for the clinician, and the clinician may be tempted to reinforce or collude with the patient's intellectualization and isolation of affect. The clinician does well to interrupt, interpret, or redirect these rambling accounts. Saying "Let's just stop for a moment. What are you feeling right now?" can refocus and set the stage for interpreting resistance.

For some obsessive-compulsive patients, clinical and transference interpretations can be quite threatening and are consequently vigorously resisted. A related transference involves individual discounting of the clinician's interpretations (Gabbard, 2005). The individual may quickly respond to an interpretation saying it is completely wrong or that he's thought about or heard it before and didn't agree with it then or now. The clinician's countertransference may range from self-doubt and cautiousness to anger and hostility at the patient's impertinence and unappreciativeness.

Pattern Analysis Strategies

Pattern analysis with obsessive-compulsive individuals involves an accurate diagnostic and clinical evaluation of schemas, styles, and triggering stressors, as well as level of functioning and readiness for therapeutic change. Knowledge of the optimal DSM-5 criterion along with the maladaptive pattern of the individual is not only useful in specifying diagnosis but also in planning treatment that is tailored to the obsessive-compulsive patient's unique style, needs, and circumstances. The optimal criterion specified for the obsessive-compulsive personality disorder is showing perfectionism that interferes with task completion (Allnutt & Links, 1996). Both planned treatment goals and interventions should reflect this theme of perfectionism.

Pattern refers to the predictable and consistent style and manner in which an individual thinks, feels, acts, copes and defends the self. Pattern analysis involves both the triggers and response—the "what"—as well as an explanatory statement—the "why"—about the pattern of a given obsessive-compulsive patient. Obviously, such a clinical formulation specifies the *particular* schemas and temperamental styles unique to a given individual rather than the more *general* clinical formulation that will be noted here (Sperry, 2006).

Triggers

Generally speaking, the "triggers" or "triggering" situations for obsessive-compulsive patients are stressors related to authority, unstructured situations, or close relationships (Othmer & Othmer, 2002). This means that when obsessive-compulsive-disordered individuals are engaging in behaviors, discussing, or even thinking about the demands of authority figures or close relationships or being in situations where expectations for them are unclear and they become distressed, their disordered or maladaptive pattern is likely to be triggered and characteristic symptomatic affects, behaviors, and cognitions are likely to be experienced or exhibited.

Schemas

Generally speaking, the underlying schemas involve a self-view of being responsible for not making errors, and a view of the world as overly demanding and unpredictable (Sperry & Mosak, 1996). Among the most frequently encountered schemas in obsessive-compulsive patients is the unrelenting/unbalanced schema. Occasionally, the emotional inhibition schema is also observed. The *unrelenting/unbalanced schema* refers to the core set of beliefs about the relentless striving to meet high flown expectations of oneself at the expense of happiness, health, and satisfying relationships. The *emotional inhibition schema* refers to the core set of beliefs that emotions and impulses must be inhibited in order not to lose self-esteem or harm others (Bricker, Young, & Flanagan, 1993; Young, Klosko, & Weishaar, 2003).

Style/Temperament

There are four unique style dimensions in the ABCDEF Profile that characterize individuals with this personality disorder: Affective, Behavioral-interpersonal, Cognitive, and Distress Tolerance. Individuals with Obsessive-Compulsive Personality Disorder have an affective style that is characterized by constriction expression. They tend to be grim and seldom express positive feelings or smile. Their cognitive style is ruminative and overly reflective, which predisposes them to preoccupation with details and minutia as well as worry. Behaviorally, their style is rigid and calculating, which, together with their ruminative style, predisposes them to procrastination and indecisiveness. Relationally, they are inhibited and ill at ease. Often, they are also deficient in empathy and other interpersonal skills (Sperry, 2003). They also tend to be distress overtolerant, which means that they can tolerate high levels of distress that results in adverse long-term consequences (Lynch & Mizon, 2011). Overall, their pattern reflects an internalizing disorder.

Pattern Change Strategies

At the outset of treatment, it would not be unusual for obsessive-compulsive individuals to have as their personal goal of treatment to become asymptomatic and more productive while retaining their maladaptive pattern. This contrasts with the therapeutic treatment goal, which is to change the maladaptive pattern. More specifically, the general treatment goal for obsessive-compulsive individuals is to achieve balance between perfectionism and drivenness and being easy going and carefree, to become introspective without preoccupation and rumination, and to better tolerate the humanness they observe in themselves and others. In other words, the goal is to "think less and feel more," which is the converse of the goal for the histrionic personality disorder (Sperry, 2006).

Treatment begins after the maladaptive pattern has been identified and analyzed in terms of schemas, style, and skill deficits. The therapeutic process involves relinquishing that pattern and replacing it with a more adaptive pattern. This pattern change process involves modifying schemas, modulating style dysregulations, and reversing skill deficits. The process of modifying the maladaptive schemas usually follows efforts to modify style and skill-deficit dimensions because schema change early in the course of treatment is often resisted by the patient. It is for this reason that, as noted in the section on facilitating collaboration, treatment should begin by using a problem-solving treatment strategy. This strategy is not only effective in establishing a collaborative relationship, but also for making initial changes in pattern. This strategy is greatly appreciated by obsessive patients because it is rational and systematic and is much less threatening and anxiety-producing than dynamic or experiential intervention strategies (Sperry, 2006).

Schema Change

The unrelenting/unbalanced standards and emotional inhibition schemas are supported by such injunctive beliefs as "Nothing I do is really good enough, I must always do better"; "I need to be in total control of my feelings"; "Details are extremely important"; "If I don't perform at the highest possible level, I'm a failure"; and "Mistakes, errors, and defects are absolutely intolerable" (Beck, Davis, & Freeman, 2015; Young et al., 2003).

In the schema change process, the clinician and individual work collaboratively to understand the developmental roots of the maladaptive schemas. Then, these schemas are tested through predictive experiments, guided observation, and reenactment of early schema-related incidents. Finally, obsessive-compulsive patients are directed to begin to notice and remember counter-schema data about themselves and their social experiences.

Style/Temperament Change

Because obsessive-compulsive individuals are characterized by an affective style of constriction and isolation of affect, emotional awareness training can be an effective intervention. Thought-stopping training can be useful in reducing ruminative thinking. Furthermore, because these patients tend to have behavioral and relational styles that are somewhat inhibited and stiff, and often have deficits in empathy, interpersonal skills training and empathy training may be indicated. Furthermore, activity scheduling (Freeman, Pretzer, Fleming, & Simon, 1990; Klosko & Young, 2004) can be effectively used in reducing procrastination and better managing time.

Medication Strategies

Currently, there are no psychotropic medications specifically indicated for treating this personality disorder (Silk & Feurino, 2012). Nevertheless, medications are used that target specific troubling symptoms associated with the disorder, such as depression, anxiety, or sleep problems. Generally, these medication are used as an adjunct to psychotherapy and skills training. Because troubling symptoms often respond to medications sooner than most psychological interventions, medications are usually prescribed at the onset of treatment (Sperry, 1995b). Unfortunately, there is little research evidence to provide guidelines for the use of such medications (Silk & Feurino, 2012).

Group Treatment Strategies

A major deficit of this disorder is the inability to share tenderly and spontaneously with others. Thus, group treatment can be particularly useful with obsessive-compulsive patients. Nevertheless, because these patients tend to be competitive and controlling, certain complications can arise which the clinician would do well to keep in mind. For instance, these patients will dominate a group with their rambling and excessive speech patterns if not redirected. Because they may initially experience the affective atmosphere in a group to be overwhelming, they may become more socially isolated or intellectually detached. Thus, the clinician does well to intervene to avoid unnecessary power struggles. When this is accomplished, these patients are usually able to vicariously model the emotional expressiveness of others in the group (Sperry, 2006).

Group therapy offers a number of advantages over individual therapy for the obsessive-compulsive patients. First, this personality pattern tends to make the individual therapy process tedious, difficult, and unrewarding, particularly early in treatment when clinicians commonly err with premature interpretations or behavioral prescriptions. Second, the group process tends to diffuse the intensity of the obsessive-compulsive patient's impact, particularly in a heterogeneous group. Third, group treatment also tends to neutralize transferences and countertransferences because patients more easily accept feedback from peers than from a clinician. Finally, group therapy activates these patients into "experiencing" their problems rather than just talking about them (Wells, Glickhauf-Hughes, & Buzzel, 1990).

There are, however, some contraindications for outpatient group therapy for obsessive-compulsive patients: severe depression or high suicidality; impulsive dyscontrol; strong paranoid propensities; acute crisis; difficulty in establishing trust; fear of relinquishing obsessive-compulsive defenses; the need to establish superiority; and the use of "pseudo insight" to avoid dealing with both hostile and tender feelings (Wells et al., 1990). Nevertheless, such patients or other lower functioning obsessive-compulsive patients may still be candidates for skill-oriented group treatment in partial hospital or day programs.

Wells et al. (1990) described a group treatment approach that is well-suited for obsessive-compulsive patients. This approach combines both interpersonal and psychodynamic interventions. The treatment process involves the following goals: modifying cognitive style, resolving control issues, expanding decision-making and action-taking capacity, modifying harsh superego, increasing comfort with emotional expression, and modifying interpersonal style.

Marital and Family Therapy Strategies

Harbir (1981) reported that obsessive-compulsive individuals usually agree to family treatment because close family members have become angry with their rigidity, procrastination, constricted affect, perfectionism, and pessimistic outlook. Likewise, the obsessive-compulsive individual may agree to couples therapy only after being threatened with divorce by their partner. Often, a threat of separation or divorce may be the only motivation to start treatment. The anxiety of the complaining partner may be the only leverage for treatment, and the clinician may need to work with that partner to deal more effectively with the other partner's obsessive-compulsive personality pattern.

Clinical experience suggests that obsessive-compulsive individuals tend to marry histrionic individuals (Sperry & Maniacci, 1998).

Salzman (1989) noted that obsessive-compulsive patients who are highly anxious may be unable to participate in marital or family therapy until their anxiety has been sufficiently quelled in individual psychotherapy or combined psychotherapy and pharmacological treatment. Even when excessive anxiety is not particularly bothersome, these patients can be tyrants in family sessions, and may immobilize other family members to such an extent that treatment is jeopardized. When this occurs, structural and strategic intervention directed at redistributing power may be particularly advantageous in such situations (Sperry, 2003).

Combined and Integrated Treatment Strategies

Salzman (1989) contended that a combined/integrated approach is essential in the treatment of the obsessive-compulsive disorder, particularly for moderately severe cases. He insisted that the various treatment modalities and methods must be viewed as mutually inclusive rather than mutually exclusive.

Combined treatments tend to be more effective when based on a protocol. Because high levels of anxiety or depression will limit participation in psychotherapy, an appropriate trial of medication may be necessary at the onset of treatment. When rituals or obsessions are prominent, specific behavior interventions are probably indicated. The dynamics of perfectionism, indecisiveness, and isolation of affect are best addressed with specific psychotherapeutic interventions. Decisions about the use of individual, group, or a modality, or a combination of modalities should be based on severity of the disorder, particular treatment targets, and specific contraindications to treatments (Sperry, 1995a, 2006).

In short, a fuller understanding and appreciation of the obsessive-compulsive personality usually requires an integration of several modalities because "the resolution of the disabling disorder demands cognitive clarity plus behavioral and physiologic alterations. Each modality alone deals with only a piece of the puzzle. A therapist who can combine all these approaches will be the most effective" (Salzman, 1989, p. 2782).

Pattern Maintenance and Termination Strategies

Termination Issues

Just as establishing a collaborative relationship with obsessive-compulsive patients can be extremely difficult, so also is terminating treatment. Assuming they have achieved some level of balance between being perfectionistic and driven and being easy going and carefree, terminating treatment can be considered. Unfortunately, ambivalence, which is a core feature of the obsessive-compulsive pattern, is commonly observed during the termination process.

Initially, these patients may press to leave treatment and function on their own. Soon thereafter, they begin expressing great reluctance to relinquish the security of therapy for the exigencies of the real world until there is absolute certainty that insurmountable problems will not occur. Consequently, they will insist on remaining in treatment. Salzman (1980) contended that these patients cannot be relied on to initiate discussion or press for termination. The clinician task is to raise the issue of readiness for termination, and then coax and prod them into the real world. Nevertheless, termination must be a gradual and empirical process. Unlike the fixed, planned termination date that might be established with the dependent personality disordered patient, some measure of flexibility is more therapeutic with the obsessive-compulsive patients. After all, clinicians' insistence on setting strict deadlines and appointment scheduling is really an enactment of the rigidity and perfectionism that they are trying to modify in these patients.

Reducing the length of a session or spacing out sessions over a reasonable period of time allows these patients to more safely reenter the real world. This reduction can begin when patients become comfortable enough to accept some uncertainty and reverses in their lives without experiencing intolerable symptoms. For many obsessive-compulsive patients, the termination process can be expected to engender anxiety and/or somatic symptoms. They must come to understand and accept that such symptoms will occasionally occur throughout life and that treatment does not guarantee symptom-free living (Sperry, 2006).

Relapse Prevention Strategies

After treatment is formally terminated, the option for occasional appointments or even brief contacts during times of crisis should be discussed. Some obsessive-compulsive patients will appreciate the offer of one or more planned follow-up visits in the subsequent 12 months. The hope, however, is that these patients will be able to function as their own clinicians. To this end, it is helpful for clinicians and patients to collaboratively develop a plan of self-therapy and relapse prevention following termination. It is recommended that these individuals set aside an hour a week to engage in activities that continue the progress made in formal treatment. They might work on selected exercises. They might look ahead at the coming week and predict which situations could be troublesome. The goal of such effort is to maintain treatment gains, particularly their newly acquired pattern. They should expect to cope much more effectively than prior to treatment because they have developed sufficient personal and relational skills to be introspective, without preoccupation and rumination, and to tolerate more of the humanness they observe in themselves and others. And when they find themselves slipping or regressing, they will know how to refocus and redirect themselves (Sperry, 2006).

The relapse plan will help them analyze specific external situations (such as persons, times, places) and internal states (such as specific obsessive-compulsive beliefs and fears) and other vulnerabilities that increase the likelihood of them responding with obsessive-compulsive behavior in the face of predictable triggers. Once predicted, a contingency plan to deal with these stressors can be developed. Clinicians may find it useful to have patients answer these questions: What can I do if I find myself ruminating? What should I do if I start placing unreasonable demands or expectations on others to be more perfect? What should I do if I start believing my old obsessive-compulsive beliefs more than my new beliefs? What should I do if I relapse? Finally, because relational demands, unstructured situations, and authority issues can trigger the obsessive-compulsive pattern, the relapse plan should also include provisions for increasing and maintaining playfulness and spontaneity (Sperry, 2006).

Case of Warren

Warren G. is a 41-year-old, married accountant who presented with his wife, Kristy G., for couples therapy. They have been married for 19 years and have an 18-year-old son who would soon be finishing high school and moving away to attend college. He complained of worsening insomnia and decreased energy. In addition, he became increasingly anxious in driving across bridges and taking escalators, especially glass elevators. He reports having to drive out of his way to get to his office building, and when there he would walk up seven flights of stairs to reach his office. He had been prescribed Ativan by his family physician but rarely used it fearing he would become addicted.

Warren reported significant strains in the marriage. He was concerned with his wife's safety, noting that she seemed more depressed and hopeless. He described Kristy as increasingly moody, unpredictable, and given to outbursts, which frustrated and frightened him. She would pursue him relentlessly with demands and all he could do was clam up and retreat. He hesitatingly admitted that it was a relief to stay late at his office so as not to face her fury. Lately, he feared he might lose his mind if this continued. His only display of emotion in the entire interview occurred then: He was briefly silent as tears welled in his eyes, but then he quickly regained composure.

Comprehensive Assessment and Diagnosis. A comprehensive diagnostic and functional assessment was completed. Warren met DSM-5 criteria for Other Specified Depressive Disorder as well as Obsessive-Compulsive Personality Disorder. Figure 10.1 portrays Warren's ABCDEF Profile.

Engagement Process—Warren

As part of the evaluation phase of couples therapy, he was scheduled for an individual evaluation session. During this session he seemed more at ease discussing concerns about the marriage than he was in the conjoint session. Nevertheless, he was somewhat reluctant in disclosing personal information. He was a methodical historian of the various details of his life. He spoke in a slow,

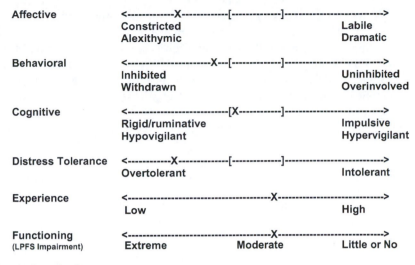

Affective	<------------X------------[-------------]----------------------------------->
	Constricted Labile
	Alexithymic Dramatic

Affective   Constricted / Alexithymic — Labile / Dramatic

Behavioral   Inhibited / Withdrawn — Uninhibited / Overinvolved

Cognitive   Rigid/ruminative / Hypovigilant — Impulsive / Hypervigilant

Distress Tolerance   Overtolerant — Intolerant

Experience   Low — High

Functioning (LPFS Impairment)   Extreme — Moderate — Little or No

[---------] = *adaptive range*

Figure 10.1 ABCDEF Profile of Obsessive-Compulsive Personality Disorder: Case of Warren

deliberate monotone with little change in affect or mood. In addition to couples therapy, individual therapy was suggested to help Warren understand the marriage relationship and the effect it was having on him. Initially, he balked at individual sessions stating that he was more concerned with his wife's well-being, and that she was his first priority. Recognizing that Warren was likely resisting individual treatment believing that he must be dutiful and unselfish, the clinician made the following observations: while it was commendable for Warren to put his wife's concerns first, Warren also had worsening symptoms that were greatly worrisome to his wife. The clinician gently reminded Warren that during their conjoint session Kristy had hoped that he would be receptive to individual sessions. Furthermore, the clinician emphasized that focusing on these matters from two perspectives, individual work and couples work, would be the most "efficient" approach. Warren liked that concept and agreed to the plan.

Engagement Process—Couple

It seemed clear that both partners wanted and needed help. However, because Kristy had been in long-term psychiatric treatment and so was perceived as a "patient," the clinician thought it necessary and useful to socialize Kristy and Warren to a systems perspective for the conjoint treatment. It was framed that neither of them were "sick" and that each was simply expressing in his or her characteristic style what neither had "permission" or "ability" to say with his or her mouth. Both responded favorably to this perspective. Warren was fascinated by the prospect that anything could occur beyond one's control. He knew it happened, he had seen it at work many times, but he never thought any such process would be going on in him without his knowing. Kristy was amused by his comment and pointed out that if he "knew" he was doing such things, he wouldn't be able to do them. She beamed at the clinician, as if waiting for a reward or praise. It was also framed that neither was "crazy" but, rather, both were attempting to communicate with the other. Not only did the receiving partner not understand the communication, the sending partner was not completely aware of the message. Thus, the first task of treatment was to accept responsibility for sending the message, that is, acknowledge that a message was being sent, and to then clarify the message. Only then, could each decide how to respond favorably to the message being sent.

Pattern Analysis—Warren

Warren described his childhood as "reasonably good," but went on to describe his father as a violent alcoholic with unpredictable mood swings, and his mother as a long-suffering woman who leaned on Warren as her sole support. Warren had a younger sister who had cerebral palsy, and he recalled his father's frequent threats to institutionalize her. He took it on as his mission to keep her out of an institution and so became her surrogate parent, teacher, and friend. He worked outside the home from the age of 15. His first job had been on a loading dock amid much squalor. These experiences led him to vow to make a better life for himself, and never lose his temper nor to drink like his father. He eventually completed a GED, went to college, studied for and passed his CPA exam, and found employment with a small accounting firm. Although he agreed that he worked too many hours, he liked his job. Although there was little room for upward mobility there, he was proud that his boss entrusted him with complicated and sensitive projects that no one else could do as well as he.

His earliest memory occurred when he was on the fire escape of the family apartment at the age of five. As he was admiring the view he heard a scream. His mother rushed out and pulled him back into the apartment, yelling that it was too dangerous to be out on the fire escape. He felt confused but vowed to be more careful and never to upset her again.

Needless to say, Warren grew up believing that he had to be careful and conscientious or bad things would happen. Gradually, the line between conscientiousness and control began to blur, and unless he controlled his, and others', lives, he sensed an uneasy, impending doom. His solution was to work harder, to control more, and to be more careful. The only dispensation he allowed himself from this rigid agenda was illness. By being afraid of heights and unable to sleep, he could ask for a break and take some time for himself without having to admit that he was shirking responsibility.

An evaluation of Warren's developmental history and clinical observation of interactions with Kristy indicated an obsessive-compulsive pattern. His pattern was notable for both the unrelenting/unbalanced and the emotional inhibition schemas. Style dimensions such as constricted affect, rigidity, empathic and interpersonal deficits, and analytic, ruminative cognitive style also suggested obsessive-compulsive pattern. Because of his own willingness and efforts to make personal and relational changes, his motivation and readiness for treatment was rated as high.

Concise Case Conceptualization. Warren's increased insomnia, decreased energy, phobic fears, and marital distress (**presentation**) appear to be his reaction to relentless demands from his wife and the anticipated loss of companionship with his son who would soon leave for college (**precipitant**). Throughout his life, Warren has striven to achieve, be conscientious, avoid mistakes, and restrict emotional expression in order to feel worthwhile as a person (**pattern**). This conscientiousness and emotional distancing is a problematic pattern for him and has negatively affected his relationship with his wife whom he increasingly avoids. It is an internalizing pattern assessed as "moderate impairment" on the Level of Personality Functioning Scale. His pattern is understandable in light of his core beliefs, skill deficits, and biological vulnerability. He views himself as hardworking, righteous, and responsible, but defective. He views others as unpredictable, overly demanding, and irresponsible. As a result, he remains vigilant and conscientious and attempts to control situations and ward off feelings of doom. He was reared by parents who were overly demanding, has had a limited social network all of his life, and lacks key social skills including relational skills, self-soothing, and stress management. His sleep problems and low energy may suggest depression for which he is biologically predisposed (**perpetuants**). Furthermore, his pattern is maintained and reinforced by his overconscientiousness and social withdrawal. A more adaptive pattern would be for Warren to become more reasonably conscientious while remaining emotionally present. Treatment goals and interventions are discussed in subsequent paragraphs (**treatment goal**).

Pattern Analysis—Couple

The interlocking dynamics gradually became clear to them. Kristy's depression was reframed as a way of asking to be cared for, and her "moodiness" as her trying to keep the relationship together. She valued love and the marriage and family, and she wanted them to be happy. She was trying to keep them together, and to look out for her husband and his health. Warren was trying to keep his family together too, and his long work hours were reframed as his way of showing caring and concern. In effect, they were told that their symptoms were serving the same purpose, just in different ways. The challenge for both of them was to communicate their desires in more direct, constructive ways.

Pattern Change—Couple

Pattern change involved rebalancing their relationship pattern. This proved exceedingly challenging, because power was rather evenly distributed: Warren was aloof, didactic, and in charge, until Kristy became upset and "hysterical," at which point she would regain power of the relationship. Then, Warren would calm the situation by arranging things the way she wanted. In the process, he would organize and structure the necessary changes and, thus, assume power again. She would allow this until she felt he cared more about his work than hers, after which and she would grow impatient, become upset, and the cyclic pattern would repeat itself. This cyclical pattern was pointed out to them. Warren immediately grasped it and its ramifications, but Kristy found it harder to comprehend. The clinician's verbal explanation was well-suited to Warren's analytic style, but did not match Kristy's more global-impressionistic style. Furthermore, their maladaptive cyclic pattern was being enacted in the session. Warren shifted into his parental mode and began lecturing her, whereas Kristy shifted into her child mode and tried but couldn't follow his explanation. At that point the clinician graphically illustrated their interaction pattern and Kristy was then able to readily grasp it.

Boundaries and intimacy were not as easily addressed. A triangle existed, with their son vacillating between being a husband-surrogate for his mother when Warren was away from home, to his acting like a friend to his father when Warren was home. His presence both fueled the maladaptive cyclic pattern and perpetuated the very problems that, without his presence, might lead to some kind of resolution. The next several weeks of conjoint treatment focused on these issues. While there might be value in switching to a family therapy mode, there were inherent dangers as well. Introducing the son into conjoint sessions would perpetuate the very issue he was helping to maintain: intruding on the couple's relationship. Instead, efforts were undertaken to strengthen the couple's bond without the son in the session. Interpersonal skills training was begun. One component of the training was for the couple to go out on a date after each session. Relating intimately had been problematic for Warren because of deficits in empathic responding. Accordingly, three conjoint sessions focused on empathy training. In addition, the clinician framed to Warren that his son needed to "have space to find himself," while Warren needed to expand his own social network. To Kristy, it was framed that by encouraging her son to "separate," she would be strengthening both her marriage as well as her son's future. Both agreed to a "weaning" process that was aided by the son's move out of the city to attend college.

Warren's controlling behavior and Kristy's emotionality were mutually complementary. She was encouraged to "teach" him to be more passionate, and he was urged to be her consultant on matters of organization. They grasped this way of working and though they still experienced some conflict they were able to become more affectionate with each other.

Pattern Change—Warren

A brief course of cognitive–behavior therapy for his phobic issues—with his wife as coach—worked very well. Within a short time, he found himself crossing bridges and riding escalators and elevators with relatively little or no anxiety. Similarly, a psychoeducational approach to insomnia was introduced. By modifying his evening schedule and attending to other aspects of sleep hygiene, his chronic insomnia was gradually replaced with restful sleep within 3 weeks. Efforts to modulate his constricted affect and reverse his interpersonal and empathic deficits were addressed in conjoint sessions. Thought-stopping training was used in individual sessions and in prescribed homework to modulate and better control his ruminations. Finally, schema change strategies were used to modify his unrelenting/unbalanced and the emotional inhibition schemas.

Pattern Maintenance and Termination—Couple and Warren

As Kristy's dysthymia became more under her control, she experienced more satisfaction in her relationship with Warren. He was encouraged to go into business for himself, and after some hesitancy, he did. He began to work out of his home, and within 6 months his accounting practice was thriving. He gained greater control over his schedule, worked less hours and more efficiently, and found more pleasure at home. These dynamics were worked on in individual and couple therapy. After 30 conjoint sessions over a period of 14 months, the couple progressed to the point of conjoint quarterly follow-up sessions. Kristy also has individual quarterly follow-up sessions. Warren has scheduled occasional individual follow-up sessions to reflect on the level of balance in his life. Each reports considerably more satisfaction with the marriage and minimal conflict. Warren has learned to be less rigidly controlling, and Kristy, while still somewhat dramatic, feels more connected and valued.

Summary

Effective treatment of obsessive-compulsive personality disorder requires that these individuals become sufficiently committed to a treatment process that is tailored and focused on modifying their maladaptive obsessive-compulsive pattern. Because these patients tend to have considerable difficulty engaging in and profiting from traditional psychotherapy, an integrative-combined approach that focuses on characterological, temperament, and skill dimensions is usually essential for effective treatment outcomes. The

Table 10.1 Treatment Strategies for Obsessive-Compulsive Personality Disorder

ENGAGEMENT	Tendency to defer to therapist and be a "perfect" client. May brings in a list or records and talks except "soft" feelings. Appears eager to engage in treatment process, but "holds back."
	Tx: Establish collaborative contract based on patient's goal and confront resistances. Structure sessions with a problem-solving focus
Transference	Tendency to ramble and get off track. Resists "loosening-up." May use job or school as a means to avoid sessions. Attempts to control sessions. May express rage, and may discount therapist.
	Tx: Interrupt, interpret, and/or redirect
Countertransference	Therapists may not feel engaged or involved in sessions. Instead, will experience feelings of annoyance, boredom, withdrawal, or anger. Unlikely to find these clients exciting to work with.
	Tx: Self-monitor
PATTERN ANALYSIS	*Triggers:* Authority; Unstructured situations; Close relationships
PATTERN CHANGE	*Treatment Goals:* "Think less, feel more"; Less perfectionistic; More spontaneous and playful
Schema/Character	Unrelenting/unbalanced standards schema; Emotional inhibition schema
	Tx: Schema change strategy; Confrontation; Interpretation
Styles/Skills	
a. *Affective Style*	Constricted/isolated affect
	Tx: Emotional awareness training
b. *Behavioral/Relational Style*	Procrastination; Empathic deficits; Rigidity; Interpersonal deficits
	Tx: Activity scheduling; Empathy training; Interpersonal skills training
c. *Cognitive Style*	Ruminative; Reflective
	Tx: Thought-stopping training
d. *Distress Tolerance*	Distress overtolerant
	Tx: RO-DBT-Distress Tolerance training
MAINTENANCE/ TERMINATION	Ambivalence about termination
	Tx: Wean and space out sessions

case example illustrated the common challenges that these patients present, and the kind of clinician flexibility and competence as well as treatment resources required. It also demonstrated the process of combining individual therapy with couples therapy for the treatment of a couple in which both presented with two different personality disorders. Table 10.1 summarizes the treatment intervention strategies most likely to be effective with this disorder.

References

Adler, A. (1956). *The individual psychology of Alfred Adler*. H. Ansbacher & R. Ansbacher (Eds.). New York, NY: Harper & Row.

Alden, L. (1992). Cognitive–interpersonal treatment of avoidant personality disorder. In P. Keller & S. Heyman (Eds.), *Innovations in clinical practice: A sourcebook* (vol. 2, pp. 5–20). Sarasota, FL: Professional Resources Exchange.

Allen, D. (1977). Basic treatment issues. In M. Horowitz (Ed.), *Hysterical personality* (pp. 283–328). New York, NY: Jason Aronson.

Allnutt, S., & Links, P.S. (1996). Diagnosing specific personality disorders and the optimal criteria. In P.S. Links (Ed.), *Clinical assessment and management of the severe personality disorders* (pp. 21–47). Washington, DC: American Psychiatric Press.

Alonso, A. (1997). The shattered mirror: Treatment of a group of narcissistic patients. *Group, 16*, 210–219.

American Psychiatric Association. (2013). *Diagnostic and statistical manual of mental disorders* (5th ed.). Alexandria, VA: Author.

Arntz, A. (2015). Borderline personality disorder. In A. Beck, D. Davis, & A. Freeman (Eds.) *Cognitive therapy of personality disorders* (3rd ed., pp. 366–392). New York, NY: Guilford.

Barlow, D., & Waddell, M. (1985). Agoraphobia. In D. Barlow (Ed.), *Clinical handbook of psychological disorders: A step-by-step treatment manual* (pp. 1–68). New York, NY: Guilford.

Baumeister, R., Vohs, K., & Tice, D. (2007). The strength model of self-control. *Current Directions in Psychological Science, 16*, 351–355.

Beck, A. (1964). Thinking and depression: II: Theory and therapy. *Archives of General Psychiatry, 10*, 561–571.

Beck, A. (1976). *Cognitive therapy and the emotional disorders*. New York, NY: International Universities Press.

Beck, A. (2015). Theory of personality disorders. In A. Beck, D. Davis, & A. Freeman (Eds.) *Cognitive therapy of personality disorders* (3rd ed., pp. 19–62). New York, NY: Guilford.

Beck, A., Freeman, A., & Associates (1990) *Cognitive therapy of personality disorders*. New York, NY: Guilford Press.

Beck, A., Freeman, A., Davis, D., & Associates. (2004). *Cognitive therapy of personality disorders* (2nd ed.). New York, NY: Guilford.

Beck, A., Davis, D., & Freeman, A. (Eds.) (2015). *Cognitive therapy of personality disorders* (3rd ed.). New York, NY: Guilford.

Beck, J. (1997). Personality disorders: Cognitive approaches. In. L. Dickstein, M. Riba, & J. Oldham (Eds.). *American Psychiatric Press review of psychiatry* (pp. 46–73). Washington, DC: American Psychiatric Press.

Behary, W., & Davis., D. (2015). Narcissistic personality disorder. In A. Beck, D. Davis, & A. Freeman (Eds.) *Cognitive therapy of personality disorders* (3rd ed., pp. 299–324). New York, NY: Guilford.

Beitman, B. (1991). Medication during psychotherapy: Case studies of the reciprocal relationship between psychotherapy process and medication use. In B. Beitman & G. Klerman (Eds.), *Integrating pharmacotherapy and psychotherapy* (pp. 21–44). Washington, DC: American Psychiatric Press.

Beitman, B., Blinder, B., Thase, M., Riba, M., & Safer D. (2003). *Integrating psychotherapy and pharmacotherapy: Dissolving the mind-brain barrier.* New York, NY: Norton.

Beitman, B., & Yue, D. (1999). *Learning psychotherapy.* New York, NY: Norton.

Bilsen, H. V., & Thomson, B. (2011). *CBT for personality disorders.* Thousand Oaks, CA: Sage

Bishop, S. (2002). What do we really know about mindfulness-based stress reduction? *Psychosomatic Medicine, 64,* 71–84.

Black, D., Zanarini, M., Romine, A., Shaw, M., Allen, J., & Schulz, S. (2014). Comparison of low and moderate doses of extended-release quetiapine in borderline personality disorder: A randomized, double-blind, placebo-controlled trial. *American Journal of Psychiatry, 171,* 1174–1182.

Bo, E., Stringer, D., & Clark, L. (2012). The schedule for nonadaptive and adaptive personality: A useful tool for diagnosis and classification of personality disorder. In T. Widiger (Ed.), *The Oxford handbook of personality disorders* (pp. 58–81). New York, NY: Oxford University Press.

Bornstein, R. (1993). *The dependent personality.* New York, NY: Guilford.

Bornstein, R. (1994). Dependency in psychotherapy: Effective therapeutic work with dependent patients. In L. Vandecreek, S. Knapp, & T. Jackson (Eds.), *Innovations in clinical practice: A sourcebook,* vol. 13 (pp. 139–150). Sarasota, FL: Professional Resource Press.

Bornstein, R. (2011). Reconceptualizing personality pathology in DSM-5: Limitations in evidence for eliminating dependent personality disorder and other DSM-IV syndromes. *Journal of Personality Disorders 25,* 235–247. doi:10.1521/pedi.2011.25.2.235.

Bornstein, R. (2012). Dependent personality disorder. In T. Widiger (Ed.), *The Oxford handbook of personality disorders* (pp. 505–526). New York, NY: Oxford University Press.

Brauer, J., & Reinecke, M. (2015). Dependent personality disorder. In A. Beck, D. Davis, & A. Freeman (Eds.) *Cognitive therapy of personality disorders* (3rd ed., pp. 155–173). New York, NY: Guilford.

Bricker, D., Young, J., & Flanagan, C. (1993). Schema–focused cognitive therapy: A comprehensive framework for characterological problems. In K. Kuehlwein & H. Rosen (Eds.), *Cognitive therapies in action: Evolving innovative practice* (pp. 88–125). San Francisco, CA: Jossey-Bass.

Buie, D., & Adler, G. (1983). The definitive treatment of the borderline personality. *International Journal of Psychoanalytic Psychotherapy, 9,* 51–87.

Cleckley, H. (1976). *The mask of sanity* (5th ed.). St. Louis, MO: Mosby.

Cloninger, C. (2004). *Feeling good: The science of well-being.* New York, NY: Oxford University Press.

Cloninger C.R. (2000). A practical way to diagnosis of personality disorders: A proposal. *Journal of Personality Disorders, 14,* 99–108.

Cloninger, R., Svrakic, D., & Przybeck, T. (1993). A psychobiological model of temperament and character. *Archives of General Psychiatry, 50,* 975–990.

Costa, P., & McCrae, R. (1990). Personality disorders and the five-factor model. *Journal of Personality Disorders, 4*, 362–371.

Costello, C. (Ed.). (1996). *Personality characteristics of the personality disordered*. New York, NY: Wiley.

Crowell, S., Beachaine, T., & Linehan, M. (2009). A biosocial developmental model of borderline personality: Elaborating and extending Linehan's theory. *Psychological Bulletin, 135*, 495–520.

Cukrowicz, K.C., Poindexter, E.K., & Joiner, T.E. (2011). Cognitive behavioral approaches to the treatment of narcissistic personality disorder. In W. Campbell & J.D. Miller (Eds.), *The handbook of narcissism and narcissistic personality disorder: Theoretical approaches, empirical findings, and treatments* (pp. 457–465). Hoboken, NJ: John Wiley & Sons.

Davis, D., & Beck, J. (2015). The therapeutic alliance with patients with personality disorders. In A. Beck, D. Davis, & A. Freeman (Eds.) *Cognitive therapy of personality disorders* (3rd ed., pp. 125–139). New York, NY: Guilford.

Diamond, R. (2009). *Instant psychopharmacology* (3rd ed.). New York, NY: W.W. Norton.

Driscoll, K., Cukrowicz, K., Reardon, M., & Joiner, T. (2004). *Simple treatments for complex problems: A flexible cognitive behavior analysis system approach to psychotherapy*. Mahwah, NJ: Lawrence Erlbaum Associates.

Eagle, M. (1986). The psychoanalytic and the cognitive unconscious. In R. Stern (Ed.), *Theories of the unconscious* (pp. 155–190). Hillsdale, NJ: Analytic Press.

Eckstein, D., Baruth, L., & Mahrer, D. (1992). *An introduction to life-style assessment* (3rd ed.). Dubuque, IA: Kendall-Hunt.

Eells, T. D. (2007). Generating and generalizing knowledge about psychotherapy from pragmatic case studies. *Pragmatic Case Studies in Psychotherapy, 3*(1), 35–54.

Eells, T. (2010). *Handbook of psychotherapy case formulation* (2nd ed.). New York, NY: Guilford.

Ellis, A. (1979). *Reason and emotion in psychotherapy*. New York, NY: Citadel.

Everett, S., Halperin, S., Volgy, S., & Wissler, A. (1989). *Treating the borderline family: A systematic approach*. Boston, MA: Allyn & Bacon.

Fawcett, J. (2002). Schemas or traits and states: Top down or bottom up? *Psychiatric Annals, 32* (10), 567.

Frances, A. (2013). *Essentials of psychiatric diagnosis: Responding to the challenge of DSM-5*. Revised edition. New York, NY: Guilford.

Frances, A., Clarkin, J., & Perry, S. (1984). *Differential therapeutics in psychiatry: The art and science of treatment selection*. New York, NY: Brunner/Mazel.

Freeman, A. (1992a). Developing treatment conceptualizations in cognitive therapy. In A. Freeman & F. Datillo (Eds.), *Comprehensive case book of cognitive therapy* (pp. 13–26). New York, NY: Plenum.

Freeman, A. (1992b). Dysthymia. In A. Freeman & F. Datal (Eds.), *Comprehensive casebook of cognitive therapy* (pp. 129–138). New York, NY: Plenum.

Freeman, A., & Fox, S. (2013). Cognitive behavioral perspectives on the theory and treatment of the narcissistic character. In J.S. Ogrodniczuk (Ed.), *Understanding and treating pathological narcissism* (pp. 301–320). Washington, DC: American Psychological Association.

Freeman, A., Pretzer, J., Fleming, B., & Simon, K. (1990). *Clinical applications of cognitive therapy*. New York, NY: Plenum Press.

Gabbard, G. (2005). *Psychodynamic psychiatry in clinical practice* (4th ed.). Washington, DC: American Psychiatric Press.

Gabbard, G. O. (1994). *Psychodynamic psychiatry in clinical practice: The DSM-IV edition*. Washington, DC: American Psychiatric Press.

Glantz, K., & Goisman, R. (1990). Relaxation and merging in the treatment of the personality disorders. *American Journal of Psychotherapy, 44,* 405–413.

Glick, I., Clarkin, J., & Goldsmith, S. (1993). Combining medication with family psychotherapy. In J. Oldham, M. Riba, & A. Tasman (Eds.), *American psychiatric press review of psychiatry* (vol. 12, pp. 585–610). Washington, DC: American Psychiatric Press.

Good, G., & Beitman, B. (2006). *Counseling and psychotherapy essential: Integrating theories, skills, and practices.* New York, NY: Norton.

Grossman, P., Niemann, L., Schmidt, S. & Walach, H. (2004). Mindfulness-based stress reduction and health benefits: A meta-analysis. *Journal of Psychosomatic Research, 57,* 35–43.

Guidano, V. F., & Liotti, G. (1983). *Cognitive processes and emotional disorders.* New York, NY: Guilford Press.

Gunderson, J. (1989). Borderline personality disorder. In T. Karasu (Ed.), *Treatments of psychiatric disorders* (pp. 2749–2758). Washington, DC: American Psychiatric Press.

Gunderson, J., & Chu, J. (1993). Treatment implications of past trauma in borderline personality disorder. *Harvard Review of Psychiatry, 1,* 75–81.

Harbir, H. (1981). Family therapy with personality disorders. In J. Lion, (Ed.), *Personality disorders: Diagnosis and management* (2nd ed.). Baltimore, MD: Williams & Wilkins.

Hayes, S. (2004). Acceptance and commitment therapy and the new behavior therapies: Mindfulness, acceptance, and relationship. In S. Hayes, V. Follette, & M. Linehan (Eds.), *Mindfulness and acceptance: Expanding the cognitive-behavioral tradition* (pp. 1–29). New York, NY: Guilford.

Hayes, S., Follette, V. & Linehan, M. (Eds.). (2004). *Mindfulness and acceptance: Expanding the cognitive-behavioral tradition.* New York, NY: Guilford.

Hooley, J., Cole, S., & Gironde, S. (2012). Borderline personality disorder. In T. Widiger (Ed.), *The Oxford handbook of personality disorders* (pp. 409–436). New York, NY: Oxford University Press.

Horowitz, L. (1987). Indications for group psychotherapy with borderline and narcissistic patients. *Bulletin of the Menninger Clinic, 51,* 248–318.

Horowitz, M. (1988). *Introduction to psychodynamics: A new synthesis.* New York, NY: Basic Books.

Horowitz, M. (1995). Histrionic personality disorder. In G. Gabbard (Ed.), *Treatment of psychiatric disorders* (2nd ed., pp. 2311–2326). Washington, DC: American Psychiatric Press.

Inderbitzin, L., & James, M. (1994). Psychoanalytic psychology. In A. Stoudemire (Ed.), *Human behavior: An introduction for medical students* (2nd ed., pp. 107–142). Philadelphia, PA: Lippincott.

Jones, S. (1987). Family therapy with borderline and narcissistic patients. *Bulletin of the Menninger Foundation, 51,* 285–295.

Kabat-Zinn J. (1994.). *Wherever you go, there you are: Mindfulness meditation in everyday life.* New York, NY: Hyperion.

Kalojera, I., Jacobson, G., Hoffman, G., Hoffman, P., Raffe, I., White, H., & Leonard-White, L. (1998). The narcissistic couple. In J. Carson & L. Sperry (Eds.), *The disordered couple* (pp. 207–238). New York, NY: Brunner/Mazel.

Keller, M., McCullough, J., Klein, D., Arnow, B., Dunner, D.L., Gelenberg, A.J., . . . Zajecka, J. (2000). A comparison of nefazodone, the cognitive behavioral analysis system of psychotherapy, and their combination for the treatment of chronic depression. *New England Journal of Medicine, 342,* 1462–1470.

Kernberg, O. (1984). *Severe personality disorders: Psychotherapeutic strategies*. New Haven, CT: Yale University Press.

Klein, R. (1989). Diagnosis and treatment of the lower-level borderline patient. In J. Masterson & R. Klein (Eds.), *Psychotherapy of disorders of the self* (pp. 69–122). New York, NY: Brunner/Mazel.

Klosko, J., & Young, J. (2004). Cognitive therapy of borderline personality disorder. In R. Leahy (Ed.). *Contemporary cognitive therapy: Theory, research and practice* (pp. 269–298). New York, NY: Guilford.

Koenigsberg, H. (1991). Borderline personality disorder. In B. Beitman & G. Klerman (Eds.), *Integrating pharmacotherapy and psychotherapy* (pp. 271–290). Washington, DC: American Psychiatric Press.

Koenigsberg, H. (1993). Combining psychotherapy and pharmacotherapy in the treatment of borderline patients. In J. Oldham, M. Riba, & A. Tasman (Eds.), *American psychiatric press review of psychiatry* (vol. 12, pp. 541–564). Washington, DC: American Psychiatric Press.

Koons, C. R., Robins, C. J., Tweed, J. L., Lynch, T. R., Gonzalez, A. M., & Morse, J. Q. (2001). Efficacy of dialectical behavior therapy in women veterans with borderline personality disorder. *Behavior Therapy, 32*, 371–390.

Krueger, R. F., & Tackett, J. L. (2003). Personality and psychopathology: Working toward the bigger picture. *Journal of Personality Disorders, 17*(2), 109–128.

Lachkar, J. (1998). Narcissistic/borderline couples: A psychodynamic approach to conjoint treatment. In J. Carlson & L. Sperry (Eds.), *The disordered couple* (pp. 254–284). New York, NY: Brunner/Mazel.

Layden, M., Newman, C., Freeman, A., & Morse, S. (1993). *Cognitive therapy of borderline personality disorder*. Boston, MA: Allyn & Bacon.

Lazarus, A. (1981). *The practice of multimodal therapy*. New York, NY: McGraw-Hill.

Levy, K. (2012). Subtypes, dimensions, levels, and mental states in narcissism and narcissistic personality disorder. *Journal of Clinical Psychology: In Session, 68*, 886–896.

Lieberman, R., DeRisi, W., & Mueser, K. (1989). *Social skills training for psychiatric patients*. New York, NY: Pergamon.

Linehan, M. (1993). *Cognitive-behavioral treatment of borderline personality disorder*. New York, NY: Guilford.

Linehan, M. (2014). *DBT skills training manual* (2nd ed.). New York, NY: Guilford.

Linehan, M., Armstrong, H., Suarez, A., Allmon, D., & Heard, H. L. (1991). Cognitive-behavioral treatment of chronically parasuicidal borderline patients. *Archives of General Psychiatry, 48*, 1060–1064.

Linehan, M. M., Comtois, K. A., Murray, A. M., Brown, M. Z., Gallop, R. J., . . . Lindenboim, N. (2006). Two-year randomized controlled trial and follow-up of dialectical behavior therapy vs. therapy by experts for suicidal behaviors and borderline personality disorder. *Archives of General Psychiatry, 63*, 757–766.

Linehan, M. M., Dimeff, L. A., Reynolds, S. K., Comtois, K. A., Welch, S. S., Heagerty, P., & Kivlahan, D. R. (2002). Dialectical behavior therapy versus comprehensive validation therapy plus 12-step for the treatment of opiod dependent women meeting criteria for borderline personality disorder. *Drug and Alcohol Dependence, 67*, 13–26.

Linehan, M., Heard, H., & Armstrong, H. (1993). Naturalistic follow-up of a behavioral treatment for chronically parasuicidal borderline patients. *Archives of General Psychiatry, 50*, 971–974.

Lynch, T. (in press). *Dialectical behaviour therapy for treatment resistant depression: Targeting emotional constriction*. New York, NY: Guilford.

Lynch T., & Cheavens J. (2008). Dialectical behavior therapy for co-morbid personality disorders. *Journal of Clinical Psychology, 64,* 1–14.

Lynch T., & Cuper, P. (2012). Dialectical behavior therapy of borderline and other personality disorders. In T. Widiger (Ed.), *The Oxford handbook of personality disorders* (pp. 785–793). New York, NY: Oxford University Press.

Lynch, T., & Mizon, G. (2011). Distress overtolerance and distress intolerance. In M. Zvolensky, A. Bernstein, & A. Vujanovic, *Distress tolerance: Theory, research, and clinical applications* (pp. 52–79). New York, NY: Guilford.

Mann, J. (1973). *Time-limited psychotherapy.* Cambridge, MA: Harvard University.

Marra, T. (2005). *Dialectic behavior therapy in private practice: A practical and comprehensive guide.* Oakland, CA: New Harbinger Publications.

McCullough, J. (2000). *Treatment for chronic depression: Cognitive behavioral analysis system of psychotherapy.* New York, NY: Guilford.

McCullough, J. (2002). What kind of questions are we trying to answer with our psychotherapy research? *Clinical Psychology: Science and Practice, 9,* 447–452.

McCullough, J., Schramm, E., & Penberthy, J. (2015). *CBASP as a distinctive treatment for persistent depressive disorder: Distinctive features.* New York, NY: Routledge.

Meichenbaum, D. (1977). *Cognitive-behavior modification: An integrated approach.* New York, NY: Plenum.

Miller, W., & Rollnick, S. (2013). *Motivational interviewing* (3rd ed.). New York, NY: Guilford.

Millon, T. (1996). *Disorders of personality: DSM-IV and beyond* (2nd ed.). New York, NY: Wiley.

Nehls, N., & Diamond, R. (1993). Developing a systems approach to caring for persons with borderline personality disorder. *Community Mental Health Journal, 29,* 161–172.

Nurse, R. (1998). The dependent/narcissistic couple. In J. Carlson & L. Sperry (Eds.), *The disordered couple* (pp. 315–332). New York, NY: Brunner/Mazel.

Othmer, E., & Othmer, S. (2002). *The clinical interview using DSM-IV-TR: Volume 1: Fundamentals.* Washington, DC: American Psychiatric Press.

Padesky, C., & Beck, J. (2015). Avoidant personality disorder. In A. Beck, D. Davis, & A. Freeman (Eds.), *Cognitive therapy of personality disorders* (3rd ed., pp. 174–202). New York, NY: Guilford.

Paris, J. (2012). Pathology of personality disorder: An integrative conceptualization. In T. Widiger (Ed.), *The Oxford handbook of personality disorders* (pp. 399–406). New York, NY: Oxford University Press.

Perry, J. (1995). Dependent personality disorder. In G. Gabbard (Ed.), *Treatment of psychiatric disorder* (2nd ed., pp. 2355–2366). Washington, DC: American Psychiatric Press.

Perry, J., Herman, J., Van der Kolk, B., & Hoke, L. (1990). Psychotherapy and psychological trauma in borderline personality disorder. *Psychiatric Annals, 20,* 33–43.

Pretzer, J. (1990). Borderline personality disorder. In A, Beck, A. Freeman, & Associates (Eds.), *Cognitive therapy of personality disorders* (pp. 176–207). New York, NY: Guilford.

Pretzer, J., & Beck, J. (2004). Cognitive therapy of personality disorders: Twenty years of progress. In R. Leahy (Ed.), *Contemporary cognitive therapy: Theory, research and practice* (pp. 299–318). New York, NY: Guilford.

Prochaska, J., & DiClementi, C. (1982). Transtheoretical therapy: Toward a more integrative model of change. *Psychotherapy, 19,* 276–288.

Reich, J. (2000). The relationship of social phobia to the personality disorders. *European Psychiatry, 15,* 151–159.

Reich, J. (2002). Drug treatment of personality disorder traits. *Psychiatric Annals, 32*(10), 590–600.

Reich, J. (2005). Drug treatment of personality disorder traits. In J. Reich (Ed.), *Personality disorders: Current research and treatments* (pp.127–146). New York, NY: Routledge.

Ronningstam, E. (2011). Narcissistic personality disorder in DSM-V—In support of retaining a significant diagnosis. *Journal of Personality Disorders, 25*, 248–259.

Salzman, L. (1980). *Treating the obsessive personality.* New York, NY: Jason Aaronson.

Salzman, L. (1989). Compulsive personality disorder. In T. Karasu (Ed.), *Treatment of psychiatric disorder* (pp. 2771–2782). Washington, DC: American Psychiatric Press.

Sank, R. I. & and Shaffer, C. S. (1984). *A therapist's manual for cognitive behavior therapy in groups.* New York, NY: Plenum.

Schmidt, N., Joiner, T., Young, J., & Telch, M. (1995). The schema questionnaire: Investigation of psychometric properties and the hierarchical structure of a measure of maladaptive schemas. *Cognitive Therapy and Research, 19*, 295–321.

Segal, Z., Williams, J. & Teasdale, J. (2002). *Mindfulness-based cognitive therapy of depression.* New York, NY: Guilford.

Segal Z., Williams J., & Teasdale, J. (2013). *Mindfulness-based cognitive therapy for depression* (2nd ed.). New York, NY: Guilford Press.

Segal, Z., Williams, J., Teasdale, J., & Williams, M. (2004). Mindfulness-based cognitive therapy: Theoretical and empirical status. In S. Hayes, V. Follette, & M. Linehan (Eds.), *Mindfulness and acceptance: Expanding the cognitive-behavioral tradition* (pp. 45–65). New York, NY: Guilford.

Sharoff, K. (2002). *Cognitive coping therapy.* New York, NY: Brunner/Routledge.

Silk, K., & Feurino, L. (2012). Psychopharmacology of personality disorders. In T. Widiger (Ed.), *The Oxford handbook of personality disorders* (p. 713–726). New York, NY: Oxford University Press.

Simon, K. (2015). Obsessive-compulsive personality disorder. In A. Beck, D. Davis, & A. Freeman (Eds.) *Cognitive therapy of personality disorders* (3rd ed., pp. 203–222). New York, NY: Guilford.

Skodol, A., Bender, D., Gunderson, J., & Oldham, J. (2014). Personality disorders. In R. Hales, S. Yudofsky, & L. Weiss (Eds.), *The American Psychiatric Publishing Textbook of Psychiatry* (pp. 851–894). Alexandria, VA: American Psychiatric Publishing.

Slap, J., & Slap-Shelton, L. (1991). *The schema in clinical psychoanalysis.* Hillsdale, NJ: Analytic Press.

Snyder, M. (1994). Couple therapy with narcissistically vulnerable clients: Using the relationship enhancement model. *Family Journal: Counseling and Therapy for Couples and Families, 2*, 27–35.

Solomon, M. (1989). *Narcissism and intimacy: Love and marriage in an age of confusion.* New York, NY: Norton.

Solomon, M. (1998). Treating narcissistic and borderline couples. In J. Carlson & L. Sperry (Eds.), *The disordered couple* (pp. 239–258). New York, NY: Brunner/Mazel.

South, S., Reichborn-Kjennerud, T., Eaton, N., & Krueger, R. (2012). Behavior and molecular genetics of personality diosrders. In T. Widiger (Ed.), *The Oxford handbook of personality disorders* (pp. 143–165). New York, NY: Oxford University Press.

Sperry, L. (1995a). *Handbook of the diagnosis and treatment of DSM-IV personality disorders.* New York, NY: Brunner/Mazel.

Sperry, L. (1995b). *Psychopharmacology and psychotherapy: Strategies for maximizing treatment outcomes.* New York, NY: Brunner/Mazel.

Sperry, L. (1999). *Cognitive behavior therapy of DSM-IV personality disorders: Highly effective interventions for the most common personality disorders.* New York, NY: Brunner/Mazel.

Sperry, L. (2003). *Handbook of the diagnosis and treatment of DSM-IV-TR personality disorders* (2nd ed.). New York, NY: Brunner-Routledge.

Sperry, L. (2005). A therapeutic interviewing strategy for effective counseling practice: Application to health and medical issues in individual and couples therapy. *Family Journal: Counseling and Therapy for Couples and Families, 13*, 477–481.

Sperry, L. (2006). Family-oriented compliance counseling: A therapeutic strategy for enhancing health status and lifestyle change. *Family Journal: Counseling and Therapy with Couples and Families, 14*, 412–416.

Sperry, L. (2010). *Core competencies in counseling and psychotherapy: Becoming a highly competent and effective therapist.* New York, NY: Routledge.

Sperry, L. (2014). Effecting change: The centrality of the case conceptualization. In L. Sperry & J. Carlson (Eds.), *How master therapists work: Effecting change from the first through the last session and beyond* (pp. 74–99). New York, NY: Routledge.

Sperry, L. (2015). Personality disorders. In L. Sperry, J. Carlson, J. Duba-Sauerheber, & J. Sperry, J. (Eds.), *Psychopathology and psychotherapy: DSM-5 diagnosis, case conceptualization and treatment* (3rd ed., pp. 27–62). New York, NY: Routledge.

Sperry, L. (in press). *Handbook of diagnosis and treatment of DSM-5 personality disorders* (3rd ed.). New York, NY: Routledge.

Sperry, L., Brill, P., Howard, K., & Grissom, G. (1996). *Treatment outcomes in psychotherapy and psychiatric interventions.* New York, NY: Brunner/Mazel.

Sperry, L., & Carlson, J. (2014). *How master therapists work: Effecting change from the first through the last session and beyond.* New York, NY: Routledge.

Sperry, L., Carlson, J., & Kjos, D. (2003). *Becoming an effective therapist.* Boston, MA: Allyn & Bacon.

Sperry, L., & Maniacci, M. (1998). The histrionic-obsessive couple. In J. Carlson, & L. Sperry (Eds.), *The disordered couple*. New York, NY: Brunner/Mazel.

Sperry, L., & Mosak, H. (1996). Personality disorders. In L. Sperry & J. Carlson (Eds.), *Psychopathology and psychotherapy: From DSM-IV diagnosis to treatment* (2nd ed., pp. 279–336). Washington, DC: Accelerated Development/Taylor & Francis.

Sperry, L., & Sperry, J. (2012). *Case conceptualization: Mastering this competency with ease and confidence.* New York, NY: Routledge.

Stein, D., & Young, J. (1992). Schema approach to personality disorders. In D. Stein & J. Young, (Eds.), *Cognitive science and clinical disorders* (pp. 272–288). San Diego, CA: Academic Press.

Stone, M. (1993). *Abnormalities of personality: Within and beyond the realm of treatment.* New York, NY: Norton.

Sungar, M. & Gunduz, A. (2015). Histrionic personality disorder. In A. Beck, D. Davis, & A. Freeman (Eds.), *Cognitive therapy of personality disorders* (3rd ed., pp. 325–345). New York, NY: Guilford.

Tarrier, N. (Ed.). (2006). *Case formulation in cognitive behaviour therapy: The treatment of challenging and complex cases.* London, UK: Routledge.

Taylor, G., & Bagley, M. (2012). The alexithymic personality dimension. In T. Widiger (Ed.), *The Oxford handbook of personality disorders* (pp. 648–673). New York, NY: Oxford University Press.

Torgersen, S. (2009). Prevalence, sociodemographics, and functional impairment. In J. Oldham, J. Skodol, & D. Bender (Eds.), *Essentials of personality disorders* (pp. 83–102). Washington, DC: American Psychiatric Publishing.

Turkat, I. (1990). *The personality disorders: A psychological approach to clinical management.* New York, NY: Pergamon Press.

Turkat, I. D., & Maisto, S. A. (1985). Personality disorders: Application of the experimental method to the formulation and modification of personality disorders. In

D. H. Barlow (Ed.), *Clinical handbook of psychological disorders*, (pp. 502–570). New York, NY: Guilford.

Turner, R. (1992). Borderline personality disorder. In A. Freeman & F. Dattilio (Eds.), *Comprehensive casebook of cognitive therapy* (pp. 215–222). New York, NY: Plenum.

Verheul, R., van den Bosch, L.M.C., Koeter, M.W.J., de Ridder, M.A.J., Stijnen, T., & van den Brink, W. (2003). Dialectical behavior therapy for women with borderline personality disorder. *British Journal of Psychiatry*, *182*, 135–140.

Wachtel. P. (1982). *Resistance: Psychodynamics and behavioral approaches*. New York, NY: Plenum.

Waldinger, R. (1987). Intensive psychodynamic therapy with borderline patients: An overview. *American Journal of Psychiatry*, *144*, 267–274.

Waldo, M., & Harman, M. (1993). Relationship enhancement therapy with borderline personality. *Family Journal, 1*, 25–30.

Waldo, M., & Harman, M. (1998). Borderline personality disorder and relationship enhancement marital therapy. In J. Carlson & L. Sperry (Eds.), *The disordered couple* (pp. 285–298). New York, NY: Brunner/Mazel.

Wells, M., Glickhauf-Hughes, C., & Buzzel, V. (1990). Treating obsessive-compulsive personalities in psychoanalytic/interpersonal group therapy. *Psychotherapy*, *27*, 366–379.

Westen, D. (2012). Prototypic diagnosis of psychiatric syndromes. *World Psychiatry*, *11* (1), 16–21.

Widiger, T. (2012). Historical developments and current issues. In T. Widiger (Ed.), *The Oxford handbook of personality disorders* (pp. 13–34). New York, NY: Oxford University Press.

Woodward, B., Duckworth, K., & Guthiel, T. (1993). The pharmacotherapist-psychotherapist collaboration. In J. Oldham, M. Riba, & A. Tasman (Eds.), *American psychiatric press review of psychiatry* (vol. 12, pp. 631–649). Washington, DC: American Psychiatric Press.

Yalom, I. (1985). *The theory and practice of group psychotherapy* (3rd ed.). New York, NY: Basic Books.

Young, J. E. (1990). *Cognitive therapy for personality disorders: A schema focused approach*. Sarasota FL: Professional Resource Exchange.

Young, J. E. (1994). *Cognitive therapy for personality disorders: A schema-focused approach* (rev. ed.). Sarasota, FL: Professional Resource Exchange.

Young, J. E., & Brown, G. (1994). Young Schema Questionnaire (2nd ed.). In J. E. Young (Ed.), *Cognitive therapy for personality disorders: A schema-focused approach* (ed. rev.). Sarasota, FL: Professional Resource Exchange.

Young, J. E., & Brown, G. (2001). *Young schema questionnaire*. New York, NY: Cognitive Therapy Center

Young, J., Klosko, J., & Weishaar, M. (2003). *Schema Therapy: A practitioner's guide*. New York, NY: Guilford.

Zanarini, M., Frankenburg, F., Reich, D., & Fitzmaurice, G. (2010). Time to attainment of recovery from borderline personality disorder and stability of recovery: A 10-year prospective follow-up study. *American Journal of Psychiatry*, *167*, 663–667.

Zimmerman, M., Rothschild, L., & Chelminski, I. (2005). The prevalence of DSM-IV personality disorders in outpatients. *American Journal of Psychiatry*, *162*, 1911–1918.

Index

Page numbers in *italics* refer to figures and tables.